Social Security and Medicare

Individual versus Collective Risk and Responsibility

Sheila Burke
Eric Kingson
Uwe Reinhardt
Editors

NATIONAL ACADEMY OF SOCIAL INSURANCE
Washington, D.C.

Copyright © 2000
NATIONAL ACADEMY OF SOCIAL INSURANCE
1776 Massachusetts Avenue, N.W., Washington, D.C. 20036

Social Security and Medicare: Individual versus Collective Risk and Responsibility
may be ordered from:

BROOKINGS INSTITUTION PRESS
1775 Massachusetts Avenue, N.W.
Washington, D.C. 20036
Tel.:   1-800/275-1447
         202/797-6258
Fax: 202/797-6004
Internet: www.brook.edu

Library of Congress Cataloging-in-Publication data

Social Security and Medicare: individual versus collective risk and responsibility/
Sheila Burke, Eric Kingson, Uwe Reinhardt, editors.
    p.   cm.
Paper presented at the 11th Annual Conference of the National Academy of Social
Insurance, held in Washington, D.C., on Jan. 28–29, 1999.
Includes bibliographical references and index.
    ISBN 0-8157-1283-9 (alk. paper)
    1. Social security—United States—Congresses.   2. Medicare—Congresses.
I. Burke, Sheila.   II. Kingson, Eric R.   III. Reinhardt, Uwe E.   IV. National
Academy of Social Insurance (U.S.). Conference (11th: 1999 Washington, D.C.)
V. Title
HD7125-S5957 2000   99-050627
368.4'3'00973—dc21   CIP

9 8 7 6 5 4 3 2 1

The paper used in this publication meets minimum requirements of the American
National Standard for Information Sciences—Permanence of Paper for Printed
Library Materials: ANSI Z39.48-1984.

Typeset in Times Roman

Composition by AlphaWebTech
  Mechanicsville, Maryland

Printed by R. R. Donnelley and Sons
  Harrisonburg, Virginia

NATIONAL ACADEMY OF·SOCIAL INSURANCE

The National Academy of Social Insurance is a nonprofit, nonpartisan organization made up of the nation's leading experts on social insurance. Its mission is to conduct research and enhance public understanding of social insurance, to develop new leaders, and to provide a nonpartisan forum for the exchange of ideas on important issues in the field of social insurance. Social insurance, both in the United States and abroad, encompasses broad-based systems for insuring workers and their families against economic insecurity caused by loss of income from work and protecting individuals against the cost of personal health care services. The Academy's research covers social insurance systems, such as Social Security, Medicare, workers' compensation and unemployment insurance, and related social assistance and private employee benefits.

Contents

Preface

WHEN THE BOARD of the National Academy of Social Insurance decided that the focus of the eleventh annual conference should be "Social Security and Medicare: Individual versus Collective Risk and Responsibility," they may not have realized just how prescient and timely they were. This dominant philosophical and ultimately practical issue of personal versus societal responsibility has become central to discussions about the future of Social Security and Medicare.

The context surrounding today's Social Security and Medicare debates has changed in other ways as well. Incremental reforms have stabilized both programs' short-term financing. In contrast to the discussions of the mid-1970s and early 1980s, there is no short-term financing crisis in Social Security. And, under the Health Care Financing Administration actuaries' central assumptions, Medicare is projected to have sufficient funds to meet its obligations through 2015.

But perhaps most interesting, unlike previous discussions, the range of solutions is not simply the traditional, incremental possibilities of some tax increases, benefit cuts, or some combination of changes (for example, treating benefits as taxable income) that no one quite could define as being either a tax cut or a benefit increase. And Medicare policy discussions are not confined to tax, benefit, and various cost-containment reforms.

Today public discussion is operating outside that box. At least for now, some significant and, many would suggest, revolutionary changes are being considered in Social Security and Medicare that would increase the level of privatization and tilt these programs away from defined benefit toward defined contribution models.

Today's policy debates present challenges and opportunities. If there was ever a time for us to be bipartisan on these issues, it is clearly now. If there ever was a time for policy researchers and policymakers alike to carefully think through the consequences of potential reforms, it is now. Prior solutions for both Medicare and Social Security have been most successful when they crossed party lines, when reforms reflected solid analytic and political thought—whether it was the 1983 solution for Social Security or the 1997 changes in Medicare.

The board thought an appropriate conference topic would be a discussion of the implications of shifting from systems that are based more on collective or community risk and responsibility, to systems that might involve more individual risk and responsibility. The session topics that were chosen and the bipartisan nature of this conference, then, should come as no surprise. The cochairs believed in the importance of looking at how the public forms judgments about these issues and how public opinion shifts. They also wanted to explore the technical and administrative consequences of changes potentially associated with public investment of the Social Security reserves in the equities markets, of moving toward a system of individual accounts in which tens of millions of workers made decisions about how to privately invest their funds, and of reforming Medicare in ways that placed greater responsibility on beneficiaries to choose their benefit packages.

The conference program mixture—including Senator Ted Kennedy (D-Mass.), Senator John Breaux (D-La.), and Representative Bill Thomas (R-Calif.)—reflected our desire to bring all views to the table to address these serious issues and find solutions. The conference gave us all an opportunity to stretch our thinking, to hear from some of the best in the field about their views and concerns, and, hopefully, to get us all better prepared to grapple with these challenging questions.

This conference, by design, raised more questions than answers. The answers are going to ultimately reflect the public's values and recognition that this set of programs is more than taxable payroll and benefits, but implies some type of a moral commitment and a sense of obligation to each other as a people. Different views of what that means needs to be discussed, arguably, explicitly.

The issues of "Individual versus Collective Risk and Responsibility" are technically very complex and morally challenging. Each generation's social ethic may be different; each may want to discuss social ethics in slightly different terms. While we may never truly settle all the questions raised it is important to have the conversation to which this conference contributed.

As the conference cochairs and editors of the proceedings, we appreciated and benefited from the efforts of Pamela Larson, Virginia Reno, Terry Nixon, and other academy staff who were so instrumental in the design of the program, the logistics of our gathering, and later in the production of this volume. They were ably assisted by Donielle Wells and Allison Watts. Kerry Kern edited the volume, Carlotta Ribar and Eloise C. Stinger proofread it, and Susan Fels prepared the index for the Brookings Institution Press. Support for the conference came from the Robert Wood Johnson Foundation, the Kaiser Family Foundation, the Health Care Financing Administration, the Agency for Health Care Policy and Research, and State Street Bank and Trust.

It is important to underscore how much we value the contributions of the conference presenters, discussants, and those who took the time to comment on their papers. The papers and discussion reflect the view of the authors and do not necessarily reflect those of their employers or other organizations with which the authors are associated, or of the financial sponsors, officers, board, staff, or members of the National Academy of Social Insurance or the Brookings Institution. We trust that their ideas will engage and stimulate your thinking, just as they did for conference participants.

Sheila Burke
Eric Kingson
Uwe E. Reinhardt

1

Introduction

Karen Matherlee

THE ELEVENTH ANNUAL conference of the National Academy of Social Insurance focused on the concept of choice in the Medicare and Social Security programs. Following up on an examination of Medicare in 1997 and an exploration of Social Security in 1998, the January 28–29, 1999, event brought the two programs together under one theme: Individual vs. Collective Risk and Responsibility. The conference probed whether choice should be introduced to the programs, how it would be defined and structured, and (if greater choice were adopted) what sorts of safeguards would be needed to protect vulnerable program participants.

Starting two days after President Bill Clinton, in his State of the Union address, had proposed infusing budget surplus funds into both the Medicare and Social Security retirement programs, the conference had a deliberate rather than an urgent tone. In part due to the healthy economy, the Hospital Insurance (HI) Trust Fund was projected to see a shortfall in 2008 (rather than 2001, as earlier predicted) and the Old Age Survivors and Disability Insurance (OASDI) Trust Fund was expected to last until 2032 before experiencing a funding gap. "We are, for the first time in a very long time, driven by long-term, rather than short-term, crisis," said Sheila Burke, executive dean of the John F. Kennedy School of Government at Harvard University. She cochaired the conference with Eric Kingson, professor of social work at Syracuse University, and Uwe Reinhardt, James Madison Professor of Political Economy at Princeton University.

For conference panelists and attendees, looking at Medicare and Social Security in terms of long-term fixes seemed a welcome change. The work of the National Bipartisan Commission on the Future of Medicare, which was featured at the conference, reinforced this view. The rhetoric of reform ranged from "tinkering" to "overhauling," as representatives from both the private and public sectors examined ways, some of them under consideration by the commission, of making the programs more responsive and cost-effective.

The reform debate inspired participants to reflect on the history of both social insurance programs. Some looked back to 1935, when Social Security was created, and others to 1965, when Medicare was added to the Social Security Act. Discussion of the relevancy of the bipartisan reform process of 1983 to current efforts to "save" the programs became particularly lively. Participants at the 1999 conference had strong views about the present applicability of the policies and politics of 1983 in establishing the prospective payment system for Medicare and in transferring trust fund dollars from Medicare to Social Security. Moreover, looking for models (both good and bad), several speakers mentioned programs in other countries, such as Chile, England, and Germany.

But choice—and the risks it brings—dominated the discussion. Experts from academia, think tanks, corporate organizations, trade associations, and government probed the nature and value of choice, the public's attitudes toward it, the tradeoffs it entails, the precautions it musters, and other topics. Even as they displayed new terminology, such as that of behavioral economics, they tended to come back to the values of the programs. They highlighted the moral commitment and sense of obligation—both to the individual and to the public as a whole—that Social Security and Medicare evoke.

In his keynote address, Robert Reischauer of the Brookings Institution bridged past and present as he explored the notion of "one size fits all" as opposed to multiple choice. He suggested that the growing interest in choice is based on four factors. The first is an increasing concern about the solvency of both Medicare and Social Security, necessitating structural change. The second consists of changes occurring in the economic and institutional environments in which Medicare and Social Security operate (for example, managed care arrangements in the health arena and investment opportunities in the pension field). The third is the state of the economy, the prosperity that the country has experienced in the 1990s. The final factor is the country's social transformation, characterized by increasing diversity.

Within this context, Reischauer offered the advantages and disadvantages of restructuring Medicare and Social Security to provide greater choice. He placed increased participant satisfaction, greater efficiency, and more flexibility on the plus side. On the minus side he put greater disparity of outcomes, increased complexity of program structure (for participants and administrators), higher administrative costs, and the risk of even more fragmentation as interests are pitted against each other. Injecting a phrase—"on balance"—that became a refrain during the conference, he asked attendees to consider all the policy ramifications of change.

Fundamental Values of Social Insurance

Retracing old ground—the history of social insurance—was necessary before staking out new ground on choice, risk, and responsibility. According to Reinhardt, who opened the session, examining why the United States has social insurance is comparable to looking at the "shovel brigade behind the private insurance sector." That is because social insurance "takes care of risks that the private sector, for some reason or other, cannot."

The session featured Edward Berkowitz, professor in the Department of History at George Washington University, who compared the creation of Social Security in 1935 with that of Medicare in 1965. Berkowitz looked first at the differences between the two times. Most prominent was the economic climate: the depression in 1935 and prosperity in 1965. Second was the locus of control of social policy: the state in 1935, as originally reflected in Social Security, and the federal government in 1965. Third was the primary objective of each new program: regulation of employment relations in 1935 and relief of distress in 1965. Last was the status of the two fields: a limited private pension system in 1935 and a well-established private health care industry in 1965. He also examined the similarities: leadership from presidents who had won by large margins (Franklin D. Roosevelt in 1935 and Lyndon Johnson in 1965) and inclusion of the social insurance provisions in omnibus bills. Putting these factors into context, Berkowitz probed the funding of both programs, particularly in terms of the debate over self- and contributory financing versus government subsidization through general revenues.

Most significantly, he focused on the fundamental values that underlie the two programs. He contended that "the United States grew into social insurance." After Social Security's enactment, "it took at least 15 years for fundamental values associated with Social Security—such as universal coverage and benefits payable as a right without a means test—to emerge as accurate descriptions of the program and as positive program characteristics." Once those values had emerged in the 1950s, Social Security became this country's most successful social welfare program, Berkowitz claimed. "The goal of universal, compulsory coverage in a wage-related program that paid benefits as a matter of right and that blended adequacy and equity in a socially acceptable manner appeared to be well in sight."

Indicating that Medicare was more difficult to negotiate than Social Security, Berkowitz said that its founders did not challenge the existing health care system because they were more interested in assuring access to care for people sixty-five and older. Rather than using the development of a new program to advance different forms of health care delivery and financing, they fashioned it according to the prevailing acute inpatient medical model.

Alicia H. Munnell, professor in the Boston College School of Management, presented the response of Robert M. Ball, former commissioner of Social Security, who was unable to participate because of illness. She conveyed Ball's general approval of Berkowitz's presentation of the social insurance programs' history, but indicated that Ball wanted to clarify one major theme: the United States did not grow into social insurance; from the start, the founders of the Social Security program were aware of the program's value-laden principles and characteristics. They were confident that the public and politicians would eventually catch on. And, Ball concluded, the public and the politicians did.

Ball included a list of the nine major principles identified with the current OASDI program: universal, earned right, wage-related, contributory and self-financed, redistributive, not means-tested, wage-indexed, inflation-protected, and compulsory. He indicated that all but one—self-financing—applied to the retirement program in 1935 and subsequent amendments of 1939 and 1950. Ball noted that Social Security "paid much higher benefits to the first generation of Social Security recipients than their contributions justified," thereby creating a permanent accrued liability, in order to gain support for the program. That accrued liability has been the focus of debate with respect to putting general revenues into the system, as is now the case with President Clinton's proposal to use surplus funds.

For Ball, the lesson of history is that "everything comes around again." As one of the founders of Social Security, he has witnessed the cycling and recycling of proposals for more than sixty years. For Munnell, accrued liability, as traced by Ball, offered a clear rationale for the administration's proposal to reach into general revenues. Speaking two days after President Clinton had unveiled the proposal, she acknowledged that there was considerable mystery about its details.

Janice Gregory, director of legislative affairs for the ERISA Industry Committee, gave an employer response to the Berkowitz paper. Referring to his Social Security chronology, she added an element, "Social insurance and employee plans grew up together." In fact, she implied that they were Siamese twins: "Social Security and employer-sponsored retirement plans are joined at the hip. When you change Social Security, pension plans will not sit still. They will change."

Gregory said that only about 15 percent of the civilian work force were enrolled in employer-sponsored plans in 1940. She reported, "In the near future, by the time the baby boom is swinging into full retirement, about 80 percent of retiring workers will have received benefits from one or more employer plans at some point during their lifetimes." She added: "In the aggregate, employer-sponsored plans today pay out more retiree and survivor benefits each year than does Social Security: $379 billion in 1997 compared to $316 billion for the OASDI program." However, given the size of the Social Security program, any changes in the program would have a dramatic impact on employer plans. For example, if Social Security were to move to individual investment accounts, participation in 401(k) and other kinds of employer plans would likely decline. If the age of initial eligibility for Social Security retirement benefits were to increase, the need for "bridge plans" to tide people over between retirement and onset of eligibility would increase.

Defending employer plans, Gregory indicated that "group savings is more effective." It is automatic, relies on professional investment management, involves painless decisionmaking, and gets immediate returns, especially if the employer matches employee contributions. However, such plans are vulnerable to regulatory burdens and administrative costs, which have caused a number of employers to drop defined-benefit pension plans. In this vein, she expressed concern about privatization of Social Security, because "most employers don't have any experience whatsoever in collecting individual employee contributions and putting them in a plan."

Individual Choices and Shared Responsibilities

With the ground staked out for a discussion of potential changes in this country's social insurance programs, Stuart Butler and Theodore Marmor debated the best reform routes to take. Butler is vice president and director of domestic and economic policy studies at the Heritage Foundation and Marmor is professor of public policy and management at Yale University. While both expressed support for social insurance, they provided divergent views on how it should be structured. Butler spoke for more individual choice; Marmor for more collective responsibility.

Butler recalled the social contracts that respectively underpin Medicare and Social Security. Contending that the contract for each program is one "that we cannot deliver," he presented three options: squeeze and trim, infuse general revenue dollars, or change and limit the contract. He supported the third option for both programs. For Medicare, Butler recommended moving from a defined benefit to a defined contribution, so participants could use a voucher or premium support to obtain health services. He also pointed to the Federal Employees Health Benefit Program (FEHBP) as a possible model for Medicare beneficiaries. For Social Security, he suggested "allowing people to put some of their contributions into savings accounts." In his view, "people being able to make choices in a competitive world is the process by which you get innovation in the future."

Marmor reframed the topic to be "the extent of economic security that is collectively provided" and the choices that are permitted and the risks that are contained because of that, rather than "putting more risk on individuals and cutting back on the collective provision of economic security." In other words, he cast the debate in terms of distribution of risk rather than individual choice versus collective decisionmaking. He contended that social insurance is a mechanism for collectively or cooperatively pooling the risk of a source of economic insecurity, such as medical expenses or loss of income from retirement. For him, entitlement means "sharing a common burden" and "pooling resources"; expansion of choice in the Medicare and Social Security programs would take away the economic security that they provide.

While both speakers saw the necessity of protecting vulnerable persons, Butler spoke for a safety net that would ensure that "nobody in this country, no matter their circumstances, should have less than this level, which will depend on the affluence, the wealth of the country, social views, and so on." Marmor advocated a platform on which people would be similarly treated regardless of cost. Whether on the issue of vulnerability or other concerns, both men agreed that this nation has to address who takes responsibility, who takes risk, to what extent risk can be managed, and what kinds of protections need to be established.

The Decisionmaking Process—A Critique of the Consumer Choice Model

Because some of the reforms being considered for Medicare and Social Security would entail greater individual decisionmaking, the academy turned to George Loewenstein, professor of economics and psychology at Carnegie Mellon University, to address psychological assumptions about the consumer-choice model. Loewenstein, a behavioral economist, began by confronting the prevailing attitude that "choice is good—the more options the better." Indicating that there are different types of choices (for example, those in the private market that are constrained by consumer taste and those brought about by government), he looked at some of the concept's benefits and costs.

Turning to the benefits, Loewenstein said that expanded choice allows people "to satisfy idiosyncratic needs and tastes." It also can "promote competition between providers and lower price or improve quality." But the latter requires well-informed, knowledgeable consumers—it is the basis of the informed-consumer model. He indicated significant costs: the time that expanded choice takes; the errors that can result; and the psychic penalty—in the form of anxiety—it may bring about if the wrong path is taken.

Loewenstein's conclusion was that expanded choice is beneficial when it satisfies "heterogeneous wants and needs" but is ill-advised when it requires "expertise that people don't possess." Applying this to Medicare and Social Security, he seemed dubious about expansion of choice in each, because of the complexity of the two programs. He also seemed doubtful of the role of experts in helping people choose, because experts require time, as well as money, and may respond to different incentives (such as the investment broker who benefits from churning stock purchases).

In responding to Loewenstein, James Lubalin, senior health services and policy researcher at the Research Triangle Institute gave a negative view of the informed-consumer model. "For consumers to use information, they have to see it, they have to understand it, and they have to recognize the larger context in which it fits," he said. He added that, in the case of Medicare, consumers have little understanding, particularly of the rudimentary concepts of managed care. "Another lesson is that providing more information won't necessarily improve the quality of decisions. In fact, people can absorb only a limited amount of information." Hence, they tend to reduce the factors. In choosing a health plan, for example, they look for a seal of approval or decide based only on cost. While he indicated that people are potentially educable about some of the issues, he expressed concern that they might be easily manipulated.

Mark Warshawsky, speaking from his experience as director of research for the Teachers Insurance and Annuity Association and College Retirement Equities Fund (TIAA-CREF), was much more sanguine about the consumer-choice model. He agreed with Loewenstein that offering choices "should entail a balancing of benefits and costs, that framing alternatives and designing defaults is critical to the success of a choice-based health or retirement program," and that the process is more natural in some areas than others. But he charged Loewenstein with underemphasizing the benefits, particularly over time. Using examples from TIAA-CREF, he described successful use of and an increased receptivity to a wide variety of investment and retirement income options by annuitants. At the same time, he underlined pension plan sponsors' responsibility to place reasonable limits on choice.

Fredda Vladeck, senior health policy consultant to the National Council of Senior Citizens, drew on her experience with International Brotherhood of Teamsters retirees in addressing individual consumers' choices and the consequences of their decisions. A social worker who believes that it is important "to start where the client is," she said that the union found that its retirees did not understand the Medicare and Social Security programs and their own union plans. In designing education initiatives for health and retirement, she discovered the most frequent—and the most difficult-to-answer—question to be "how much money do I need?"

During this segment, presenters and attendees raised various questions that invited further research. Examples include the effects of greater choice on participant satisfaction with the Medicare and Social Security programs; the extent of interest of members of the public in exercising control over their health plans and retirement accounts; and the differences in returns—in quality, services, and volume—from the social insurance programs for different groups of the population, such as minorities, women, and low-income people. Another was the efficacy of consumer education approaches—for instance, the 800 number, printed information, and the one-on-one counselor.

Regulation to Ensure the Markets Deliver on Their Promise

Turning to what type of regulation is needed to help the markets deliver, a panel consisting of current and former regulators explored the types of mechanisms that would protect consumers if Medicare reform continues in the direction of market-based options and Social Security moves to mandatory retirement accounts. A federal regulator, Paul Carey, drew on his work as commissioner of the Securities and Exchange Commission (SEC) in focusing on investor protection in the Social Security program if it moves to private accounts. "While Social Security reform has not been a traditional area of expertise for the SEC, many of the issues that arise, such as investor education, financial literacy, corporate governance, disclosure of material information (including expense information), and sales practices, have long been concerns for us." He saw the need for regulation of two kinds of plans: those in which part of an individual's payroll tax or contribution would be invested in a private account and those in which the government would invest some or all of the Social Security trust fund in the market.

Carey also focused on investor education. He urged that consumers be educated about the relationship between risk and return, the administrative costs of investing, the managers of the accounts, the investment choices permitted, and the types of investment switches allowed. At the same time, he admitted that there are various unknowns that require research: how government shares would be voted, who would vote them, what type of impact a huge influx of capital would have on the market, and what effects market fluctuations would have.

William Niskanen, a former federal official who is now chairman of the Cato Institute, indicated that no regulation is necessary, other than the provisions of commercial law, "when people are informed, when they face a range of choices, and when they bear the marginal benefits and costs of their own choices." He agreed, however, that, in the absence of a working consumer-choice model, certain rules become essential.

In terms of Medicare, he contended that "the customers are poorly informed, have few choices, and pay very little for the services they receive." He viewed this as an invitation to "futile, ineffective regulation" and called for changes in the program to "increase the information, the choice, and the incentives of both the suppliers and the consumers." He suggested a three-part plan to transform Medicare from a comprehensive to a catastrophic insurance plan in which the consumer's deductible would be proportional to income.

In terms of Social Security private investment accounts, Niskanen saw a rationale for regulation to "provide some safety net for those who, for whatever reason, do not accumulate a socially adequate retirement annuity." He would like to see the federal government approve a number of broad-based stock and bond funds, according to certain risk criteria. Once a consumer had met a certain investment standard, there would be no further regulation of that person's incremental investments. Consumers who had not qualified would be subject to safety-net protections.

Kansas insurance commissioner Kathleen Sebelius, responsible for regulating more than 2,000 companies and 32,000 agents in the state, responded that Niskanen's scenario sounded good but was unrealistic, because it was based on an imaginary marketplace. Commenting on Medicare+Choice, she said that beneficiaries lacked options—that in parts of Kansas health maintenance organizations were not offered. While stating that nationally some health plans had reduced their service areas or had withdrawn entirely from the program, she added that money drives the system—"market players won't play in a system where they can't make money." Sebelius advocated that the Medicare program take steps to educate consumers by utilizing counselors in local communities. She also commented on problems in the implementation of provider-sponsored organizations, which were authorized under the same legislation—the Balanced Budget Act of 1997—as Medicare+Choice.

The Policy Environment—Views from Capitol Hill
and the Administration

Senator John Breaux (D-La.), ranking member of the Senate Special Committee on Aging; Senator Edward Kennedy (D-Mass.), ranking member of the Senate Committee on Health, Education, Labor and Pensions; and Representative Bill Thomas (R-Calif.), chairman of the House Ways and Means Committee Health Subcommittee, addressed the likelihood of Medicare and Social Security reforms. Breaux was the statutory chairman and Thomas the administrative chairman of the National Bipartisan Commission on the Future of Medicare. (The panel was scheduled to give its recommendations on Medicare reform a month after the conference but was unable to reach consensus.)

Breaux referred to a package of reform proposals that he had offered the commission. He said that adoption of the proposals would require eleven votes in the commission to pave the way for consideration in the House and Senate. Among the proposals was a plan to model Medicare after the FEHBP. He reviewed the Medicare board, the minimum benefit package, and the consumer education program that would be created under the plan. He contended that the new configuration would address the four Medicare problems that Reischauer had posed earlier: insolvency, inadequacy, inefficiency, and inequity.

As to the financing, Breaux said that he had worked that out, too. In determining the premium, the board "would calculate the national weighted average of all of the plans" that submitted bids to cover the core basic benefit package. In most cases, the federal government would pay 88 percent and the Medicare beneficiary 12 percent. For higher income beneficiaries, the ratio would be 75 percent and 25 percent, respectively. Age of eligibility would be the same as for full Social Security retirement. Mechanisms would have to be explored to fund the prescription drug provision. "So the board would not be regulating prices," Breaux added, "but certainly regulating what is being offered to the beneficiaries to ensure that what they are being offered across the board meets the needs of the Medicare beneficiaries in this country. And then the marketplace would be able to compete to see who can do it the best."

Kennedy emphasized the social underpinnings of Social Security and Medicare. "It is said that the measure of a society is how well it takes care of its most vulnerable citizens, the very young and the very old." Saying that Social Security benefits keep more than a million children out of poverty and fund more than half the income of two-thirds of senior citizens, he accused opponents of exaggerating the Social Security program's long-term financial problems. He backed President Clinton's proposal to use surplus funds for Social Security, which he said would close most of the shortfall.

Contending that a shift from public assumption of risk and responsibility toward a system of individual accounts "would put the risk on each individual instead of spreading the risk across the work force," Kennedy expressed concern about altering the progressive benefit structure that had been the mainstay of the program for so long. The only role he saw for such accounts was supplementary to the current system.

Turning to Medicare, Kennedy outlined three problems: an outdated, inadequate benefit package; insufficiency in providing the highest quality care; and a precarious trust fund. He singled out Medicare's lack of coverage of prescription drugs as its biggest gap, a problem he hoped to see addressed in the current Congress. Other problems that he identified were misuse of prescription drugs, the rare use of clot-dissolving drugs for stroke patients, inadequate vaccination for influenza and pneumonia, and the need for more prevalent screening for cervical and breast cancer. He also expressed concern about long-term financing to preserve benefits for the baby boom generation.

Thomas reflected on the political environment with respect to Medicare, which he characterized as being, just five years ago, "the third rail of American politics—touch it and you die." Today, he said, it is essential "to figure out how to fairly balance those individual and collective resources to provide an adequate health care policy for our seniors that not only incorporates today's technology in health care delivery changes, but also creates a mechanism in which tomorrow's technology and health care delivery structures can be integrated in a cost-effective manner." He singled out one of the proposals: coverage of outpatient prescription drugs. Indicating that "65 percent of all seniors had some form of supplemental drug payment in 1995" and that coverage provided under managed care had increased that percentage, he said it was important to focus on those seniors without any drug benefit.

In reviewing the proposals that were before the commission, Thomas joined Breaux in stressing the importance of a public-private partnership. "We're not saying that the private sector's going to solve the problem," Thomas insisted. "We think a healthy competition between the private and the public monitored by the public sector is the best chance of integrating technological and health delivery changes in a timely and efficient fashion."

White House and Department of Health and Human Services officials, joined by trade association and union representatives, also provided perspectives on the reforms. Kenneth Apfel, commissioner of the Social Security Administration, discussed President Clinton's Social Security reform proposals and emphasized the opportunity provided by the federal budget surplus to "partially advance more of the Social Security system." Advocating that 62 percent of the federal budget surplus be transferred to Social Security over the next fifteen years, Apfel contended that "there could be no better use for this historic surplus than ensuring retirement security for future generations." He urged diversification of the Social Security trust fund portfolio to include "a modest portion of stocks" and said that the choice was between that and a lower benefit structure, which to him was no choice at all. Calling President Clinton's proposal "a solid framework for ensuring retirement security through the first half of the next century," Apfel also underlined the importance of Americans' increasing their own retirement savings "above and beyond Social Security."

Nancy Ann DeParle, administrator of the Health Care Financing Adminis-tration (HCFA), reviewed some of the agency's activities, especially the programs it is implementing as a result of Balanced Budget Act mandates. She mentioned the Child Health Insurance Program, expansion of the Medicare prospective payment system, program integrity safeguards, and Medicare+Choice. Admitting that HCFA needs more administrative resources and greater man-agement flexibility, she insisted, "We shouldn't do anything that erodes the government's role here in overseeing such a massive program that is funded by the taxpayers and provides important protections for beneficiaries."

DeParle urged that the program be strengthened: by ensuring a guaranteed benefit package that includes prescription drug coverage, modernizing fee-for-service Medicare, providing clear and adequate support for low-income ben-eficiaries, and maintaining a stable and adequate level of financial support. In terms of the latter, she mentioned the portion of the budget surplus that President Clinton proposed go to the HI Trust Fund. "The president's frame-work would reserve 15 percent of the projected surpluses, so around $650 billion to $700 billion over the next 15 years would go to the Medicare trust fund. Because the funds could not be used for other purposes, they will ensure that the money goes to help meet the health care needs of older and disabled Americans, and extend the solvency of this trust fund," she concluded.

"The stars must be in alignment," Sharon Canner began, noting the budget surplus, bipartisan leadership, and public support for both Medicare and Social Security. Vice president for entitlement policy at the National Association of Manufacturers (NAM), she noted that contributing 15 percent of the budget surplus to the HI Trust Fund would be a "good start." She expressed caution, however, on raising the age for Medicare eligibility in line with the phasing of eligibility for full Social Security retirement benefits. She indicated that it might force employers out of the retiree health care market.

Referring to her eighteen years with NAM and the program reforms she had seen over the years, Canner praised the Clinton administration for its plan to use the budget surplus for Social Security, but wondered if the funds would materialize. On Social Security trust fund investment, she advocated letting "individuals invest rather than collective investment." She stressed that "we at NAM would keep a safety net, a basic benefit. And when we talk about privatizing, the government is not going to get out of the system. No politician worth his salt would let a system go unregulated, so there will still be government regulation." For her, "the word privatization really is a misnomer."

John Rother, director of legislation and public policy at the American Association of Retired Persons (AARP), praised President Clinton for transforming the Social Security debate. Indicating that the president was not just looking at solvency, he commented: "He's really looking at how Social Security fits in a total scheme to strengthen the economy so that when we get to 2020 or 2030, we have a stronger base from which to finance our own retirement." Rother also drew attention to Republicans' attempt to focus on the proverbial three-legged stool: the importance of Americans' having pensions and savings along with Social Security retirement payments. "I think that whether it's called a USA account or something else, a mechanism that would let more ordinary Americans, particularly those of moderate low income, start to put together real retirement savings on top of Social Security is a very important step that we should not let slip from our grasp this year." Rother expressed concern about stock market investment, however, because of difficulties he saw in insulating it from political manipulation.

Regarding Medicare reform, Rother was hesitant about premium support but indicated that it was premature to offer judgment on it. He said that in the past Medicare had been framed as a budget issue. He thought the president had reframed the debate to focus on the program's inadequacy and inefficiency and the need to fix it. He then centered on what reform would mean for beneficiaries, which is key to the AARP. He talked about the services beneficiaries receive (or he thinks they should receive, such as coverage of prescription drugs) and the out-of-pocket costs they pay. Ultimately, the question is: "How can we move this whole system to take more seriously the challenge of delivering health care and keeping the population healthy into the 21st century?"

Dismissing outright the idea of premium support for the Medicare program, David Smith, director of public policy at the American Federation of Labor-Congress of Industrial Organizations (AFL-CIO), concentrated instead on Social Security. He said that President Clinton had framed two issues: replacing the social insurance system with an individual account system, and finding new revenue or cutting benefits. Reflecting the suspicion of the AFL-CIO and other unions toward what he called the substitution of an individual investment account for a defined benefit in the Social Security program, he contended:

"They want to transform a defined benefit system into a defined contribution system. They want to shift the risk from all of us to each of us." Calling Social Security "the bedrock of retirement security for American working people," he recommended that reformers start by considering "the earnings cap and possible adjustment."

An International Perspective on the Issues

Uwe Reinhardt offered an international view of health care. Making global comparisons at a conference at which panelists and attendees had brought up Chile's experience with investment accounts and various European countries' pension systems, he compared U.S. and European cultural values regarding health care. "No European would ever finance health care the way we do, because European social ethics are based in health care practice (not in the health professions themselves)—quite different from ours. I think social ethics have less to do with how you deliver care than how you finance it—whether the provider is for-profit or nonprofit, privately owned or public." He implied that social ethics are imbedded in the financing of health care—whether health care is a social good or, as in Germany, a mix of a public utility and a "private consumption good."

Reinhardt categorized the health systems of other countries as being government-financed, government-run, or statutory social insurance systems. He described the United States as having "a private insurance system with public fallbacks." Whatever the system, it involves trade-offs; in the United States, the trade-offs seem to operate to the detriment of the needy, he contended.

An ongoing critic of greed in the U.S. system, he was especially critical of providers. "A health system has two objectives: to enhance the quality of life of the patient and to enhance the quality of the provider's life." In this respect, he contended that U.S. health care costs are 40 percent higher than those of Germany. Having just come from an international conference, Reinhardt commented on almost universal dissatisfaction across the globe with health care. Why? "Health care is economically illegitimate." "It is simply illegitimate because . . . people who receive the care don't pay for it and the benefit-cost calculus isn't right." While most of his comments were tongue in cheek, he had a clear message: "It is really imperative to shift the supply curve down so that kindness is once again affordable in America and we don't blanch every time we say, 'Let's give some children health insurance or let's help the elderly not have to trade off drugs against food.'"

Public Readiness for Medicare and Social Security Reform

Whether the public is ready for choice—whether it knows the advantages and disadvantages of social insurance programs that incorporate choice and is prepared to move forward—is a key question. Benjamin Page, professor in the political science and communications studies departments at Northwestern University, addressed this question, casting it in terms of the political feasibility of entitlement reform. He contended that collective policy preferences tend to be stable over time. Since 1984, for example, "more than 90 percent of Americans have regularly indicated a desire to keep the [Social Security] program the same or expand it." He also indicated that collective public opinion tends to have coherence, reflecting basic underlying values and beliefs. At the same time, he discounted the media, which he characterized as being interested in dramatic stories that tend to be misleading or wrong about public opinion. In this vein, he advocated paying close attention to the media's interpretation of statistics and responses to survey questions, including the wording of the questions themselves.

Addressing public opinion on Social Security, Page explained that it "shows higher information levels than other programs" and "enjoys extremely high support among the American public." In terms of specific changes, he cited public resistance to benefit reductions, both in existing payments and in future increases to account for inflation. He also indicated opposition to extending the retirement age and increasing the payroll tax, although "large majorities of the public say they prefer tax increases to benefit cuts." However, he reported that "a large majority of Americans favor cutting benefits for the well-to-do." He was less certain of public opinion on some other changes, such as using general revenues to bolster the Social Security trust fund and removing the "cap" on earnings subject to the payroll tax. Finally, he said that privatization—moving to private investment accounts—is "an area in which opinions are much less well formed," with more time and more data needed.

Three experts responded to Page: Willis Gradison of the law firm Patton Boggs LLP; Beth Kobliner, journalist and author; and William Spriggs, director of research and public policy at the National Urban League. Gradison, bringing to bear his long tenure as a member of Congress and president of the Health Insurance Association of America, contested Page's confidence in public readiness and even the importance of public opinion on the details of Medicare and Social Security reform. As ranking minority member of the House Ways and Means Committee Health Subcommittee when the Social Security Amendments of 1983 were passed, he suggested the bipartisan process that occurred then as a model for current reform. He said that it was based more on coalescing political and interest groups than on marshaling public support. Gradison also said he backed "a modest carve-out for private accounts" as a means of increasing support for the Social Security system, especially among young people.

Carrying the standard for Generation X (persons born between 1965 and 1976), Kobliner went against the common wisdom that its members are "leading the charge for stock market investments and individual accounts." She contended that the actual opinions of the generation "may be closer to those of the general public than we think." Citing the wording of questions in two polls, she also agreed with Page's views on the presentation of public opinion. "The way questions are framed can lead to results which are presented as being representative of a generation's opinion and subtle word differences can make a huge difference." She depicted Generation X as being similar to other generations in its support for "some sort of minimum, guaranteed benefit."

Spriggs also endorsed Page's comments on the importance of public opinion, the extent to which the public is informed on the present Social Security program and changes proposed to it, and the depth of public support for the program. He challenged how much experts know about the program and how readily opinion leaders point to intergenerational conflict. Indicating that only minor changes are needed, he stressed the Social Security system's moral underpinnings for people of all ages.

Whether from the panelists and respondents or attendees who posed questions, this part of the conference raised numerous topics for further research. Many of the topics focused on the extent of public knowledge of Medicare and Social Security, awareness of the status of the HI and OASDI Trust Funds, exposure to proposed changes, and receptivity to those changes. Others centered on consumer education, particularly in terms of the structuring of choice and the efficacy of different approaches.

Conclusion

As the National Academy of Social Insurance's eleventh annual conference unfolded, there was point-counterpoint among presenters and attendees alike on the topic of individual risk and responsibility versus collective risk and responsibility. The major themes of introducing, defining, and structuring choice and of providing consumer safeguards were presented, dissected, questioned, and challenged.

Underlying this activity, which was the main purpose of the conference, was the reaction, pro and con, to President Clinton's dramatic proposal earlier in the week to infuse both the HI and the OASDI Trust Funds with budget surplus dollars. Even as the National Bipartisan Commission on the Future of Medicare was struggling to reach some sort of consensus on its proposals (an effort that failed), the idea of putting general revenue dollars into the contributory Medicare hospital and Social Security programs meant that all bets were off. Some welcomed the proposal as an easy way out of a dilemma. Others saw it as pulling the rug out from under meaningful Medicare and Social Security reforms. Still others decided to wait and see.

As the Clinton administration and Congress address the program and fiscal problems of Medicare and Social Security, the contributions in this volume give parameters to the debate. In the final year of the twentieth century, they reflect the range and diversity of views from which agreement may emerge to shape these two hallmark social insurance programs for the decades to come.

2

Bridging Past
and Present

THIS CHAPTER presents a look at the similarities and differences, advantages and disadvantages, among choice-oriented reform options in Medicare and Social Security. Robert Reischauer explores the notion of "one size fits all" programs versus the growing interest in multiple choice.

Choice and Social Insurance
Robert D. Reischauer

FOR HALF A CENTURY after Social Security was enacted and a quarter of a century after Medicare was passed, policymakers, taxpayers, and beneficiaries seemed fairly content with uniform structures for the nation's two largest social insurance programs. They did not object to the fact that participants were offered no significant choices—that the same benefit and tax rules were applied to everyone. No one considered it a drawback that, as far as social insurance was concerned, one size was expected to fit all.

Starting about a decade ago, however, interest began to develop in reforms that would introduce a degree of participant choice into these basic social insurance programs. Under these approaches, individuals would be able to exercise some control over the way in which their promised social insurance protections were delivered, managed, or structured.

With respect to Social Security, this interest manifested itself in a growing number of reform proposals that would add a defined contribution or individual retirement account component on to the nation's mandatory defined-benefit pension system. Although these proposals differ greatly in detail, all would give participants far more personal control over the disposition of at least a portion of the contributions they are required to make to support the

19

government-mandated retirement pensions. Some plans would give workers a great deal of control over who manages their personal retirement account, what assets are held by these accounts, the level of contributions made to these accounts, and the form and pace at which balances can be withdrawn upon retirement. Others would provide only a modest amount of individual discretion on these matters but, nevertheless, the accounts would be considered to be owned by the individual worker.

In Medicare, the movement has gone far beyond mere proposals. The Tax Equity and Fiscal Responsibilities Act of 1982 provided beneficiaries with an alternative way of obtaining their benefits. Starting in 1983 they were given the choice of receiving their Medicare-covered services either through the traditional, indemnity system, which pays a portion of charges for unmanaged fee-for-service (FFS) care, or through an approved health maintenance organization (HMO) that would be paid a capitated amount.

For the first few years, this choice was more promise than a reality for many Medicare participants because no approved HMOs were available in their communities. As recently as 1992, there were no-risk plans—as the capitated HMOs were called—offered in twenty-four states, and only 4.4 percent of all beneficiaries were enrolled in one of the ninety-six plans that were available.[1] In the mid-1990s, this situation began to change rapidly. By 1997 just more than two-thirds of Medicare beneficiaries lived in a county where at least one of the 307 approved HMOs was available and, in that year, some 13 percent of Medicare participants had elected to receive their benefits from such plans.

The Medicare+Choice (M+C) program, which was a component of the Balanced Budget Act of 1997 (BBA), further expanded the choices available to Medicare participants. Starting in January 1999, this program expanded the types of capitated plans that could be offered to participants and modified the payments to these plans in ways that were intended to increase their availability in low cost and rural areas where few or no plans had been offered previously. In addition to the traditional FFS and HMO delivery options, under Medicare+Choice beneficiaries would be able to have their Medicare services delivered through coordinated care plans such as preferred provider organizations (PPOs) and provider-sponsored organizations (PSOs), private FFS plans, or even catastrophic insurance policies supplemented with medical savings accounts (MSAs). For all but a handful of participants, these new options are not yet available because very few of these new types of delivery organizations have applied to the Health Care Financing Administration (HCFA) for permission to provide services. However, this situation should change gradually over the next few years.[2]

In an effort to increase the availability of M+C plans in areas where the low level of capitated payments has left participants with no choice other than FFS Medicare, the BBA of 1997 established a minimum capitated payment level ($380 per month in 1999), guaranteed that capitated payments in all areas would rise by at least 2 percent a year, and adopted measures that would blend local and national costs in determining each area's capitated payment. By the end of 1998 roughly one participant in six—about 16 percent—had signed up with one of the 346 Medicare+Choice plans that were available in counties containing almost three-quarters of all participants.

To help set the stage for the other papers presented at the National Academy of Social Insurance's eleventh annual conference on "Social Security and Medicare: Individual versus Collective Risk and Responsibility," this chapter examines several of the reasons why there has been a surge of interest in participant choice in Social Security and Medicare. It then provides an overview of some of the broad issues that are raised when participant choice is introduced into the world of social insurance.

Why Choice Now?

At least four factors have contributed to the burgeoning interest in providing expanded participant choice in Social Security and Medicare. Foremost among these is the growing appreciation among policymakers and the public that, as currently structured, both Social Security and Medicare are headed for insolvency and that neither can be saved from this fate through modest tweaking of its benefit structure or a small boost in payroll tax rates. Instead, more far-reaching structural changes will be required to achieve long-run solvency in the face of the retirement of the baby boom generation, improved life expectancy, and the inexorable increase in the capability and cost of medical care. This reality has opened up the policy debate to a reexamination of the current program structures—structures that have not been altered in any fundamental sense since these two programs were initiated, even though much has changed in the intervening years in the worlds of retirement saving, pensions, and health insurance. The broadened scope of debate has encouraged consideration of entirely new approaches to meeting the core objectives of these social insurance programs and many of the new approaches that have been proposed incorporated greater participant choice.

A second factor that helps explain the interest in choice is the changes that have occurred in the broader economic and institutional environments within which Social Security and Medicare operate. On these dimensions, conditions are far different from what they were a decade or two ago, let alone when these two programs were first conceived. Approaches dismissed as unworkable when the structures of Social Security and Medicare were being designed are now feasible.

With respect to Social Security, there would certainly be no discussion of private retirement accounts if there had not developed over the past few decades a mature and efficient mutual fund market through which small investors can easily purchase and sell diversified portfolios of stocks and bonds without incurring excessive transaction costs. Nor would the nation be having a discussion of personal retirement accounts if a sizable portion of the working population had not had some experience with defined contribution retirement saving vehicles such as individual retirement accounts (IRAs), 401(k) and 403(b) plans, and Keogh plans. Estimates from the 1995 Survey of Consumer Finances suggest that, in that year, 30 percent of employees participated in a 401(k) and 403(b) plan and 39 percent of the adults had an IRA or Keogh plan.[3]

Yet these are fairly recent developments. Mutual funds did not become widespread until the 1970s. In fact, as recently as 1980 the *New York Times* listed the prices of fewer than 500 such funds; in January 1999 that newspaper listed the closing net asset values for more than 5,000 different funds and the mutual fund industry reported that 7,314 separate funds were available to the public in 1998. Furthermore, it was not until 1976 that the first index fund was offered to the public. The Revenue Act of 1978 created 401(k) plans and IRAs became widespread only after passage of the Economic Recovery Tax Act of 1981.

With respect to Medicare, the issue of providing participants with a choice of the type of organization through which they might obtain their health care was a relatively meaningless one until the late 1980s because virtually all health coverage for the under age sixty-five population took a form—indemnity insurance for FFS care—similar to that offered by traditional FFS Medicare. Today, however, with the under age sixty-five population being offered care through a wide variety of plan types—group and staff model HMOs, HMOs with point of service options, independent practice associations, PPOs, and FFS indemnity plans—consumers of health insurance have more choices and experience with a variety of plan types.

For both programs, one cannot imagine that structures with participant choice would be being considered if there had not been an explosion in computing power and a sharp decline in the costs of processing information and data. Without inexpensive computers, there would be no workable way to keep track of how and where participants in a program offering individual choice were obtaining their social insurance protections. Without computers, government could not know whether participants were making their required contributions or premium payments in a timely fashion to the appropriate account or plan. In short, without the recent advances in information technology, it would be impossible to implement many of the approaches that advocates of choice are proposing today.

A third factor that has contributed to the current climate in which many citizens seem willing to consider the introduction of some measure of participant choice into the nation's bedrock social insurance programs is the long period of prosperity that the nation has enjoyed. As the White House is fond of pointing out, the nation is now enjoying the longest peacetime expansion in its history; if growth continues through January 2000, the qualifying word *peacetime* will be dropped from that statement. Unemployment is lower than at any point since mid-1970. The fraction of the adult population that is employed is at an historic high. Incomes are rising across the board. One has to go back to the mid-1960s to find two consecutive years in which the inflation rate was below 2 percent, as was the experience of 1997 and 1998. In this sunny economic climate, Americans seem to be more willing to consider shouldering the greater risk that inevitably accompanies increased individual choice.

The long expansion and the passage of time seems to have dulled Americans' appreciation of the adverse consequences that normal economic fluctuations can have even on those who play by the rules—consequences against which social insurance, as traditionally structured, has provided significant protections. For most Americans, the hardships caused by the Great Depression may be as remote as the Great Plague. After all, 85 percent of today's population was either not born or a child under the age of five when World War II pulled the economy out of the Great Depression. Similarly, the economic uncertainty that the double-digit inflations of 1974, 1979, 1980, and 1981 injected into lives of many Americans, particularly those living on fixed incomes, may have been erased by the extremely subdued price level increases the nation experienced during the last half of the 1990s. The suffering that the 9.5 percent unemployment rates of 1982 and 1983 brought to those who lost high-paying manufacturing jobs—jobs that provided adequate pensions and health benefits—also seem to have been largely forgotten.

No discussion of the economic climate that underlies the enthusiasm for more participant choice in the nation's core social insurance program would be complete without mentioning the stock market, which, no doubt, has caused visions of sugar plums to dance on the virtual balance sheets of those who advocate carving personal retirement accounts out of existing Social Security payroll tax. Whether one considers the situation since 1995 or the longer bull market that started in the early 1980s, the recent record is breathtaking. Since

1990 the Dow Jones average has ended every year higher than it began the year. Many investors and noninvestors who favor privatizing Social Security seem to think that the laws of nature require that the market rise each year. They also seem convinced that market corrections will always be short and sweet as the last two—in 1987 and 1998—were. At the close on the last trading day in December 1987, the market was higher than it had been on the first trading day of that year and the precipitous 25 percent drop in market values that occurred in October of that year had been erased within two years. Similarly, a rising market obliterated the correction that took place in mid-1998 by the end of that year.

Few seem to recall that the Dow Jones Industrial Average was lower in 1980 than it was in 1965 or that the Standard and Poor's Index for 1978 was below its 1968 level—and these figures do not account for the inflation that eroded the value of a dollar. One wonders whether a lively discussion of the merits of privatizing a portion of Social Security would be taking place if markets had simply risen over the past four years at their historic rate of about 7 percent faster than inflation. If that had been the case, the Dow Jones average would have been around 5,500 on January 27, 1999, the day of the National Academy of Social Insurance's eleventh annual conference, rather than 9,200, which was its actual level on that date.

A final factor that helps to explain the support for reform approaches that encompass some element of participant choice is the transformation that has occurred in society. The nation no longer celebrates conformity. It no longer strives to march to a single drumbeat, one whose cadence is set by elite opinion makers or the corporate culture. Diversity is in. What is good for the Joneses is not automatically assumed to be best for the Smiths, the Sanchezes, or the Wongs. Unions, the traditional advocates of public policies that reinforce social solidarity, have declined in importance. From a postwar peak of 27 percent of the work force, union membership declined to 14 percent in 1998. In this new social environment, the argument that the uniform structures of Social Security and Medicare are desirable because they provide all Americans with a common or shared experience that helps to bind a diverse nation of individuals together may no longer be as convincing as it was during the Great Depression, World War II, or the cold war years.

This brief and undoubtedly incomplete review of some of the factors that have spawned interest in structural reforms that would introduce greater participant choice and individual control in social insurance suggests that this development is not likely to be ephemeral. Interest in more flexible and individualized arrangements is likely continue to grow in the foreseeable future.

Some Consequences

There are many possible ramifications of restructuring Medicare or Social Security in ways that would increase participant choice and control over the way in which they obtain their social insurance protections. At a general level, these consequences are familiar to those who have been actively engaged in recent policy debates. Generalizations, however, are difficult to make because many specific proposals contain ingenious features that are designed to overcome some of the more obvious drawbacks of social insurance program structures that offer choice to participants.

In theory, structures that offer choice have a number of advantages. Foremost among these is the possibility that the level of participant satisfaction might increase if beneficiaries are given the ability to choose from among a number of different structures the one that best meets their individual needs and circumstances or the one that best reflects their values and preferences.

A second potential advantage of structures that offer choice is that, if properly designed, they can be more efficient. In other words, they have the potential to deliver the social insurance protections society deems essential at a reduced cost to the government.[4] This might be accomplished by facing participants with incentives to act in cost-effective ways or by letting private sector agents, subject to market forces, manage the program in ways that government agencies, subject to political pressures, cannot.

The premium support structure that the National Bipartisan Commission on the Future of Medicare considered employed both of these approaches. It provided new incentives to participants. Those who selected health plans with above average costs—presumably plans that were less efficient or provided more generous benefits than Medicare mandated—would be required to bear the higher costs of their decisions.[5] Those selecting less expensive plans would benefit from reduced Part B premiums. In addition, private health plans operating in a premium support system presumably would be able to negotiate lower payment rates with providers than those paid by the HCFA through its system of administered prices, a system whose flexibility is severely limited by congressional dictates.

A third advantage of social insurance structures that offer some degree of participant choice is their flexibility. Such systems tend to be less rigid and more capable of evolutionary change than those with a unitary structure. They may be better able to adjust to the rapidly changing world in which we live because, as participants gravitate away from some options and toward others, policymakers and interest groups will be given signals about the desirable direction and pace of change. Furthermore, change may be less threatening because it can involve no more than adding on a few new options, ones that reflect the revealed preferences of participants.

These advantages are but one side of a coin, for there are also potential disadvantages to increasing participant choice. Greater choice inescapably means that there will be a greater disparity of outcomes for participants who are similar in every respect save the choices they made when faced with their social insurance options. If disparities in outcomes reflect the preferences of the decisionmakers—the participants, that is—no one should complain. In other words, if risk-averse individuals choose to invest their individual account balances conservatively with full knowledge that their returns are most likely going to be lower than those of more aggressive investors, there should be limited dissatisfaction if the expected outcome is realized. But that will not always be the case, both because of the unpredictable nature of the economy and because the unforeseeable character of an individual's future economic circumstances and health care needs ensures that many, in retrospect, will wish that they had made different choices. Structures intended to increase participant satisfaction could end up generating considerable discontent among a sizeable portion of the beneficiaries.

Under a system that offered choice, a rational individual would probably look at his or her past health care utilization, modify this experience by expectations for the upcoming year, and choose the health plans that would maximize that individual's expected benefits. When struck by some unexpected health problem, however, many such rational consumers will discover that they would have been much better off had they selected a different health plan—for example, one with the richer prescription drug benefit; lower copayments for physician visits; or more individual, rather than group, therapy sessions. Faced with this situation, some will be dissatisfied and unwilling to accept responsibility for their rational, but ex post incorrect, choice of a plan.

Similarly, if an individual had followed financial experts' advice to invest the preponderance of his or her personal retirement account in stock funds, how would he or she react if the stock market stagnates, as it has done from time to time, during the decade preceding the individual's retirement? Human nature being what it is, that individual is more likely to blame the financial advisers or "the system" than to chalk up the poor returns to bad personal judgment or bad luck. Such a reaction would be even more likely if a relative, close friend, or colleague from work had invested in bonds and, as a result, realized significantly higher returns.

Inevitably, disparities in outcomes will create new pressures on the government to help those whose choices have been unwise or those who have simply been unlucky. Added costs could be imposed on safety net programs—such as

Supplemental Security Income and Medicaid—if inadequate social insurance benefits cause some to fall below the floors society has established for these basic protections. Deciding who is deserving of such compensation and who should be asked to live with the adverse consequences of their decisions is likely to be a contentious issue. Those who regard their reduced circumstances to be capricious or largely the result of forces over which they had little control will demand redress. In addition, pressure will build to allow individuals to revisit their decisions frequently even though the efficiency and costs of many structures with choice may depend on locking participants into their decisions for some minimum length of time—as the Medicare+Choice rules have recognized.[6]

Increased choice unavoidably also means greater complexity of program structure. For some, this complexity will cause confusion. Much of the discussion of the advantages of reforms with increased participant choice has been carried on as if the average participant in the Social Security and Medicare programs were a college-educated individual with the computer and Internet dexterity of a Silicon Valley teenager, the experience of a self-employed businessman who has made benefit decisions for several decades, and a home library containing a complete collection of books on prudent market investing.

This caricature, of course, is far from the real world. Many workers have little interest in exercising control over their retirement accounts or choosing among a variety of complex health plans. As Arthur Levitt, chairman of the Securities and Exchange Commission, pointed out in a speech at Harvard University, many have little experience with or knowledge of financial market matters.[7] Most retirees have had their health plans chosen for them by their employers. Others have delegated all financial and health coverage decisions to a spouse who may be deceased. Some, particularly those over age eighty, are cognitively impaired. This suggests that any reform that introduces participant choice must be accompanied by a massive education and counseling effort. It also suggests that choices must be both structured and limited.

Social insurance structures encompassing choice would put added burdens on policymakers and program administrators as well as new responsibilities on participants. Lawmakers have not always had an easy time dealing with the unitary structures of Social Security and Medicare. Multiple structures might subject them to a wider variety of political pressures and create more problems than they can handle. Similarly, the jobs of program administrators could be made much more complex if there were a wide degree of participant choice in Social Security and Medicare. Administrative costs would almost certainly rise as new burdens—such as structuring and managing the markets for health plans, in the case of Medicare, and regulating or even managing personal retirement accounts, in the case of Social Security—were placed on federal program administrators.

Finally, introducing participant choice could alter the political dynamic that has sustained support for Social Security and Medicare over the years. Interests are likely to become more fragmented, identifying with the various options and possibly pitting one choice against another. Support for the core social protections afforded by Medicare and Social Security may start to erode. Demands may grow to allow participants to integrate their social insurance benefits with similar benefits they receive from their employers. Over the long run, this could result in the most economically secure workers and retirees easing their way out of the redistributive contributions they now make to the basic social insurance programs. The durability of broad public support for the goals of the existing social insurance programs should be a prime consideration as the nation considers whether Social Security and Medicare can be reformed in ways that would introduce more participant choice into programs.

Conclusion

Introducing participant choice into the nation's basic social insurance programs could bring benefits, but it also entails certain risks. Before charging headlong down this road it would be best to address the following key questions:

—What specific objectives would the nation be attempting to achieve by introducing greater choice into social insurance? Are those objectives likely to be attained in Medicare? In Social Security?

—If, on balance, more choice would be desirable, how much choice would be optimal? How should that choice be structured? How should it be limited?

—What adverse consequences are likely to arise, in the short and long runs, from structures involving more participant choice and what precautions should be taken to minimize these unavoidable adverse repercussions?

Notes

1. Health Care Financing Administration, *A Profile of Medicare, Chart Book*, May 1998, p. 60, and Committee on Ways and Means, *1998 Green Book*, p. 174. There are also plans with cost contracts that are reimbursed on the basis of costs incurred. In 1992 such plans enrolled 2.2 percent of beneficiaries.

2. As of September 1999 only one PSO and no PPOs, private FFS plans, or MSA/ catastrophic plans had been approved to offer Medicare services.

3. Federal Reserve Board (http://www.federalreserve.gov/pubs/oss/oss2/95/ SCF95home.html).

4. For a discussion of how choice need not lead to these outcomes see Henry J. Aaron, "Medicare Choice: Good, Bad, or It All Depends," in Andrew J. Rettenmaier and Thomas R. Saving, eds., *Medicare Reform: Issues and Answers* (University of Chicago Press, forthcoming).

5. This is the case only if a mechanism can be developed that accurately adjusts capitated payments for the input price differences faced by competing plans and the differences in the underlying health conditions of the plans' participants.

6. After 2002, Medicare+Choice participants will be locked into their plan for the balance of the year after a three-month trial period. If new Medicare enrollees wish to drop the plan, they will be permitted to revert to fee-for-service Medicare.

7. Arthur Levitt, "The SEC Perspective on Investing Social Security in the Stock Market," John F. Kennedy School of Government Forum, Harvard University, October 19, 1998.

3

Why We Have
Social Insurance

SOCIAL SECURITY AND MEDICARE reflect a particular set
of answers to fundamental questions of individual choice,
risk bearing, and the relationship between the individual and society. How did
we as a nation arrive at the answers embodied in our existing programs? Why
are these fundamental questions being asked anew in today's debate on how to
shape retirement policy and health care for the future? Are there lessons of the
past that ought to influence the choices we make for the future?

History and Social Security Reform
Edward D. Berkowitz

FOR A TIME in the spring of 1999 it looked as though Social
Security would come to the head of the legislative agenda and be the object of
comprehensive reform. For a historian this circumstance posed the challenge
of determining what in Social Security's past might be relevant to its future. In
other words, what can past periods of reform tell us about the present one? How
did the basic characteristics of Social Security (considered in this chapter to be
the Old Age Survivors and Disability Insurance and Medicare programs) come
to be formed and how susceptible are they to change?

As is often the case, these matters make better questions than answers. Even
a cursory examination of Social Security's history reveals that many of the
major characteristics of Social Security have evolved over time, rather than
being contained in the program's founding legislation. Contrary to public

The author would like to thank Eric Kingson and Robert Ball for their helpful
comments, as well as the students at George Washington University who did research in
the Murray Latimer Papers.

belief, Social Security has not always formed the third rail of American politics. Indeed, for a substantial portion of its history, the program has been characterized as much by the indifference of its friends as by the passion of its enemies. At critical junctures, policymakers have failed to anticipate significant future trends, changing the course of the program's history. All other things being equal, there is no reason to expect today's policymakers to fare any better. At best the historian can only make policymakers aware of some of the differences between expectations and outcomes that have arisen over the years.

Comparing Then and Now

Some basic comparisons help draw out historical lessons. A robust economy, such as we have now, does not appear to be a precondition for reform. In 1935 the Social Security program started during a severe depression that diminished people's faith in the capabilities of the American economic system and discredited many of the financial agents of capitalism, in particular the stock market and the banking system. In 1965, by way of contrast, the country felt flush enough to begin the Medicare program. In other words, the program owed its existence to the Great Depression but enjoyed its most significant expansions during periods of prosperity. The postwar economic boom made possible the 1950 amendments that settled once and for all the question of whether welfare or social insurance would be America's major form of income maintenance. Continuing prosperity led to the passage of disability insurance in 1956, Medicare in 1965, and the creation of inflation protection in 1972, not to mention the increases in basic benefit levels that occurred in 1952, 1958, 1969, and many other years as well.

If the current discussion is about privatization, then we can say that such a discussion could never have taken place in 1935. At that time the few private pension plans that existed had many problems meeting their obligations, and the stock market did not enjoy the confidence of the American public. With prosperity, however, came a renewed acceptance of the private market's vigor and potential. It became fashionable to talk of a partnership between public and private pensions and between public financing and private provision of medical care. The 1935 law was about strengthening the public presence in a heavily privatized world. Today, due to the force of the economy and the bull market in stocks, the terms of the debate have been reversed.

Whatever the economic conditions, fundamental reform of the Social Security system requires political will. The conditions that have led to this political will in the past and produced the 1935 Social Security law and the

1965 Medicare law have featured Democratic presidents with a strong legislative agenda facing Congresses with large Democratic majorities. In particular, President Franklin D. Roosevelt's strong victory in the congressional elections of 1934 paved the way for legislation in 1935.[1] President Lyndon Johnson scored a landslide victory in 1964 that he translated into the legislative gains of 1965.[2] But other political patterns have also produced major changes in Social Security. Disability insurance and the cost of living adjustments were the products of a Republican president and a Democratic Congress. Indeed, the one pattern that has not led to major legislation is the present one: a Democratic president and a Republican Congress. The Republican 80th Congress—the one that launched President Harry Truman on the way to his 1948 victory by, in Truman's view, doing nothing—managed to make only some minor adjustments to the program, nearly all of which had the effect of decreasing the program's size.[3]

This sort of broad-based historical comparison advances the discussion only a little. The historian has to do more than simply read the past into the present; analogies need to be probed for their accuracy and relevance.[4] The 106th Congress, for example, is not likely to follow the pattern of Truman's 80th Congress. The current Congress faces a Social Security program that is significantly different from the one that existed in 1947, and this Republican Congress does not have the burden of overcoming the effects of Franklin Roosevelt's four terms.

Forgotten Aspects of the 1935 Law

Change every bit as much as continuity characterizes Social Security's history. To underscore that point one has only to compare the 1935 law and today's program. Much about the circumstances that produced this law has faded from public memory.

The Social Security Act of 1935, an omnibus piece of legislation that included many different types of social welfare programs, emphasized values different from those that later generations would come to associate with Social Security. For example, the original legislation placed a heavy emphasis on state, rather than federal, action. The programs within the legislation that attracted the most attention and gained the most congressional support contained means tests. The social insurance programs, unemployment compensation and old-age insurance, were the least popular parts of the program and came the closest to being rejected by Congress. Coverage under these programs was far from universal, and the notion of self-financing the old-age insurance program, without contributions from general revenues, found few proponents among those who designed the legislation. Of course, such highly touted values of the modern program as protecting benefits against inflation were not even on the conceptual map in the deflation-ridden 1930s.

By way of contrast, state control of social policy formed a major motif of the rhetoric associated with the creation and passage of the Social Security Act. The four people who played the most important roles in the creation of the Social Security Act—President Franklin Roosevelt, Labor Secretary Frances Perkins, Committee of Economic Security staff director and University of Wisconsin professor Edwin Witte, and Assistant Secretary of Labor Arthur Altmeyer—all got their starts in state government. They were reluctant to disturb the tradition of local primacy over social policy. In a June 8, 1934, statement on economic security, President Roosevelt emphasized "a maximum of cooperation between states and the federal government." The report of the Committee on Economic Security, chaired by Perkins and written by Witte and Altmeyer, preceded congressional introduction of the legislation and contemplated the return of "primary responsibility for the care of people who cannot work to the State and local governments."[5] The report also suggested that there be considerable variation in the design of unemployment compensation programs so that the states could act, in Supreme Court Justice Louis Brandeis's phrase, as the laboratories of reform. The planners hoped to learn "through demonstration what is best."[6]

The Social Security Act allowed two exceptions to the expectation that general relief for the poor, as contrasted with such activities as social insurance, public health, or vocational rehabilitation, would remain the permanent financial responsibility of the states and localities. One concerned the very young, and the other involved the very old. For the very young, the act included a program of grants to the states for the continuation of what the states had called widows' pensions and what the new act labeled "Aid to Dependent Children." For the very old, the act contained the old-age assistance program that consisted of grants to the states for the continuation and extension of what the states had called old-age pensions. Each of these programs featured means tests, since everyone anticipated that they would pay benefits only to people in financial need. As a result, the Social Security Act, remembered for the start of a program in which means tests were anathema, included welfare, with its attendant means tests.

The presence of welfare programs in an act devoted to social insurance reflected institutional continuity and the politics of the depression. Twenty-eight states already ran old-age pension programs in 1935, and in the session immediately prior to the one that produced Social Security, Congress had spent time on a bill that would have provided partial federal funding for these state-run programs. As a consequence, Congress took a proprietary interest in federal aid for state old-age pension programs and included this in the Social Security bill. In a similar sense, most of the states had widows' pension laws, and a federal agency—the Children's Bureau—maintained a vested interest in preserving and improving these laws. Aid to Dependent Children was, in any event, a minor portion of the Social Security Act and constituted a small percentage of the nation's social welfare expenditures.

In comparison, old-age assistance lay at the heart of Social Security politics in 1935. Its inclusion in the Social Security Act stemmed from the realization that old-age insurance, with its contributory features, offered little or no help to people already old. In the depressed labor market of the 1930s, the need for immediate monetary grants appeared urgent, particularly since the Townsend Movement publicized the plight of the elderly in hard times.

The fact of the matter was that members of Congress found voting for old-age assistance easier than voting for old-age insurance. In general, the Social Security Act offered two sorts of programs. The social insurance programs featured payroll taxes, always unpopular with employers, and required long start-up periods before they could gather enough funds to pay benefits. The rest of the programs in the Social Security Act fell into the category of federal grants-in-aid, which meant that they offered fiscal relief to the states, almost always a popular cause, for such purposes as the provision of public health services or the payment of Aid to Dependent Children or old-age assistance. Such programs could begin almost as soon as the money started to flow. Not surprisingly, then, members of Congress praised the grant-in-aid programs or complained that they were not lavish enough.

The social insurance programs met with a much less cordial reception. In a typical bit of congressional rhetoric, Congressman Daniel Reed, a conservative Republican from New York, argued that both old-age insurance and unemployment compensation should be eliminated from the bill. "They are not relief programs, and they are not going to bring any relief to the destitute or needy now nor for years to come," he said.[7]

No wonder, then, that the creators of old-age insurance sweated through the passage of the bill. "The gossip I have been receiving . . . has suggested the elimination of all of the provisions of the Security Bill touching insurance, . . . both the unemployment compensation payroll tax and the old age insurance scheme and the retaining of only the subsidy provisions of the Security Omnibus bill," wrote one of the authors of the old-age insurance plan to another in March of 1935.[8] Her correspondent replied that, "As for the prospects for the bill as a

whole I regret to say that chances look rather slight. . . . [T]he Congressmen . . . feel a little wonder at why they go ahead when the date for beginning
of taxes is set for 1937 and payments begin only in 1942."[9]

Although most members of Congress agreed with Daniel Reed and would
gladly have jettisoned what we now regard as Social Security from the Social
Security Act, the managers of the bill managed to keep its titles together and to
make the legislation, in effect, an all-or-nothing deal. To get old-age assistance—the welfare program—they tolerated the presence of old-age insurance. And their tolerance was the result of heavy pressure from the White
House, calling in its chits in the wake of its impressive victory in the 1934
elections.

Whatever the political situation in 1935, the congressional reaction under-
scored the difficulties of starting an old-age insurance program without an
initial government subsidy. The system needed to mature before it could pay
adequate benefits, yet, as it matured, it faced criticism from people who
compared it to a noncontributory system and found it wanting. In this manner,
the politics of transition cut in the opposite direction from the way it would
later. In 1935 erecting an old-age insurance program involved substantial
costs, such as payroll taxes with no immediate returns. Once the system was in
place, however, the situation was reversed. Disassembling the system became
a costly venture, since benefits needed to be assured to present beneficiaries
and to those on the verge of receiving benefits. Hence, the residual costs of the
old system had to be included in whatever new system was being proposed, an
important factor in making liberal versions of privatization plans, ones that
continued benefits for present beneficiaries, less politically attractive than they
might otherwise have been.[10] Put another way, history teaches that change of a
fundamental sort—whether moving from a private to a public or a public to a
private system—involves costs that require extraordinary circumstances to
overcome. It is therefore prudent to bet against fundamental change.

Despite the barriers to fundamental reform, people care deeply about Social
Security because so many people participate in the program. More than ninety-
five percent of people over 65 either receive benefits or will do so as soon as
they retire or reach age seventy. In the future, this percentage should rise, rather
than fall.[11] Hence, changes in the program affect nearly everyone. We need to
bear in mind, however, that the nearly universal coverage achieved by Social
Security represents a post-1935 development.

Designed as a piece of labor legislation rather than a form of general relief,
old-age insurance originally applied to wage and salary workers who were on
a payroll. It did not cover those who were their own bosses, such as farmers,
tenant farmers, owners of a small business, or independent contractors, such as

domestic workers. As a result, the program covered less than half the labor force. Historians, who, as often as not, have been critics of the program, would later interpret these omissions as signs of racial discrimination in the legislation. To exclude domestic workers and tenant farmers, after all, was to exclude a significant percentage of the African American population in an era where the vast majority of this population still lived in the South. In my opinion, the initial gaps in coverage reflected indifference on the part of such groups as farmers as much as racial discrimination.[12] In this spirit Representative Robert Doughton (D-N.C.) told Social Security administrator Arthur Altmeyer in 1939, "Doctor, when the first farmer with manure on his shoes comes to me and asks to be covered, I will be willing to consider it."[13] As the quotation from Doughton implies, the "universal" coverage much praised by Social Security advocates did not come about until the 1950s and only then after a painful series of adjustments to make Social Security benefits more adequate.

The Slow Triumph of Social Security

Limited coverage in the old-age insurance program only exacerbated the problem of competing with old-age assistance. Old-age assistance held the potential to reach all the elderly who were poor, depending on how individual states decided to administer the program. Between 1935 and 1950 some states, such as Louisiana and Colorado, proceeded to interpret "need" in a very liberal manner; as a result old-age assistance reached a high percentage of the elderly in those states. Over the objections of the Social Security Board, the states blurred the distinction between a program based on need and one that awarded benefits as an earned right.[14]

If the coverage restrictions were not enough to cripple old-age insurance, there was also President Roosevelt's insistence that the program be self-financed. The designers of old-age insurance looked upon the financing of benefits for the elderly as a delicate balancing act. If the nation relied upon general revenues to pay for noncontributory pensions, the committee estimated the cost to the federal government would be $1.3 billion by 1980.[15] The high cost reflected depression-era pessimism that bad economic conditions would continue. Since the planners regarded this cost as prohibitive, they recommended that a contributory program be started at the same time. While this would reduce future expenditures from general revenues, it would also lead to its own sorts of problems. In particular, payroll taxes would steadily increase as the percentage of elderly eligible for contributory pensions increased. Pessimism about the future made the problem appear particularly stark. It caused planners to believe that the birthrate would never recover from the low levels of the 1930s, which meant that for many years the elderly would form a relatively high percentage of the population, increasing the pressure on workers from the lower birthrate cohorts to fund the system. To ease the problem, the planners recommended gradually rising tax rates and, once the principle of contributory pensions had become established, a contribution from the federal government in the form of general revenues. As long as income from contributions and interest on the accumulated reserves exceeded payments, no federal subsidy would be necessary, but the planners believed that such a subsidy would be required by the middle of the 1960s. When Franklin Roosevelt learned of this subsidy, he ordered the planners to rework the tax rates, making the rates even higher than originally contemplated, thereby increasing the size of the reserve necessary to fund the program in the future and compounding the program's political dilemmas.

Long-term financing of the program would again become a problem in the 1970s and under somewhat similar circumstances. As before, a decline in fertility rates following a baby boom complicated the problem of paying future benefits. The problems foreseen during the depression were eased by the arrival of postwar prosperity and the accompanying baby boom. As the members of this baby boom prepared to retire, people once again predicted grave problems that could not easily be remedied through reserve financing. In both cases, however, people's views on the severity of the long-range crises depended on how pessimistic they were about the country's long-term economic prospects. It was natural for people to carry their depression-era pessimism forward. In this spirit, Robert Ball, a noted program defender, chastised Carolyn Weaver, a noted program critic, for her lack of faith in the economy at the end of the Jimmy Carter era. "You seem to take at face value, as if given," he told Weaver, "that our immigration policies will be the same, that disability rates will rise, that fertility rates will not go above the replacement rates. . . . I tend to agree with some of those assumptions but they are by no means certain."[16] History demonstrates the strength of this truism: the future is never certain. It is therefore a temptation to accept the assumptions that bolster one's predetermined case.

The self-financing feature of the program, first proposed by Franklin Roosevelt in 1935, became another of its celebrated virtues. Before that happened, however, the program broadened the range of its benefits to include family and survivors benefits in 1939 and expanded its coverage and raised its average benefits in 1950. Only after 1950 did Social Security, as the old-age insurance program came to be known, triumph over old-age assistance. Even then the self-financing nature of the system was a value more celebrated by the congressional proprietors of the program than by program administrators or policy experts.

Along the way to the triumph of social insurance over welfare, each adjustment to the program required program administrators to determine the right mix of adequacy and equity. Although the 1939 decision to include a benefit for a recipient's spouse made economic and political sense, for example, no inherent scientific method could determine the relationship between a basic benefit and a spousal benefit. One idea, which reemerged in the modern era by way of conservative economists such as Michael Boskin, was to condition the receipt of a spouse's benefit on a means test.[17] To do so, however, violated the fundamental ideology of the old-age insurance program. To maintain the distinction between welfare and social insurance and to make benefits payable as a matter of right were central tenets of that ideology. In 1939 the government simply mandated a spouse's benefit of 50 percent based on estimates of what the system could afford and on implicit notions that married couples required more money than did single retirees—but not twice as much, since contemporary planners assumed that women could live more frugally than men. In a similar manner, a "widow's" benefit was pegged at three-quarters of a regular benefit. Each of the family benefits strained the concepts of equity and the notion of a wage-related benefit. Even with family benefits in place, the system still struggled against the coverage restrictions, which worked against husbands and wives alike, and the generally low benefit level, whatever percentage a spouse received.

Although the program's blend of adequacy and equity soon became one of its celebrated virtues, this did not exempt the program from making hard decisions that, in retrospect, were subject to criticism. In a familiar historical process, choices made in 1939 about family structure became points of criticism as circumstances changed. When married women entered the labor force as a matter of course, for example, questions were raised about awarding a spouse's benefit to a woman who had never worked outside the home or the volunteer sector of the economy. After the depression of the 1970s made program financing a central issue, points of criticism became points of vulnerability. The more the system looked to be the result of subjective judgments, the less it could be protected from change. The more Social Security could be portrayed as an anachronism, the easier it became to dismantle.

Before the triumph of social insurance over welfare, people tended to combine the two programs into one large package, and often they included unemployment compensation and the other programs in the Social Security Act in the mix. As a result, public opinion polls did not sharply distinguish between welfare and social insurance, and Congress tended to accept both types of programs.[18] In sum, it took at least fifteen years for fundamental values associated with Social Security, such as universal coverage and benefits payable as a right without a means test, to emerge as accurate descriptions of the program and as positive program characteristics. Nor could it be said that the nation "chose" social insurance as its fundamental approach to social welfare policy in 1935. It would be more accurate to say that the United States grew into social insurance.

Forgotten Alternatives of 1935

Historians assess the consequences of what happened but also of what did not happen. In the case of Social Security, there are any number of forgotten alternatives that, had they been adopted, would have changed the course of the nation's social policy. One needs to be cautious in thinking of these matters because there is no way to determine just how close they came to being implemented. As Frances Perkins remarked about the notion of linking unemployment benefits with the provision of a job, President Roosevelt favored it because "it sounded so good." She noted, however, that Edwin Witte, who was in charge of writing the Social Security Act, realized "it was not necessarily a part of an insurance scheme and in insurance the important thing is that it should be sound and practical."[19] Whatever the reason, the employment assurance plan died, and historians and social planners would forever lament the lack of an employment guarantee in the American economy.[20] We did adopt the WPA, which brought American social welfare spending to the highest level in the world during the 1930s, but we never really extended the idea.[21] Subsequent efforts to revive it, such as the 1946 Employment Act or President Carter's Program for Better Jobs and Income, failed.[22]

If liberals objected to the omission of a jobs program from our Social Security program, conservatives could complain about the failure to pass the Clark Amendment.[23] As proposed by Senator Bennett Champ Clark (D-Mo.), the amendment would have given employees a choice between the federal old-age insurance plan and the employer's private plan, provided that the employer's plan was "not less favorable" than the federal plan. In other words, the amendment would have given employees in industries with established pension plans the chance to opt out of the Social Security system. At least one hundred large companies supported this amendment in the summer of 1935.[24] Unlike the idea of employment assurance, the Clark Amendment, with a tangible and powerful constituency behind it, came close to passage.

Social Security planners condemned the amendment for the harm it would do to Social Security. If younger and more affluent workers dropped out of the system, the cost to the system would become much greater because of the subsidies to older and less affluent workers contained within the system. In a political sense, an already vulnerable system would become that much more vulnerable. Instead of working to expand the system, unionized and other comparatively advantaged workers and employers would concentrate on the expansion of private pensions and neglect Social Security. In fact, something like that happened between 1935 and 1950. With the Clark Amendment the process might never have stopped. As it turned out, the administration mustered its political strength and defeated the Clark Amendment in conference after it had been passed by the Senate.

Even so, the deletion of the Clark Amendment took Social Security insider Edwin Witte by surprise. Exhausted by his work with the Committee on Economic Security, Witte spent the summer of 1935 on vacation in Europe. As he traveled, he heard little about the progress of the Social Security bill through Congress. Finally, after the August 14 passage of the bill, he received a wire from America. "I feared," Witte noted, "that it would be necessary to take the Clark Amendment in some form; but it is certainly much better that it has been eliminated, even if (as I am told here) there is some sort of an understanding that the Clark Amendment is to be introduced as a separate bill."[25]

Despite Witte's worries that the Clark Amendment would be reintroduced, the issue faded. In 1936, the year after the passage of the Social Security Act and the year before the system started to collect payroll taxes, supporters from the private pension industry tried once again to pass a version of the amendment. This time they met with little success. Eastman Kodak's Marion Folsom, who was regarded as an authority on social insurance in the business field, began as a supporter of the amendment in 1935 but decided in 1936 that the existence of Social Security hardly posed a threat to firms such as Kodak. "In the future," Folsom said, "the employee will accumulate part of his annuity with the insurance company and part with the government."[26] Folsom's prediction proved to be right. The compatibility of private and public pensions became another of Social Security's celebrated virtues. Indeed, public and private pensions expanded together. Employers appreciated the subsidies for low-income workers and the presence of employee contributions in the Social Security program. Still, passage of the Clark Amendment in 1935 might have changed that. Its existence showed just how fragile Social Security was in its early stages.

The Triumph of Social Security: A Summation

Despite the initial problems and missed opportunities, Social Security emerged as America's most popular and most successful social welfare program in the 1950s. By 1954, after the Republican Eisenhower administration had endorsed the program, the goal of universal, compulsory coverage in a wage-related program that paid benefits as a matter of right and blended adequacy and equity in a socially acceptable manner appeared to be well in sight.

To be sure, contradictions in the complex program abounded. For example, Social Security encouraged work by linking the entitlement to benefits to participation in the labor force. At the same time, Social Security discouraged work among the elderly by reducing the benefits for those beneficiaries still working. It gave spouses, particularly in affluent families, little extra incentive to work because their benefits were conditioned on their place within the family, not within the labor force. It also proved to be a strong force in encouraging early retirement after the addition of disability benefits in 1956 and early retirement benefits—for men—in 1961. The program emphasized the value of work but also encouraged people to retire. It was a tribute to the program's managers, many of whom remained in office from the program's founding in the summer of 1935 to the beginnings of the Eisenhower administration in 1953 (some, just below the level of political visibility in the agency, stayed even longer), that they handled the political challenges to the program and adjusted the program's internal tensions (work-retirement, adequacy-equity) so effectively.

The Politics of Medicare

Medicare represented a departure from the traditional Social Security program that was portrayed as an incremental expansion. The very success of Social Security encouraged proponents to move the program beyond its original objective of paying retirement benefits. Hence, thirty years after the passage of the Social Security Act, Medicare arrived. Despite the fact that it was a new sort of program, one that financed services provided in disparate locations across the nation, the structure of its original legislation bore a resemblance to the 1935 legislation. Medicare Part A, which paid hospital benefits, borrowed the form, if not the content, of old-age insurance; participation was compulsory and financing came from payroll taxes. Medicaid expanded the traditional welfare system. It functioned similarly to the old-age assistance program in 1935 in that it provided health insurance for those outside of the social insurance system. Medicare Part B, a separate program to pay the doctors' bills of Medicare beneficiaries, was both voluntary and financed in part by the elderly themselves; it bore a resemblance to a program of voluntary old-age annuities that was part of the original Social Security proposal but never made it through Congress. So, whether or not policymakers realized it at the time, Medicare fit a historical pattern. Without a doubt, policymakers played upon Social Security's heritage as a means of reassuring Congress and its constituents that Medicare was not "socialized medicine," something ugly and alien, but rather a desirable and straightforward extension of the trusted Social Security program. In 1961, for example, Wilbur Cohen described the Kennedy administration's Medicare proposals as demonstrating the "conservative and responsible" Social Security approach.[27]

Even with such reassurances, Medicare proved difficult to sell to Congress, in part because it was so different from the rest of Social Security. The 87th and 88th Congresses that convened in 1961 and 1963 both rejected it, despite the entreaties of Presidents Kennedy and Johnson. It took the exceptional events of 1963 and 1964—the Kennedy assassination and Johnson's landslide victory— to generate the political will necessary for the passage of Medicare. Even then, the bill bore the earmarks of four years of congressional bargaining, the direct stamp of history on our social policy. As passed, the legislation had what might be described as a permissive cast, with the government agreeing to intrude as little as possible on the practice of medicine. One section, for example, asked that the government make payments to hospitals that included "both direct and indirect costs" based on "the principles generally applied by national organizations."[28]

The contents of Medicare reflected the repeated guarantees of Social Security administrators that the government would not tell doctors how to practice medicine or hospitals how to deliver care. The 1965 legislation traded upon the fact that, although Medicare was controversial, the Social Security Administration had nonetheless built up a stock of congressional goodwill. Hence Congress felt comfortable leaving many of the details of the program to the bureaucracy. In contrast to laws passed later, therefore, Medicare contained relatively loose and imprecise language, with many of the details settled by the regulatory, rather than the legislative, process. That was in part because members of Congress wished to use ambiguity as a way of defusing political battles that might undermine consensus. But it was also because they did not feel the same need to tie the bureaucracy's hands, as they would in a later era when the executive and legislative branches were controlled by different parties. One might even say that the largely permanent Congress that made Social Security legislation trusted the largely permanent Social Security bureaucracy to implement the law in a responsible manner. As a consequence, members of Congress relied on the bureaucracy to interpret such concepts as what constituted "reasonable costs" or the "reasonable charges" that were to be paid to doctors.[29]

The bureaucrats who implemented Medicare were themselves schooled by the history of Social Security. They took their cues both from congressional instructions and from their own policy experiences. In particular, the implementation of the disability insurance program paved the way for the initiation of the Medicare program. The same people who had put disability insurance into operation after 1956 also worked on Medicare after 1965. In the disability program, for example, Social Security officials such as Arthur Hess learned to work cooperatively with doctors. Hess helped to set up a medical advisory committee, and as he noted, "it was a very reputable group of men. . . . We said to them, 'Let's forget about all this socialized medicine stuff. We've got a professional job to do. How do you do it? How can we work with the medical societies and the medical profession?'" By the time Medicare came along, Hess "knew on a first name basis some of the biggest guys in the AMA [American Medical Association] and in the state medical societies."[30] The disability insurance program therefore helped to lay the groundwork for the Medicare program. As one of Arthur Hess's colleagues later remarked, "what Art was so good at was sitting down with a bunch of doctors who hated him when he walked in the door and wound up saying, 'This guy—if that's what our government is going to be like, it might not be so bad.' Art had that facility to kind of win people over by just clearly being a reasonable sort of person."[31]

The disability program also taught Social Security administrators how to work through intermediaries. In the case of disability, these intermediaries were state-run rehabilitation offices. In the case of Medicare, these intermediaries were Blue Cross, Blue Shield, and private insurance companies that were given the responsibility for the day-to-day operations of the program. The notion of utilizing those intermediaries came up in the course of the legislative bargaining that occurred between 1961 and 1965. In June 1962, for example, Wilbur Cohen, the chief link between the Kennedy administration and the Social Security Administration and Congress, suggested to Kennedy staffer Ted Sorensen that the administration's proposal be altered to allow hospitals to designate private insurance carriers "(1) to determine the amount of payments due upon presentation of their bills for services and (2) to make such payments."[32] Essentially, that provision went into the final law, and people like Hess, guided by his previous experiences in the bureaucracy, implemented that law. The fact that the experience of working with states on disability insurance had proved successful suggested to key officials in the Social Security Administration that they could achieve similar success working with insurance companies on Medicare.

Medicare and Critiques of Medicine

Just as in 1935 when there were suggestions that, if adopted, would have changed the nature of old-age insurance, so alternatives to Medicare existed in 1965 that might have altered its permissive cast. Not everyone accepted the idea that the government should simply pay into the existing medical system on behalf of the elderly. To be sure, Medicare began in the context of a well-established and widely acclaimed system of private medical care. The situation, in other words, was quite different from that of 1935 in which old-age insurance operated against the backdrop of a private system of provision that was limited in scope and enjoyed little popular confidence. Still, critiques of the medical care system existed in 1965, but the legislative process did not permit them to be heard.

For one thing, the field of health services research, led by such individuals as Kerr White of Johns Hopkins University, was questioning the level of the quality of care, even in such technologically and scientifically advanced settings as university medical centers. Health care researchers also sought to promote what they described as "primary care" and argued that the medical schools neglected training in this area and instead brought students into contact with hospital patients who were not typical of the people the students would see in private practice. Led by White and his colleagues, a campaign to create a National Center for Health Services Research and Development that would presumably have advanced some of these ideas coincided almost exactly with the effort to pass and implement Medicare.[33]

White's campaign had little effect on the legislative proponents of Medicare, despite the fact that each side—the health service researchers and the Social Security advocates—would have expressed admiration for the basic objectives of the other. In part, this situation reflected the relative isolation of the Public Health Service and the field of public health more generally from questions related to health care financing.[34] In part, this situation stemmed from the intensely political atmosphere in which Medicare was passed. The founders of Medicare did not want to challenge the conduct of medical care so much as they wanted to assure access to that care on the part of the elderly. They accepted the structure of health care and of medical education—the very things that White and his colleagues critiqued—and proposed only to alter some of its financing arrangements. What mattered was political bargaining in order to pass the legislation. One direct consequence was that little of what might be described as health services research went into the design of Medicare. As Wilbur Cohen, the official of the Department of Health, Education, and Welfare [HEW] who was perhaps the central Kennedy and Johnson administration figure in the fight for Medicare, noted, "There was only a limited amount of experience with large-scale, nationwide, health reimbursement programs. There was a good deal of rhetoric and little empirical information. There was an extensive outpouring of ideology and a limited amount of research."[35]

For another thing, the founders of Medicare refused to give an advantage to what Paul Ellwood would later describe as health maintenance organizations (HMOs). By emphasizing preventive services and primary care, these organizations sought to lower the rate of hospital admissions and improve the quality of care and, at the same time, to reduce the cost of care. Many of the Washington-based leaders of the Medicare coalition, such as Lane Kirkland of the AFL-CIO, HEW's Cohen, and Robert Myers of the Social Security Administration, belonged to the Group Health Association of Washington, D.C. Although they received their health care from an HMO, they resisted forcing elderly Medicare recipients into "managed care," to use the expression of a subsequent decade.[36] On the contrary, the founders of Medicare wanted the elderly to enjoy the benefits of the same expansive system as did the majority of other Americans. As a consequence, they did not use the legislation as a vehicle to advance the cause of alternative forms of health care financing and delivery.

The Development of Medicare

If there were flaws in Medicare that resulted from the hasty effort to get it enacted during the short window of congressional tolerance for such ventures, many people thought these imperfections could be eliminated through regulation and subsequent legislation. Reading the history of old-age insurance into Medicare, one might even have taken an expansive view in 1965. One could have predicted that coverage would expand—perhaps to encompass different age groups in incremental strides toward national health insurance—in an analogous way to which coverage had been extended to a growing number of occupational groups under Social Security. One could foresee the triumph of Medicare over Medicaid just as old-age insurance had triumphed over old-age assistance. One might also have anticipated that the benefits would become more adequate, perhaps encompassing long-term care as well as hospital stays, in a similar manner to the way in which disability insurance had been added to old-age insurance.

In this spirit, Cohen, who had as deep an appreciation of the history of Social Security as anyone, took a first step toward Medicare's incremental expansion early in 1968: he proposed "kiddycare" to pay for prenatal and postnatal care of all mothers, as well as the costs of delivering the baby and the baby's care during the first year of life. Using the reasoning he had learned over the course of his professional career, Cohen advised that kiddycare should not be limited to the poor and that the plan's benefits should be funded through the payroll taxes to create a "contributory, earned right." It was important, he said, to give people the "psychological feeling that they have helped to pay for their protection."[37] Philip Lee, a prominent health care official in the Johnson and Clinton administrations, later commented that he and many others believed that kiddycare would become the vehicle to move national health insurance forward. "We thought by 1975 there would be national health insurance," he said.[38]

Once again reasoning by analogy failed, and the future failed to arrive on schedule. Medicare expanded in a predictable manner between 1965 and 1972, so that by the time of President Richard Nixon's second term it paid for kidney dialysis for people of all ages and covered the recipients of Social Security Disability Insurance. After that, Medicare, like the rest of the Social Security program, became enmeshed in the economic setbacks of the 1970s, and the drive toward the incremental creation of national health insurance stalled.

Dilemmas of the 1970s

Social Security suffered financing crises and a loss of political confidence during the 1970s because the system was not designed to accommodate changes in economic conditions. The problems stemmed in large measure from the fundamental revisions made to the program in 1972. The notion of a cost-of-living adjustment (COLA) that was put in place during that year, as part of the so-called automatic provisions, represented such a fundamental shift in the system that, like Medicare, it strained the concept of incremental reform. Where previously Congress had legislated benefit increases in the old-age insurance program, often spending "unanticipated" surpluses that were the result of increased revenues from rising wage levels, it decided in 1972 to abandon this ad hoc system.[39] The result was an unanticipated crisis that changed the outlook for the future of Social Security.

Oddly enough, the cost-of-living adjustments that led to tremendous expansions in benefit levels were the product of a Republican White House. In 1969 the Nixon administration produced a series of innovative reforms in social welfare policy. Almost all followed the suggestions of economists who wanted to control the growth of large entitlement programs, encourage work, and put a curb on the expansionary appetites of members of Congress in Washington and street-level bureaucrats such as social workers. In this way the administration hoped to substitute a "rational" for a "political" approach to social welfare policy and create a set of liberal but disciplined programs that had a distinctively Republican stamp.[40] The Family Assistance Plan, Nixon's proposal for the welfare reform system, attracted the most publicity, but the idea of indexing Social Security benefits to the rate of inflation fit the general pattern. In a practical sense, a cost-of-living adjustment would stop a system by which the Democrats, presumed to be the majority party far into the future, could outbid the Republicans on the level of Social Security benefits and take the credit with voters.

In September 1969, the White House announced that Social Security recipients should not bear the brunt of inflation. "The way to prevent future unfairness," the Nixon White House stated, "is to attach the benefit schedule to the cost of living." White House counselor and noted economist Arthur Burns explained that "the President expects that we can now proceed more rationally in . . . Social Security legislation in the future, rather than wait for an election year and have the two parties compete and have individual Congressmen compete. So the automatic adjustment should make for more rational revision of Social Security legislation in the future." At the same briefing, Social Security Commissioner Robert Ball noted that introducing a cost-of-living adjustment into the program did not require any increase in taxes. It was simply a matter of adjusting the taxable wage base. As long as the wage base went up to reflect increases in average wages, then the system would be sound because, "over the years wages go up more than the cost of living goes up."[41]

It took nearly three years for Congress to accept President Nixon's suggestion. The delay reflected Congress's preference for the old system in which it gained direct credit for benefit increases, and was tied to presidential politics leading up to the 1972 election. In 1972, however, Wilbur Mills (D-Ark.), the chairman of the Ways and Means Committee and himself a candidate for president, engineered a spectacular 20 percent increase in benefit levels, accompanied by a change to the new system in which future benefit increases would be related to increases in the cost of living as defined by the Consumer Price Index. Robert Ball, nearing the end of his tenure as Social Security Commissioner, pronounced himself pleased with the changes. When combined with the benefit increases beginning in 1968, he wrote, the changes "have so greatly improved the program that it seems to me quite proper to speak of 'Our New Social Security Program.'"[42] Leaving office in 1973, Ball turned his attention toward what he regarded as the next logical step: national health insurance. The cash side of the program no longer demanded such close attention. Early in 1974, for example, Ball, now ensconced as a visiting fellow at the National Academy of Science's Institute of Medicine, told a correspondent that he was content with the financing of Social Security benefits: "We have a program which is now going to be kept automatically up to date . . . with the cost of living and the present contribution rates in the law are approximately sufficient to maintain the cash program on into the next century."[43] The system appeared to be working, and Social Security looked to be headed on its usual incremental course.

Things deteriorated quickly after that. By the summer of 1974 the trustees of the Social Security Trust Funds had revised their estimates about Social Security financing in a downward direction. The actuaries adopted a lower birthrate that had the effect of increasing the estimated ratio of retirees to workers in the next century. In addition, the actuaries changed their assumptions related to inflation, predicting a higher inflation rate in the near future, and altered their tables to reflect a higher incidence of disability among the working-age population.[44] Each of these things spelled trouble for Social Security financing. At base, the actuaries were predicting a slower rate of economic growth than they had previously. A staff member on President Gerald Ford's Domestic Council explained to the president that, "If the increase in real wages, the difference between the nominal wage increases and the inflation rate, is below expectations, then the cost of the system as a percentage of taxable payroll will be higher than expected." Furthermore, the staff member was pessimistic about ever again obtaining the levels of real growth that characterized the 1950s and 1960s. In a society that attempted to internalize environmental costs, increase the level of safety for workers, and compensate for an increase in the cost of raw materials such as oil, "we must realistically expect to see lower growth rates in real output than we have experienced in the last 25 years."[45] In 1977 Social Security actuary Haeworth Robertson, who would go on to become a prominent program critic, noted that the situation still had not improved. "Factors such as declining birthrates, improving mortality rates, double-digit inflation, high unemployment, and the fact that we have experienced approximately zero net gain in real covered wages since 1971 have had (appropriately in my opinion) a significant impact on the way we view the future," he told Robert Ball.[46] Or, as Arthur Burns's staff members told him in 1977, "the excess of social security benefit payments over receipts that began in 1975 is expected to continue without interruption during the remainder of this century. Funds are expected to run out in 1981."[47]

High inflation, lagging productivity, and high unemployment created financing problems for the program in the short run; predictions of slow growth rates and low fertility rates made the already difficult problem of funding the retirement of the baby boom that much worse. Furthermore, the problems were linked. Short-term crises led to a loss of confidence in the system's ability to overcome its long-term problems.

After 1972, presidential administrations faced difficult choices on Social Security. Gerald Ford, who presided over the first cost-of-living adjustment in 1975, suggested that no COLAs be paid over 5 percent, regardless of the changes in the cost-of-living index. He worried that rising Social Security benefits would only serve to fuel inflation (the reverse of the fear that Social Security taxes would fuel deflation in the 1930s).[48] In 1979, Stuart Eizenstat, President Carter's domestic adviser, received a memo from Robert Ball, the veteran Social Security policymaker, in which Ball advised him that under current economic conditions the amounts needed to keep Social Security solvent "are so large that there is no way to deal with the problem by a series of minor adjustments."[49] A new law would be needed, even though President Carter had already signed a law in 1977 that raised tax rates and was expected to keep the program solvent into the foreseeable future. Eventually, a law was passed in 1983 that put the system on solid financial footing, but the damage had been done. A program once considered beyond controversy—people had long since forgotten the controversies of the 1930s—had shown a financial vulnerability that made people uneasy.

Toward the Present

In retrospect, we can see that the 1970s were a watershed in American history, just as the 1930s had been. In the 1930s people reacted to the adverse consequences of deflation and looked to the government to stimulate the economy through public expenditures. In the 1970s people worried about the ill effects of inflation and sought ways of decreasing government expenditures. It was not surprising, therefore, that government spending programs were initiated in the New Deal. During the 1950s and 1960s, favorable economic conditions led to the expansion of those programs, such as Social Security, that survived the depression. Once considered part of the solution, these programs became perceived as part of the problem in the inflation-ridden 1970s, as Americans sought ways to control the growth of entitlements.

If Social Security was a problem, then it made sense to consider alternatives. Ideas such as those of Ronald Reagan about privatizing Social Security slowly gained respectability in the 1970s and 1980s. During the 1990s, the economic boom, combined with an ideological climate much changed since the days of LBJ and the advance of the baby boom cohort into middle age, brought this notion from the conservative fringes to the edge of the mainstream. When

Ronald Reagan first suggested that Social Security funds be invested in the stock market, for example, Republican politicians, such as his rival Gerald Ford, ridiculed him for it. In time even some of Social Security's staunchest defenders adopted the idea. In 1964 Reagan asked, in an unconscious imitation of the Clark Amendment, "can we introduce voluntary features that would permit a citizen to do better on his own, to be excused upon presentation of evidence that he had made provisions for the non-earning years?"[50] By asking that question, Reagan exposed himself to political difficulties that lasted for the next twenty years. In the 1990s it became eminently respectable for a politician to ask such a question.

Conclusion

Policymakers have a selective historical memory. They choose to highlight those aspects of the past most congenial to their political preferences. Policymakers in Social Security's expansive era chose to ignore Social Security's initial failures. They offered the Social Security Act as proof of the popularity of social insurance when, in fact, the social insurance provisions of the act were its most unpopular features. An omnibus law, the Social Security Act did not provide a referendum on the popularity of wage-related, contributory social insurance with benefits payable as a right. Perhaps that referendum took place in 1950 or 1952 or 1954, but the laws passed in those years failed to make much of an impression on the public imagination. Policymakers in more recent years, highlighting their visions of future doom with the retirement of the baby boom generation, chose to ignore Social Security's considerable success in the period between 1950 and 1972. Never before had such a successful vehicle for reducing poverty among the elderly or maintaining the income of people with disabilities been created. The fact that the system encountered so many initial problems made its ultimate success all the more remarkable. The economic problems of the 1970s tended to blot out that success, in part because policymakers with vested interests in dismantling the system played upon the financial insecurities of baby boomers, who were old enough to be concerned about their future but young enough not to remember Social Security's initial travails and ultimate triumphs.

What stands out is that so often in Social Security's history policymakers have been wrong about future developments. Contrary to expectations, the depression and the problems it posed for starting up Social Security did not become a permanent condition of American life. Prosperity raised fertility rates, wage levels, and employment rates, all of which changed the outlook for Social Security.

Once in an era of prosperity, some policymakers thought it would go on forever. Such expectations bred a series of expectations. Policymakers made the implicit assumption that Medicare, begun as a limited program for retirees, would expand into a comprehensive health insurance program for people of all ages. In the expansive new era, policymakers believed, Social Security benefits would continue to rise and beneficiaries would receive protection against inflation. In the 1970s the conventional wisdom changed again. Stagflation, with its price increases driving up benefit levels beyond the system's means and with its high unemployment contributing to a more or less permanent baby bust and decreasing system revenues, made planning for the retirement of the baby boom a task so formidable as to lead to suggestions for a major system overhaul. But the return of prosperity, although it has legitimized proposals to invest Social Security funds in the stock market, has also diminished the urgency of the problem and caused Congress to approach Social Security reform very gingerly.

At the risk of oversimplifying, one might synthesize this historical narrative into a series of short observations. Policymakers tend to incorporate their understanding of the past into the policies they create. As they do so, they hope to influence the future. Hence, many Social Security advocates had trouble accepting the dire economic predictions of the 1970s. As Robert Ball put it in 1974, "the trustees are getting everyone pretty excited about [something that] may be only a possibility rather than a probability."[51] Some twelve years later his colleague Wilbur Cohen noted, "I part company with those who take a pessimistic view of the future of the American economy. . . . It seems to me that these nay-sayers lack a historical imagination. . . . Periods of expansion and periods of recession alternate, but the general trend has been upward."[52]

Even the most gifted policymakers, however, have difficulty seeing around corners. Points of discontinuity cause policies to develop in unexpected ways. Fundamental reform of social welfare policy comes only rarely because of the difficulties of generating the political will necessary to make the change. As a consequence, we tend to live with past policies that have been modified in response to unexpected contingencies. Often the reasons for the modifications become obscured with the passage of time. It falls to historians, therefore, to explain how the past solutions have become today's problems and to warn policymakers, in Social Security and other fields as well, of the differences between expectations and outcomes that have characterized our past and, quite likely, our future as well.

Notes

1. In the 1934 elections, the Democrats gained nine seats in the House and nine in the Senate, augmenting the large majorities the party had obtained in the 1932 election. The best source that describes the passage of the 1935 Act is Edwin Witte, *The Development of the Social Security Act* (University of Wisconsin Press, 1963).

2. On a straight party basis (ignoring the presence of conservative southern Democrats), President Johnson enjoyed a majority of 155 seats in the House and 36 seats in the Senate in 1965. For a view of LBJ's legislative mastery see Robert Dallek, *Flawed Giant: Lyndon Johnson and His Times, 1961–1973* (Oxford University Press, 1968). A good source on changes in the political composition of Congress is Michael Barone, *Our Country: The Shaping of America from Roosevelt to Reagan* (Free Press, 1990).

3. See Arthur J. Altmeyer, *The Formative Years of Social Security* (University of Wisconsin Press, 1968), pp. 152–68.

4. Richard Neustadt and Ernest May, *Thinking in Time: A Guide for Decision Makers* (Free Press, 1988).

5. *Report of the Committee on Economic Security* (Government Printing Office, 1935), p. 7; President Roosevelt's statement and other basic documents related to the Social Security Act are contained in *50th Anniversary Edition: The Report of the Committee on Economic Security of 1935* (Washington, D.C.: National Conference on Social Welfare, 1985).

6. *Report of the Committee on Economic Security*, p. 5.

7. Representative Daniel Reed (R-N.Y.) in the *Congressional Record*, 74 Cong. 1 sess., 1935, p. 5990.

8. Barbara Armstrong to Murray Latimer, March 15, 1935, Murray Latimer Papers, George Washington University, Washington, D.C.

9. Murray Latimer to Barbara Armstrong, March 23, 1935, Murray Latimer Papers.

10. On this point see Edward M. Gramlich, "How Does Social Security Affect the Economy?" and Robert M. Ball and Thomas N. Bethell, "Bridging the Centuries: The Case for Traditional Social Security," in Eric Kingson and James Schulz, eds., *Social Security in the 21st Century* (Oxford University Press, 1997), pp. 147–55, 259–94.

11. Ball and Bethell, "Bridging the Centuries," p. 259.

12. For a historical discussion of the relationship between Social Security coverage and race see Robert C. Lieberman, *Shifting the Color Line: Race and the American Welfare State* (Harvard University Press, 1998).

13. Altmeyer, *The Formative Years*, p. 103.

14. See Blanche D. Coll, *Safety Net: Welfare and Social Security, 1929–1979* (Rutgers University Press, 1995).

15. *Report of the Committee on Economic Security*, p. 28.

16. Robert Ball to Carolyn Weaver, July 30, 1980, Robert Ball Papers, National Academy of Social Insurance, Washington, D.C.

17. Michael J. Boskin, *Too Many Promises: The Uncertain Future of Social Security—A Twentieth Century Fund Report* (Homewood, Ill.: Dow Jones-Irwin, 1986).

18. Virginia P. Reno and Robert B. Friedland, "Strong Support but Low Confidence: What Explains the Contradiction," in Kingson and Schulz, eds., *Social Security in the 21st Century*, p. 179.

19. Frances Perkins's "Foreword" to Edwin Witte, *The Development of the Social Security Act*, p. vii.

20. See, for example, Linda Gordon, *Pitied but Not Entitled: Single Mothers and the History of Welfare* (Free Press, 1994).

21. Edwin Amenta, *Bold Relief: Institutional Politics and the Origins of Modern American Social Policy* (Princeton University Press, 1998).

22. Margaret Weir, *Politics and Jobs: The Boundaries of Employment Policy in the United States* (Princeton University Press, 1992).

23. Carolyn L. Weaver, *The Crisis in Social Security* (Duke University Press, 1982).

24. "Companies Known to Favor Clark Amendment to Social Security Act," Dr. Rainhard B. Robbins, "Confidential Material Collected on Social Security Act and Clark Amendment," July 11, 1935, Murray Latimer Papers.

25. Witte to Latimer, August 11, 1935, Murray Latimer Papers.

26. Marion Folsom to Rainhard B. Robbins, December 18, 1935, Murray Latimer Papers.

27. Wilbur J. Cohen to editor, *Milwaukee Journal*, March 3, 1961, Box 74, Wilbur Cohen Papers, Wisconsin State Historical Society, Madison, Wisconsin. For more on Cohen and his role in the passage of Medicare see Edward D. Berkowitz, *Mr. Social Security: The Life of Wilbur J. Cohen* (University Press of Kansas, 1995).

28. Quoted in Herman Miles Somers and Anne Ramsay Somers, *Medicare and the Hospitals: Issues and Prospects* (Washington, D.C.: Brookings, 1967), p. 138.

29. See Somers and Somers, *Medicare and the Hospitals*, p. 36, and Marilyn Moon, *Medicare Now and in the Future* (Washington, D.C.: Urban Institute Press, 1993).

30. Interview with Arthur Hess in Charlottesville, Virginia, July 8, 1996, conducted by Edward Berkowitz, Health Care Financing Administration (HFCA) Oral Interview Collection, Baltimore, Maryland. These interviews are available at the HCFA library or on the web at the Social Security history website.

31. Interview with Paul Rettig in Washington, D.C., August 14, 1995, conducted by Edward Berkowitz, p. 10, HCFA Oral Interview Collection, Baltimore, Maryland.

32. Wilbur Cohen, June 8, 1962, "Health Insurance Benefits—Use of Blue Cross and Other Private Organizations to Facilitate Payments to Hospitals and Other Providers," Theodore Sorensen Papers, Box 36, Subject Files 1961–64, Medical Care for the Aged, 6/2/62–6/13/63, John F. Kennedy Library, Boston, Massachusetts.

33. Interview with Kerr White, March 12, 1998, Charlottesville, Virginia, conducted by Edward Berkowitz as part of a series of interviews for the National Library of Medicine on the development of Health Services Research.

34. A fact noted by historian John Parascandola on pages 491–92 of his entry on the Public Health Service that appeared in George Thomas Kurian, ed., *A Historical Guide to the U.S. Government* (Oxford University Press, 1998).

35. Wilbur Cohen, "Reflections on the Enactment of Medicare and Medicaid," *Health Care Financing Review,* 1983 Annual Supplement, p. 3.

36. See Edward Berkowitz and Wendy Wolff, "The Origins and Consequences of Medicare," in Jonathan D. Moreno, ed., *Paying the Doctor: Health Policy and Physician Reimbursement* (New York: Auburn House, 1991), pp. 143–56.

37. Cohen to Joseph Califano, January 19, 1968, Box 95, Wilbur Cohen Papers.

38. Interview with Philip Lee, November 27, 1995, Washington, D.C., conducted by Edward Berkowitz as part of a series of interviews on the history of health care financing, HCFA Oral Interview Collection, Baltimore, Maryland. These interviews are available at the HCFA library or on the web at the Social Security history website.

39. On the adoption of cost-of-living adjustments, see Martha Derthick, *Policymaking for Social Security* (Washington, D.C.: Brookings Institution, 1979); R. Kent Weaver, *Automatic Government: The Politics of Indexation* (Washington, D.C.: Brookings Institution, 1988); and Julian Zelizer, *Taxing America: Wilbur D. Mills, Congress, and the States* (New York: Cambridge University Press, 1999).

40. On the liberal side of Nixon's domestic policy see Joan Hoff, *Nixon Reconsidered* (Basic Books, 1994).

41. White House press release and transcript of press briefing, September 25, 1969, Arthur Burns Papers, Box A20, Gerald Ford Library, Ann Arbor, Michigan.

42. Robert M. Ball, *Social Security: Today and Tomorrow* (Columbia University Press, 1978), p. 18.

43. Robert Ball to Wendell Coltin, February 12, 1974, Robert Ball Papers.

44. "Briefing Notes for James B. Cardwell," June 4, 1974, Pamela Needham Files, Box 3, Gerald Ford Library.

45. Robert S. Kaplan and Roman L. Weill, "Executive Summary of an Actuarial Audit of the Social Security System," September 1974, in Pamela Needham Files, Box 3, Gerald Ford Library.

46. Haeworth Robertson to Robert Ball, April 6, 1977, Robert Ball Papers.

47. Helmut Wendel, Jim Fralick, Josh Greene, and Mary Stevens to Chairman Burns, June 6, 1977, Arthur Burns Papers, Box B-96.

48. W. Andrew Achenbaum, *Social Security: Visions and Revisions* (Cambridge University Press, 1986), p. 65.

49. Robert Ball to Stuart Eizenstat, November 15, 1979, Stuart Eizenstat Papers, Box 277, Jimmy Carter Library, Atlanta, Georgia.

50. On Reagan's Social Security positions in his prepresidential years, see the article in the *Los Angeles Times*, January 25, 1965, which is collected, along with other materials on Reagan, in "Social Security Fact Sheet," no date but clearly 1980, in Stuart Eizenstat Papers, Box 277.

51. Robert Ball to Kermit Gordon, August 19, 1974, Robert Ball Papers.

52. Wilbur J. Cohen, "Social Security in 1995: The Future as a Reflection of the Past," in Edward Berkowitz, ed., *Social Security after Fifty: Successes and Failures* (Greenwood Press, 1987), pp. 150–51.

Comment by Robert M. Ball

Old Arguments and New

I am very glad the organizers of this conference included a session on history. I love to study the early days of our social insurance system. I find it interesting to see how persistent the problems of such a system turned out to be and what the founding mothers and fathers of the system proposed for dealing with the problems. I am amazed at how much they anticipated. And I am grateful to Ed Berkowitz for doing such a good job in analyzing the past and the relevance of old arguments to arguments today.

There is one point he makes, though, that I would give a different emphasis to. It is true, as Berkowitz says in his opening piece of this chapter: "In sum, it took at least fifteen years for fundamental values associated with Social Security, such as universal coverage and benefits payable as a right without a means test, to emerge as accurate descriptions of the program and as positive program characteristics."

But I would not want Ed's words to be interpreted to mean that the founding mothers and fathers themselves were unclear about program principles or the program's positive characteristics. They knew what the principles of social insurance were and why they preferred a system for the long run based on them rather than the more immediately effective means-tested old-age assistance programs. When the system started few others than the mothers and fathers themselves and the representatives of labor and employers who had been on advisory groups understood what the program was all about. However, the mothers and fathers and their supporters were confident that the public and politicians would come in time to support the principles in which they devoutly believed. Roosevelt from the beginning had a vision of an insurance policy issued at birth to cover the major risks of life from the "cradle to the grave." (He resented that later this phrase was attributed popularly to Lord Beveridge rather than to him!)[1] Of the nine major principles identified today with the current Old Age Survivors and Disability Insurance program—universal, earned right, wage-related, contributory and self-financed, redistributive, not means-tested, wage-indexed, inflation-protected, and compulsory (see appendix)—all applied to the Old-Age Benefits Program in 1935, subsequent amendments, and the program as it is today. The fact that during a transition period reliance on means testing, for example, in separate federal and state programs was supported by the founding mothers and fathers did not indicate any confusion about the nature of social insurance. The United States did not so much "grow into social insurance," as Berkowitz noted, as it had to decide whether the program based on clear principles from the beginning should be kept.

In 1947–48, as staff director of an advisory council to the Senate Finance Committee, I worried a lot about whether Congress might not drop the whole thing because it was so ineffective, with only about 20 percent of the elderly eligible for benefits and the benefits averaging only about $25 a month, much less than Old-Age Assistance was paying. I think that the council and the Social Security Administration saved the program at that time by recommending the extensions of coverage, the increase in benefits, and the liberalization of eligibility requirements in the 1950 amendments. But the principles of social insurance were always clear; they were not being invented. The issue was whether the country was to keep a program with such principles or reject it in the late 1940s as being ineffective. The case for flat payments out of general revenues, which would be immediately effective, was pressed from many quarters from the Townsend plan on, and the double-decker idea was quite popular.

But in this discussion it seems more important to me to address one of the nine principles enumerated in the appendix about which there was disagreement then and now, rather than to focus on what may be a nuance of emphasis between Ed Berkowitz and me.

A totally self-financed system was not a universal Social Security principle in 1935 and this fact is recognized by reference to different principles in some foreign systems in the summary of principles listed in the appendix. Self-financing has been a practice in the United States but certainly not a "principle of Social Security." In 1935 when the staff-prepared proposal on old-age benefits was about to go to Capitol Hill (Roosevelt had announced that it would be transmitted the next day), the president stopped it and sent it back for a rewrite. In so doing he highlighted differences of view on the use of general revenues for Social Security that will probably surface again in the developing debate over President Bill Clinton's current Social Security proposals.

In recommending an eventual government contribution, the Committee on Economic Security's three-member staff on old-age benefits thought they had the answer to a basic dilemma that arose in getting the insurance system started. The staff members on old age (certainly influential among the founding mothers and fathers) were Barbara Nachtreib Armstrong, the leader of the group, professor of law at the University of California; Doug Brown, director of the Industrial Relations Section at Princeton; and Murray Latimer, an expert on industrial pension plans and the first chairman of the Railroad Retirement Board. They knew that for this program to be acceptable, it would have to pay

benefits in the first generation that would exceed what the first generation of
workers and their employers paid in.

The problem was that most workers were already well advanced in their
careers. There were middle-aged workers and older workers to whom benefits
would need to be paid but who did not have a full career remaining over which
their contributions could be accumulated. To give them only what their
contributions could have paid for would have meant a very unsatisfactory
benefit level for all but the very young and a long postponement of any
contribution old-age insurance might make to the problem of old-age security.
Few would have voted for such a proposal.

So the plan paid much higher benefits to the first generation of Social
Security recipients than their contributions justified. In doing so the staff
recognized that they were creating a permanent accrued liability for the system,
and that concerned them. They feared that those starting to pay in the 1960s and
beyond would complain about not getting their "money's worth" if the full cost
of the earlier liability was to be paid from earmarked Social Security contributions, the payroll tax. Doug Brown described their reasoning in a 1972 book,
An American Philosophy of Social Security:

> The staff members of the Committee on Economic Security responsible
> for the planning of the old age insurance system were convinced that
> eventual government contributions would be necessary. To provide a
> reasonable level of benefits for those retiring in the early years of the
> system would require paying more in benefits to the retired worker than
> the worker and his employer had contributed. The difference, drawn from
> the contributions of younger workers, would need to be reimbursed to the
> system as these younger workers became old. . . . In private insurance
> terms, the system assumed an accrued liability in paying adequate ben-
> efits to those retiring in the early years of the system. . . . It was the
> conviction of the staff that the accrued liability within the system was a
> proper charge upon the government. Millions of aged workers who would
> otherwise require needs-test old age pensions, entirely financed by the
> state and federal governments, would be receiving benefits instead from
> the contributory social insurance system. It seemed entirely reasonable to
> ask the government to reimburse the system the amount it would save
> through reduced old age assistance payments.[2]

The staff suggested that the government contribution should be paid when
it was needed and not before and estimated that under their approach the first
government contributions would begin in 1962.

The chair of the Committee on Economic Security, Secretary of Labor Frances Perkins, and the executive director, Edwin Witte (along with then-assistant secretary of labor Arthur J. Altmeyer, the other important members of the founding mothers and fathers group), went along with this reasoning, but Perkins and Witte were not nearly as interested in the old-age provision as they were in unemployment insurance. At the last minute Roosevelt intervened, probably at the instigation of Secretary of the Treasury Henry Morgenthau, and said "no," the program should be completely self-financed in the sense that the earmarked contributions had to cover the whole cost down the road—not just at the beginning. Roosevelt wanted to avoid any burden on the general treasury. The only way he would let the staff plan go forward was to say that this was just one approach. Later the administration submitted a plan without general revenue, and this is how the bill passed.[3]

But those concerned about the payroll taxes going "too high" and the program becoming unpopular unless there was some general revenue to meet the cost of the accrued liability did not give up. Doug Brown chaired the advisory council in 1937–38 and was a member of the 1947-48 council, and many others after that. He never changed his mind and kept pushing for eventual general revenue support. Both the 1937–38 and the 1947–48 advisory councils and most Social Security experts agreed with him.

I did, for example. I wrote an article for the July 1949 issue of the *Social Security Bulletin* (I was out of government then) called "What Contribution Rate for Old Age and Survivors Insurance?" in which I argued that workers should pay a contribution rate matched by employers that was estimated to pay for the benefits of their generation—what the government actuary in the United Kingdom called the "actuarial rate"—and that the cost of the accrued liability was fairly borne by the general taxpayer.

Support for a general revenue contribution slacked off in the late 1950s, although I kept advocating it as late as in a book I published in 1978. But then I changed my mind. I just could not see a commissioner of Social Security, as I had been, successfully arguing before Congress for the huge amounts of general revenue the accrued liability rationale required. It would have shifted financing to about one-third from the employees, one-third from the employer, and one-third from the general taxpayer and would have been in competition with all the other demands for federal financing. Considering the great resistance on the part of the public to general taxes, I was fearful that sufficient general revenue would not be voted. On the other hand, the public generally seemed quite willing to pay a hefty tax earmarked for Social Security, so I and most other experts gave up on general revenue financing and adopted the "self-financed" principle (as stated in the appendix at the end of this chapter).

But times have changed. President Clinton has proposed $2.7 trillion for Social Security out of general taxes down the road, in addition to the roughly $2.7 trillion excess in Social Security taxes plus interest over benefits estimated for the next fifteen years under present law. This is only about one-third of what Doug Brown's rationale would call for, but it is certainly a major commitment in this direction.

I am astounded after some thirty years of advocating such a policy and then abandoning it, but I am pleased—I think. The pledge for later general support will be backed by gradually placing interest-bearing bonds in the trust funds over the period of the next fifteen years, except that about one-fifth of this $2.7 trillion infusion devoted to Social Security from general revenues will be used to buy equities up to a maximum of 15 percent of the Social Security funds. This is being done with the full support of Secretary of the Treasury Robert E. Rubin, who is looked to on Wall Street with at least as much deference as Chairman of the Federal Reserve System Alan Greenspan, who opposes this move. I could not be more pleased than I am about the breakthrough on equity investment, which is new and has no historical precedent.[4]

There are other rationales for government contribution than the one urged by Doug Brown. Some have argued that the cost of modifying the equity principle of quid pro quo to carry out a social purpose—the weighted benefit formula, for example—ought to be carried by the general taxpayer, not solely by the better-off contributors. Some have just left the argument at the point that Social Security is an extremely important institution in American life and the government should pay part of the cost, leading to a somewhat more progressive way of raising the funds, while still keeping strong reliance on the contributory principle.

So far the Clinton administration has not taken the risk of leaning on any particular rationale. They seem to be saying, rather, in my words, "We anticipate these large surpluses in the unified budget over the next fifteen years, let's use a large part of it to pay down the debt held in private hands and increase the debt held by Social Security and Medicare—more bonds in these trust funds to be cashed later as needed. Let's just give a big part of these anticipated surpluses to Social Security and Medicare, thus avoiding much of the need for substantial Social Security benefit cuts or Social Security tax increases." No particular rationale is offered or apparently needed.

Reducing the size of the federal debt held in private hands and instead increasing the size of the debt held by Social Security will give the Treasury more flexibility in meeting future Social Security and Medicare obligations. For example, the bonds could be paid off by increased general taxes or by borrowing from private lenders once again. (It is necessary, of course, that future general revenues to the amount of the promise—$2.7 trillion or its equivalent in percent of payroll, in the case of Social Security—be actually committed to Social Security, with bonds and stocks representing the commitment put in the trust funds. The actuaries could hardly be expected to estimate the ability of the system to pay full benefits until 2055 instead of 2032, as under present law, on a vague commitment of 62 percent of whatever the unified budget surplus turns out to be over the next fifteen years!)

Eventually everything comes around again. Clinton's proposal for U.S. government annuities supplementary to Social Security was part of the Roosevelt plan in 1935, although bargained away in the negotiations over the 1935 bill. The Clinton plan is in somewhat different form with more appeal to conservatives. The proposal in 1935 looked like a competitive threat to insurance companies and other private sellers. The Clinton plan looks more like an incentive for middle-income workers to put more into private investments.

In an interesting informal comment by Altmeyer, the second chairman of the Social Security Board and the first commissioner for Social Security (and perhaps the most influential father of all the founding mothers and fathers of Social Security) actually proposed to Republican Social Security leader Senator Arthur Vandenberg that because of his opposition to a big fund buildup he might want to put some Social Security money in stocks, but Altmeyer never pursued the idea.[5]

Berkowitz has shown in this chapter how history throws light on the current Social Security debate in many ways.

And further debate is needed. To get rid of the entire long-range 2.19 percent of payroll deficit reported by the trustees in 1998 we need changes beyond the Clinton proposal, amounting to about 0.85 to 0.90 percent of payroll, more when the interaction among proposals is taken into account. One big step in that direction would be to raise the maximum earnings base to where it makes taxable about 90 percent of earnings in covered employment as it used to, instead of 86 percent as at present. This would result in a 0.58 percent payroll reduction in the Social Security deficit. (Under the assumptions in the 1999 Trustees Report, this change alone is just about enough on top of the president's proposal to eliminate the entire seventy-five-year deficit.)

We do not have to invent everything all over again. There were a lot of good ideas developed in the past that are applicable today. What seems clear is that we need to know enough history to preserve what is good, but we must also be willing to embrace new ideas like equity investment as they come along and are shown to be useful.

Appendix

The Nine Principles of Social Insurance

These principles are discussed on page 94 of the "Report of the 1994–1996 Advisory Council on Social Security."

1. *Universal:* Social Security coverage has been gradually extended over the years to the point where 96 out of 100 jobs in paid employment are now covered, with about 142 million working Americans making contributions in 1996. The goal of complete universality is now within reach—and, as previously discussed, the last step should be taken to reach that goal.

2. *Earned right:* Social Security is more than a statutory right; it is an *earned* right, with eligibility for benefits and the benefit rate based on an individual's past earnings. This principle sharply distinguishes Social Security from welfare and links it, appropriately, to other earned rights, such as wages, fringe benefits, and private pensions.

3. *Wage-related:* Social Security benefits are related to earnings, thereby reinforcing the concept of benefits as an earned right and recognizing that there is a relationship between one's standard of living while working and the benefit level needed to achieve income security in retirement. Under Social Security, higher-paid earners get higher benefits—while, at the same time, the lower-paid get more for what they pay in.

4. *Contributory and self-financed:* The fact that workers pay earmarked contributions from their wages into the system also reinforces the concept of an earned right and gives contributors a moral claim on future benefits above and beyond statutory obligations. And, unlike many foreign plans, Social Security is entirely financed by dedicated taxes, principally those deducted from workers' earnings matched by employers, with the self-employed paying comparable amounts. The entire cost of benefits plus administrative expenses (which are only eight-tenths of one percent of income) is met without support from general government revenues.

This self-financing system has several advantages. It helps protect the program against having to compete against other programs in the annual general federal budget—which is appropriate, because this is a uniquely long-term program. It imposes fiscal discipline, because the total earmarked income for Social Security must be sufficient to cover the entire cost of the program. And it guards against excessive liberalization: contributors oppose major benefit cuts because they have a right to benefits and are paying for them, but they also oppose excessive increases in benefits because they understand that every increase must be paid for by increased contributions. Thus a semiautomatic balance is achieved between wanting more protection versus not wanting to pay more for it.

5. *Redistributive:* One of Social Security's most important objectives is to pay at least a minimally adequate benefit to workers who are regularly covered and contributing, regardless of how low-paid they may be. This is accomplished through a redistributional formula that pays comparatively higher benefits to low-paid than to high-paid earners. The formula and the idea behind it make good sense. If the system paid back to low-wage workers only the benefit that they could reasonably be expected to pay for on their own, millions of retirees would end up on welfare even though they had been paying into Social Security throughout their working lives. This would make the years of contributing to Social Security worse than pointless, since the earnings deductions would have reduced their income throughout their working years without providing in retirement any income above what would be available from a welfare payment. The redistributional formula solves this dilemma, and, in so doing, reduces the burden of welfare for everyone: those who would otherwise end up on it and the rest who must pay for it.

6. *Not means-tested:* In contrast to welfare, eligibility for Social Security does not depend on the beneficiary's current income and assets; nor does the amount of the benefit. This is a crucial principle. It is the absence of a means test that makes it possible for people to add to their savings and to establish private pension plans, secure in the knowledge that they will not be penalized by having their Social Security benefits cut back as a result of having achieved additional retirement income security. The absence of a means test allows Social Security to provide a stable role in anchoring a multitier retirement system in which private pensions and personal savings can be built on top of Social Security's basic, defined protection.

7. *Wage-indexed:* Social Security is portable, following the worker from job to job, and the protection before retirement increases as wages rise. Benefits at the time of initial receipt are brought up to date with recent wages, reflecting improvements in productivity and thus in the general standard of living. Without this principle, Social Security would soon provide benefits that did not reflect previously attained levels of living.

8. *Inflation-protected:* Once they begin, Social Security benefits are protected against inflation by periodic Cost-of-Living Adjustments (COLAs) linked to the Consumer Price Index. Inflation protection is one of Social Security's greatest strengths, and one that distinguishes it from other (except federal) retirement plans: no private pension plan provides guaranteed protection against inflation, and inflation protection under state and local plans,

where it exists at all, is capped. Without COLAs, the real value of Social Security benefits would steadily erode over time, as is the case with unadjusted private pension benefits. Although a provision for automatic adjustment was not included in the original legislation, the importance of protecting benefits against inflation was well understood, and over the years the system was financed to allow for periodic legislation to bring benefits up to date.

9. *Compulsory:* Social Security compels all of us to contribute to our own future security. A voluntary system simply wouldn't work. Some of us would save scrupulously, some would save sporadically, and some would postpone the day of reckoning forever, leaving the community as a whole to pay through a much less desirable and less efficient safety-net system. With a compulsory program, problems of adverse selections—that is, individuals deciding when and to what extent they want to participate, depending on whether their individual circumstances seem favorable—are avoided (as are the problems of obtaining adequate funding for a large safety-net program serving a constituency with limited political influence).

Notes

1. Arthur J. Altmeyer, *The Formative Years of Social Security* (University of Wisconsin Press, 1968), p. 5.

2. J. Douglas Brown, *An American Philosophy of Social Security* (Princeton University Press, 1971), pp. 97–99.

3. Altmeyer, *The Formative Years of Social Security,* p. 29.

4. The plan described was the president's first proposal. In October 1999 he submitted a substitute designed to gain more support. The new proposal did not include investments in stocks and proposed an annual general revenue contribution beginning in 2011. For the years 2011 through 2016, the contribution would be the estimated amount of interest saved in those years on the publicly held debt because of reduction made in that debt beginning in the year 2000 as the growing Social Security surpluses were used to buy back debt from the public. From 2016 on, the amount of the annual payment would be fixed at the 2016 level. The payments would end with 2044, the estimated exhaustion date for the non-Social Security budget surplus.

5. Altmeyer, *The Formative Years of Social Security,* p. 89.

Comment by Janice Gregory

Employers' View

Ed Berkowitz has given us a different response to the question, "Why do we have social insurance?" In his narrative, the emergence of social insurance seems almost accidental, and its fundamental tenets grew and developed over time.

In fact, his discussion tells us more about how social insurance came to be than about what it is today or why it is there at all. But in so doing, his article is extremely instructive because "accidental" and "development over a period of time" are attributes that also can be applied to one of the great companions of our social insurance programs. That great companion is one that I know a fair amount about—the benefit plans provided voluntarily by employers for their employees.

When Berkowitz said there was little confidence in the private system in the late 1930s, it may be because the system was too limited to have much impact on most individuals. For example, in 1940 only about 15 percent of the civilian work force was participating in any kind of an employer-sponsored retirement plan. By contrast, in the near future, when most of the baby boom cohort will reach full retirement, about 80 percent of retiring workers will have received benefits from one or more employer plans at or before their retirement. For a totally voluntary system this is extraordinary.

The explosion of the employer-sponsored plan system may have been triggered as an offshoot of the wartime wage restraints—hence the "accidental" nature of its growth, but the timing of the growth of these plans is also closely tied to the creation of social insurance.

Social insurance and employee plans grew up together. That is an important fact because we tend to examine social insurance programs in general, and Social Security in particular, as though the program exists in a world separate from everything else.

If you do not remember anything else from what I say, remember this: Social Security and employer-sponsored retirement plans are joined at the hip. When you change Social Security, pension plans will not sit still. They will change.

Almost all the analysis of Social Security reform proposals assumes that the pension world keeps going as though nothing had changed. This is an enormous mistake.

Benefits from employer-sponsored plans are the largest source of retirement income, other than Social Security, for the middle three quintiles of the population. In the aggregate, employer-sponsored plans today pay more retiree and survivor benefits each year than does Social Security—$379 billion in 1997 compared to $316 for the Old Age and Survivors Insurance program.

A failure to take into account the impact of Social Security reform on employer plans means that millions of workers will see their retirement dreams wither. We may save Social Security, but we will worsen the chances for millions of individuals to find their *retirement* security.

Berkowitz provides ample examination of the truth of the interconnection of our programs by reminding us how much of the Social Security Act was, from the beginning, a multititled act, and arguing that the Social Security program as we call it and know it today was not the most important nor even the most popular in the beginning.

The current academy project that is examining the interconnection of all programs that bear on risks faced by older workers—their overlaps and their gaps—is exactly on target, too, in revealing how the separate programs that we create here and there never wind up being very separate.

I am going to provide a few examples of how Social Security and pensions are linked, make a couple of additional comments about the Berkowitz article, and conclude by answering the question "Why do we have social insurance?" from an employer point of view.

First the examples: (1) Depending on how they are designed, the creation of individual accounts in Social Security can cause participants in 401(k) plans and other types of employer savings plans, particularly lower-paid partici-pants, to reduce their contributions to those plans. If this happens, not only will many suffer a net loss of retirement assets, but the plans in which they formerly participated may fail the nondiscrimination rules and will have to be discontin-ued or scaled back. (2) Imposition of a means test for the receipt of Social Security benefits would be a disaster for pension plans. Employers would not know how to structure their plans to provide similar benefits at different wage levels, and employees will not want to participate in plans that might jeopar-dize their Social Security. (3) An increase in the age of initial eligibility—currently age sixty-two—will have a direct and dramatic cost impact on plans that provide bridge payments until an individual becomes eligible for Social Security. On the other hand, it might also cause employees to work longer, which might reduce pension costs and might also result in a lot of other changes in the work force. (4) Elimination of the earnings test would eliminate one, but by far not the only, barrier that makes it difficult today for employers to set up phased retirement plans for their older workers. (5) Finally, the administration of individual accounts can have a significant impact. Most employers do not have 401(k) plans. I think that many policymakers think the 401(k) plan is the only type of plan out there, but there are about 700,000 plans and only about 200,000 401(k) plans. Moreover, these 700,000 plans are spread among 6.5 million employers. So add it up. Most employers have no experience whatsoever in collecting individual employee contributions and putting them in a plan. Thus, if we set up Social Security individual accounts, thinking that we can force employers to administer them, it is going to be a nightmare, to say the least.

Looking again at the Berkowitz article, he sees the modern crisis of Social Security as something that grew out of the economic fluctuations of the 1970s, and I certainly agree with that. I want to mention another important and compelling factor that is at play now, and that is demographics—longevity, specifically. And that is no secret to this group.

Many have said that the current buildup in the trust funds was set in motion on purpose in the 1983 financing amendments as a way to prefund the baby boomers' retirement. But there were a lot of other considerations at work in how the 1983 amendments were structured. If you go back and look at the sensitivity analysis in the 1983 trustees report you will discover that, if an extended or severe recession had occurred in the years just after 1983, not only would the surplus we are enjoying today have gotten a slow start, but we could easily have been forced to enact further short-term changes to the program toward the end of the 1980s. That was not, for those of us who were there at the time, a pleasant prospect.

The Social Security program got lucky demographically after the mid-1940s, and it got very lucky economically after the 1983 amendments.

But we still have a demographic issue out there, and I think that has to be included in any equation or debate in the pension world, as well as in the social insurance world.

Second, I note the similarity between Berkowitz's argument that policymakers in the 1930s saw the creation of a contributory program as necessary to reduce future federal outlays and the arguments advanced today for the creation of individual accounts.

Finally, I address the question "Why do we have social insurance?" While I acknowledge—and, in fact, given my prematurely gray hair, I emphasize—that I was not there in 1935, I take issue with the Edwin Witte quote that the social insurance programs were created not with the primary objective of relieving distress but rather as a form of the "regulation of employment relations in the interests of the public welfare."

This sounds too much like bureaucratic tidying up. In fact, all such programs are created with an objective somewhere underneath them of relieving distress. Witte is addressing a question of how you structure going after that purpose. One is a question of purpose; the other is a question of organization.

Indeed, employer plans also have this same underlying purpose. An employer does not want to see his or her former employees lying around in a gutter somewhere homeless and destitute. For starters, it is not good for the company image. Banding together to relieve distress improves morale, provides the employer with important tools to manage the work force, and, most believe— although it is difficult to prove—increases productivity.

But this is what makes the questions of organization so interesting. Why do we have social insurance? Why band employees together in an employer-sponsored plan? Why not just give everybody a copy of the Individual Retirement Account (IRA) ads from the newspaper and be done with it?

The answer is because group savings are more effective. It is estimated that half the elderly population would be in poverty without Social Security, and, while some without Social Security would have been motivated to provide and would have succeeded in providing for themselves, the experience of the employer plan world indicates that most would not.

Employer-sponsored plans have been far more effective than individual arrangements such as IRAs in setting aside larger amounts of retirement savings for individuals at younger ages. This includes plans that offer individual savings opportunities, like 401(k) plans. Let me draw some comparisons.

Of the 59 million households eligible to make deductible contributions to an IRA in 1992, only 3.9 million did so. Even during the 1981 to 1986 period, when IRAs were universally available, the maximum number of tax returns claiming an IRA deduction was 16.2 million in 1985. By contrast, in 1993 when there were 106 million civilian workers, 25.2 million were making contributions to a 401(k) plan, even though 401(k) plans were far from universally available to those 106 million workers.

Moreover, 401(k) plans attracted participants at younger ages: 52.6 percent of the 401(k) participants were age forty or under compared to 37.7 percent for IRA contributors. I think similar patterns will evolve if Social Security individual accounts are made voluntary.

There are several reasons for the effectiveness of employer-sponsored plans. Not all of what I am going to say applies to every type of private sector plan, but each statement applies to some private sector plans. Why do these plans work?

—Savings is automatic in most plans. This is true in almost all defined benefit plans and also occurs in many defined contribution plans where the profit-sharing contribution is made by the employer, not the employee. Under defined benefit plans the participant's benefits are also guaranteed. The employer pays the benefits or the Pension Benefit Guaranty Corporation pays the benefits.

—Investments are professionally managed, certainly in defined benefit plans, but even in defined contribution plans where employees have a professionally chosen selection of investments options.

—Plans offer painless decisionmaking. Once the employee makes the decision to make a payroll deduction contribution, it just happens. The individual does not have to think about it every time.

—The employee gets immediate and substantial investment returns if he or she is participating in a program that has a matching employer contribution.

—Finally, the employee gets useful assistance—he or she is more likely to have access to benefits forecasting, somebody to talk to, and so on.

In a world where mergers and acquisitions are commonplace, we are moving toward a world of virtual companies where who my employer is can change overnight. As a result, employers are encouraging employees to take more responsibility for managing their own retirement.

But it is still responsibility within a group context. What the group does to provide retirement security for its members is changing, but there is still a belief that we need each other in order to do a good job of providing for ourselves.

We should not conclude from this, however, that group plans are "always going to be there." For example, between 1982 and 1994 Congress enacted laws that added regulation on top of regulation and repeatedly imposed new and restrictive limits on retirement plans in general and defined benefit pension plans in particular. The administrative costs to operate defined benefit plans went right through the roof. As a result, there are no more defined benefit plans in the small employer market. They do not exist there anymore. It is too expensive.

Thus, employer-sponsored plans can disappear. They are flexible.

This is an important time. The debate is wide open. What is often portrayed is a transition from the idea of a pure group—such as exists in the defined benefit world or in a welfare scheme, where the responsibility is a total group responsibility—to the idea of the "pure" individual who manages his or her own assets through IRAs or other similar vehicles.

But what is really happening in the world is that we are seeing more of a spectrum. We see this in the private sector through, for example, 401(k) plans. Under these plans, individuals have separate accounts, but administrative costs, investment options, and other similar features of the plan are shared. Employees might also receive a matching payment from the employer. So you have a hybrid type of plan—the individual within the group.

Thus, when we ask why we have Social Security, I think we have to factor in this new spectrum of what people might be defining social insurance to be.

And we also have to remember, finally, that if we move to some kind of a hybrid social insurance system or a hybrid Social Security system, the private world will also move. Perhaps the private retirement system will move more toward a defined benefit system—precisely the opposite of where it is headed now—but it will move.

4

Individual Choice versus Shared Responsibility: Debate on Social Insurance Reform

Stuart Butler and Theodore Marmor

T HIS CHAPTER PRESENTS a debate between two authorities on social insurance—one in favor of more individual choice and one who supports more collective responsibility. They discuss the various paths that Medicare and Social Security reform may follow in the coming years and the potential risks. The debate was moderated by Marilyn Moon.

Marmor: This is not going to be *Crossfire* in the sense of trying to scream and shout at one another. It is going to be an effort to clarify our differences as well as our common ground—a pact we made some months ago out of our common dissatisfaction with the public discussion of Social Security and Medicare.

I have six points I want to make by way of an opening, all of which are necessarily elliptical and which will be part of the back and forth.

The first is the stipulation that the purpose of today's debate is to clarify the differences between a social insurance advocate of a rather traditional kind, like myself, and someone who is a critic of some aspects of social insurance, in this case Stuart Butler. I want to separate out where we disagree on the facts, from where we disagree on economic philosophy, from where we disagree on moral premises.

The second point is that it is extremely easy to miscast a debate about Social Security and Medicare in the current context, if you frame the topic as a matter of individual choice versus collective provision. What I mean by that is, both in Social Security and Medicare, the debate is about the extent of economic security that is collectively provided—and the choices that permits as well as the risks that are insured—versus the advantages of putting more risk on individuals and thereby cutting back on the collective provision of economic security, in the hope of serving other purposes.

So it is the distribution of risk (not simply and crudely individual choice) versus collective decisionmaking that really frames the debate.

The third point has to do with ways of understanding the classic conception of what social insurance is expected to do. Now, a classic conception is not the only conception, so that normatively I am advancing a preferred way of thinking about it. Let me try to clarify.

It is important to understand the fundamental premise of social insurance worldwide. It is a device for collectively pooling funds to deal with risks of economic insecurity—whether it is the loss of income from retirement, the loss of income from the threat from medical expenses, the loss of income because of disability, and the like. It generally uses contributions as one basis of entitlement, but that is no bar to sources of income from other places. The key notion about contribution is not that it has to be universally the financial source, but rather that there has to be some link between what one gives and what one gets, that is, participation in a common enterprise.

It is also important to understand that the public is involved in that enterprise in such a way that people regard the receipt of the protection against risk when it arises as something they as citizens are entitled to, not something they receive as charity. Anything that threatens that sense of "deservingness" is a threat to social insurance. It does not follow from this that the word *entitlement,* in budgetary terms, communicates the sense of entitlement I'm talking about. That sense of entitlement comes by sharing in a common burden, pooling those resources, and distributing them in ways that people feel they are entitled to and done in such a way as to preserve their dignity.

The fourth point about the current arrangements is that it is not at all clear, certainly to me, if the problem requires anything like a fundamental restructuring of the program—either in Social Security or in Medicare. In the case of Social Security pensions, for instance, without recommending one solution or another anybody can list relatively marginal, sometimes called "technical changes," which would produce actuarial balance as far as the eye can see.

So the argument cannot be that we cannot afford Social Security pensions. It has to be that we have some disagreements about who should get what, under what auspices, what degree of private risk bearing there should be, and what degree of collective risk spreading there should be. I think Stuart would agree with that. Mind you, the fact that we do not have a crisis or that the problem is not overwhelming us is not an argument against adjustments. The collective spreading of risk certainly ought to require constant adjustments in line with those purposes, but that is not the argument about "saving" Social Security. What I want to know is—save Social Security from what danger?

This is true in Medicare, too, although because its outlays depend not simply on the number of elderly persons or disabled persons or people with renal failure, but also on the rate of inflation in medical care costs and the rate of increases in utilization, so it raises tougher problems of cost control.

In the interest of time, I am going to state the last two points quickly: one on economic philosophy and the other on feasibility.

On economic philosophy and choice, my view can be stated simply. Those people who would legislate choice in the name of what is called expanded choice, and take away economic security from Americans—either in Social Security or Medicare—are confusing the matter. Choice in Medicare today is extensive as far as the ability of beneficiaries to select their providers, and that is the choice most Americans fundamentally care about. Choice in Social Security is extensive, too. No one constrains what you do with your benefit check after you have the Social Security's economic protection.

It seems to me crucial that the difference is not more choice in the new proposals, but different conceptions of who should bear what risk and how we distribute the burdens of the choices that are made. Calling a plan "Medicare +Choice" is propagandistic rhetoric, not realistic definition.

Butler: I agree with Ted very much. As he has made clear on this and on many other occasions, we are both concerned that we have a public discussion going on which I have described as wretched in terms of the kinds of the bogus options that people are presented with in order to chart out the future of the Social Insurance programs: Social Security and Medicare. I want to take my time to highlight what I feel to be the fundamental choices that we really have to make. What I will say overlaps with a lot of the things that Ted mentioned.

I just want to stress that this is not a debate about the principle of social insurance. As Ted said, it is a debate to some extent about the scale of social insurance, the balance of risk, and how we discharge the objectives of social insurance.

But it is not a question of being either "for" or "against" the principle of social insurance. It is also a debate about trust fund projections, as he quite rightly said. I would take the view that even if we had a situation where the fiscal integrity of both Social Security and Medicare was sound as far as the eye could see, we should still be talking about fundamental changes and reforms. It seems to me this is a debate really about three fundamental questions.

First, what is the nature of the social insurance contract between the generations? Second, does the pension element of Social Security today actually provide the retirement security that people need and expect? And third, what system—what ideological system, if you like, central planning or a market-based system, is most likely to achieve the objectives we have in Medicare and Social Security?

All these questions are part of the public debate and show up occasionally, but really only implicitly. Ted and I feel they should be explicit; that they should be presented as fundamental and put on the table. We should be talking about them. Given the time constraints, and at the risk of being simplistic, let me deal with each of them quickly.

First, when we look at the social contract in both Social Security and Medicare, I believe we have a contract that we cannot deliver. We have essentially committed ourselves as a nation to a system based on forcibly taking contributions throughout people's lives in order to give them a good pension, a good retirement pension, good insurance, and state-of-the-art retirement health care benefits. But we cannot continue to simply say that and achieve it without making some changes in the system—both in terms of risk, and the assignment of the assurance of services.

It seems to me that, being able to fulfill our commitments, in terms of this contract we have three directions that we can go. One is to squeeze—to trim here and there and to slightly make the promise less real in the future than it was in the past. The second is to end any pretense that this is really a social insurance-based system where people as a group contribute through their working lives in order to get what they paid into the system. This to me means just simply committing ourselves to put in as much general revenue as necessary—an unlimited commitment. That is one of the big concerns I have about what President Clinton has said. He has, in my view, breached the dam on that issue. Third, we can explicitly change and limit the social contract in social insurance. This means we must talk about where the risk should be; discuss to what extent the general taxpayer and future generations should carry all the risk and to what extent the risk should be shared in some way. That in turn means we ought to be discussing, too, the fact that we cannot provide an adequate contract to the poor under the current arrangements if we are trying simultaneously to give a very good contract to everybody else. We really have to talk about the welfare element of social insurance, and talk about it explicitly.

Let me go on to the Social Security issue—specifically, whether Social Security provides adequate retirement security. I believe we should recall the vision that President Roosevelt had, in terms of what constitutes full retirement security. He talked about the three-legged stool of retirement security—through Social Security, through employer pensions, and through other types of pensions and savings. He saw these as the three elements necessary for a secure future.

But the fact is, if we look at Social Security in terms of its contribution as a critical leg of the stool, it is surely lacking, and we need to talk about some fundamental changes.

Retirement security must contain three elements—insurance against catastrophic events like disability or death; the assurance of a predictable and secure retirement income on a monthly basis; and the ability to create wealth, both to enjoy during retirement and to pass on to the next generation.

Social Security in my view does an adequate job of the first in terms of insurance. Social Security, however, does an increasingly less good job in doing the second—of giving you a good, solid retirement income, and I think if we look at that we see it is getting worse and worse as the years go by. Just look at the rates of return. Finally, Social Security does not even try to allow people to build wealth during their working years for their retirement. That is why there is increasing concern about Social Security's impact on wealth creation and generation among lower-income Americans and minorities. This is why people like Senator Daniel Patrick Moynihan (D-N.Y.) have drawn attention to the importance of changing the basic structure of Social Security to permit people who currently lack capital to be able to build that through their working lives within Social Security. And that is why I believe that we need to look at a refinement of Social Security as it is currently structured, which means allowing people to put some of their contributions into savings accounts, in order to deal with that lack of a tool for wealth creation.

This is something that other countries are doing—countries like Australia or the United Kingdom. It is a general change that is being undertaken in these social insurance programs to permit wealth creation. Even in Sweden, where everybody looks like a blond version of Ted Marmor; even in countries that have, without question, a complete commitment to social insurance, they recognize this deficiency and are reforming programs to deal with it.

Let me just end, given the time, by saying a few words about Medicare. We have a Medicare system today, in which we have promised specific benefits to seniors without regard to the burden and risk that places on others. And we have tried to provide those benefits in a structure of central planning, which inherently is economically inefficient.

We are currently seeing and debating those twin problems now in Medicare. We have been trying to provide very detailed benefits, recognizing that these not only are difficult to provide under a centrally planned system, but the selection of benefits is necessarily politicized under our legislative system. This is why we have intense debates in the national legislature of the United States about how many doctor visits you can have.

This is not the way to run a railroad or a Medicare system. So we need to have a debate, a national discussion, about what is the commitment of the public-at-large, in real resources, to the health care of the retired population.

We need to discuss where the risks should be and who should make decisions. I favor moving toward some kind of hybrid defined contribution system—you can call it a premium support, which is now the term in vogue, or a voucher, or whatever. I think we can have a discussion about how to do that in ways and design that meet the understandable concerns of people with regard to risk and whether they can afford future benefits.

Finally, we need to have a real discussion about whether to move to a much more generalized commitment of benefits and a much more individualized choice within that, in order to encourage the evolution of benefits, and the improvements of benefits that you get in the program that covers members of Congress, the Federal Employees Health Benefits Program (FEHBP), by the process of continuous innovation through competition and choice. This is not to shift burdens, but to encourage improvement over time. That is an economic strategy that is a much more effective way of achieving our objectives.

Marmor: Stuart, as he said, raises a number of points on which we do not differ. He is not an opponent of a major role for social insurance, so I will concentrate on the ways in which we differ and select two to try to get at a principal difference.

Let me go backward from his last point, which was about Medicare. There is a sharp difference between what is technically called the *defined benefit program*—the assurance of services to be covered by a public program—and a *defined contribution*, or voucher premium support, which is a down payment on a set of services.

But that is just the technical way of describing it. Much more important for our philosophical differences is the extent to which the Medicare program was conceived as a stepping-stone to an arrangement by which Americans would take medical care largely out of market relations among patient, physician, and hospital, and substitute nonmarket criteria about who should get what from whom.

As soon as one uses a voucher in a program like Medicare—even if there is a defined benefit package—there will be greatly increased differences in the treatment of similarly situated beneficiaries. Vouchers are options to buy varying packages from varying institutions, not a common insurance plan in which older Americans are in the same boat. Over time a voucher program communicates the idea that Americans will not be in the same boat regarding medical care when they are disabled or over sixty-five.

Now, you can talk around this a bit. You can even criticize the current Medicare program for not putting people exactly in the same boat. That is true. We have failed to enact the program that we expected to extend in 1965, either to new population groups or by expanding the benefits.

It is also the case that the benefit package is too narrow and limited now. There is no question about that. Modern medicine has changed. But that does not change the philosophical point. We need to improve Medicare's performance; we don't need to transform Medicare.

The difference between us, really, is that Stuart wants a world in which there is a medical down payment that is a safety net that protects everybody. I want a platform on which most people who are, roughly speaking, similarly ill are similarly treated, and where the size of their wallets does not make a bit of difference. That is an important philosophical difference between us, and it is important to clarify.

The second area that Stuart raised is a little harder to argue with unless it is unpacked. What can we say about retirement security? How well does Social Security do at providing retirement security? He says it does pretty well, although he can imagine a future state of affairs that gets worse. If we can do it pretty well, that is a pretty good argument for keeping it going. If you turn the question to: Does the American Social Security system directly add to the wealth of the country by supporting investment? No. If it does it at all it does it indirectly by affecting what the interest rates would have been otherwise because of our holding those bonds. Or, it does it because we give citizens the kind of economic security that lets them take on risks that they would be unwilling to do if it were a dog-eat-dog scene, and if our parents or our children viewed us as being a future burden for the very base of Social Security.

Third, and last for now, Stuart said that defined contribution plans would be the way to wealth. I just want to challenge the seeming obviousness of that point in two ways. One, it is true that if you have individual accounts you will increase savings in those accounts. But it does not follow that net savings rise necessarily. And two, it does not follow that net savings increases necessarily lead to productive investment; otherwise Japan would be the leading economic example of that right at the moment.

So, the easy connection between individual accounts and wealth creation is partly a product of the recent remarkable boom in the stock market. And if you believe that the stock market boom is going to continue for the next thirty years in the twenty-first century, you and Garrison Keillor should get together in Lake Wobegon.

Butler: Let me deal with a number of Ted's points, not necessarily in order. First, I want to distinguish between what I would call myth and reality.

The myth is that today we really are all in this together, all in the same boat, and all getting the same. I come from Britain, a country where that idea was a stated but fraudulent goal for the way the country functioned. The reality is, we may be all in the same social insurance boat, but some of us are sinking faster than others and some of us are rowing harder than others. Moreover, it turns out that the ways in which people end up being treated differently in this boat are a lot less fair than people assume. When we look at the way in which Medicare and Social Security function, it turns out that there are big differences between the returns on their Social Security taxes different groups of the population get and the quality of Medicare different people get.

It is a myth that we currently are all in a nice boat and all we need to do is trim it here and there. The changes I am talking about would allow wider discretion, allow more individual choices, and so forth, within the system. This would encourage more innovation and is precisely designed to deal with the fact that we are not in the same boat and we are certainly not all getting the same services under those programs.

Ted is right when he says I take the view that we ought to rethink to some degree the social insurance component of both Medicare and Social Security and focus more on a safety net. *Safety net* is a term people tend to think of as meaning way down at the bottom. What I mean by it is simply that we ought to be looking at a core component of both retirement security, in terms of income, and health care, which nobody in this country should lack, no matter what their circumstances. The scale of their care will depend on the wealth of the country and the social views of the people.

We should focus on delivering that solid core, rather than the comprehensive but leaky boat that everybody is in today.

The second point I want to make concerns personal accounts and Social Security. It is important to distinguish in the debate what can and should take place between macroeconomics and personal economics. This is really an issue of individual and personal circumstance and personal wealth and personal views of the future.

Today you have a situation where large segments of this country—particularly in the African American or the Hispanic community—face a huge capital shortfall that affects their ability to save through their lives and to build for the future. You have entire communities that are held back when you have a lack of savings by those communities. I feel that Social Security has been an unindicted coconspirator in the wealth gap and the income gap that has occurred in this country. So one of the things we must achieve with Social Security reform is to change the program—not so that people can gamble on the stock market or see themselves as individuals and devil take the hind-most—but in order to create a process of wealth generation within communi-ties that the Social Security system leaves out of the mainstream today. That is a fundamental reason why we need these reforms. When you look at other countries—particularly my native country, Britain—over the long term, such reform has led to changes in wealth accumulation and distribution, particularly to the benefit of people who previously could not look forward to building up wealth for themselves and for their children.

There is also a fundamental economic dispute between us—and probably throughout this organization—between those of us who feel that allowing people to make health care choices in a competitive world is the best process to get innovation in the future: in the design of benefits, in the way benefits are provided, and in how a benefits package can change over time. I believe that is fundamentally better, more effective, and has a better outcome than trying to do this through the political process, where we try to define precisely what people are going to get. I would argue that clearly the Medicare system has fallen behind its initial state-of-the-art condition pre-cisely because of that political process of trying to establish benefits. And that is why we need to move toward greater innovation through individual choices.

Marmor: Four quick points. One, I am sorry I introduced the concept of a boat. I see a promiscuous, metaphorical move here; assertions of leakiness without evidence to support the view. I did not say for Social Security that being in the same boat meant everybody receives the same thing. I said there was an egalitarian element in Medicare. In fact, what happens in Social Security, as Stuart well knows, is that there is a redistribution from higher earners to lower earners, but it is muted. We keep the same distribution of income but we squeeze the range. That is the way we ought to be talking about it. And if we care about those at the bottom of the income distribution, ex post, then we ought to have a scheme that, ex ante, arranges somewhat more redistribution. I do not think that is on the agenda as the major topic of Social Security at the moment, but it may be.

Second, a safety net. I will make a point here to clarify—not to attack but to clarify. It is important to think about the metaphor of a social safety net, because there is an ambiguity about whether a net is there to catch people when they fall, or if a net is there held taut to hold people up that they can count on. I worry about thinking about social insurance in social safety net terms—the size of the holes and the depth of it. I think the metaphorical point we ought to be making is that this is not a legal guarantee. This is a political social guarantee in which the political risk is minimized if we agree together that this is for all of us. That is the sense in which I meant all in the same boat.

Let me concentrate on Medicare in the last few points. It is absolutely crucial to unpack the current discussion of Medicare, as Stuart started to do. I concede right at the outset that if people had vouchers for medical care the diversification and innovation in the medical care industry would probably increase even further. The number of spas for upper-income people would increase, as well as specialized clinics for sports—lots of variety, Stuart.

So I think you are right on that point. Markets reward innovation; no question. But it is the case that most social insurance versions of medical care in the world, and in Medicare if properly reformed, would have a wide benefit package in which providers would compete for customers on the basis of the presumed quality and appropriateness of their care, while the consumer's cooperative, the unitary system, would negotiate on price.

That is the proper vision. It is not about central planning, which is insensitive to the circumstances of recipients. After all, there are two forms of accountability. One is accountability that arises through exit from a system, and the other is the accountability that involves protest, voice. Anybody who thinks that we do not have channels of voice in Medicare would be wrong. I think that the last twenty-five years have been marked by Medicare reformers, progenitors, and supporters not regularly in power. I would hope we have an opportunity for the return of Medicare's original vision and the expansion of it.

And finally, it makes a difference that we are talking about Medicare, and not talking about the Yale Health Plan. Medicare is for people who are particularly ill-suited to be shopping around for insurance plans.

I can tell you on the basis of being the faculty representative at Yale, an educational campaign is the necessary condition for the promotion of choice among plans. Stuart, I think the IQ of Yale professors is adequate to the task, but their capacity to work through what it means to choose within the FEHBP indicates the need for keeping a common plan that gives us wide choice of physician, doctor, and so on, and gets reform by adding prescription drugs.

Butler: Let me make two or three quick points.

This is, indeed, a debate about risk and responsibility, or risk and burden. And it should be, and we should have a real debate about it. I think the concern that both Ted and I have, whether we take different views on it or not, is that the debate is not happening. We are seeing instead the mythology of saying you can have it all; just get rid of waste and fraud and abuse and everything will be fine, everybody can get everything, and we can have new benefits. Do not worry. That illusion has got to be shattered.

We have got to talk in hard terms about who takes the responsibility, who takes the risk, to what extent can the risk be managed, and who is less able to take risk and needs more help? That is what the debate is about.

Second, I will say that on the issue of choices and innovation and so on, Ted is right. If you do nothing more than say, "Here's some cash. Go spend it on medical care," you will get all kinds of innovation and much of it will be of the type that he suggested. That is why I do not support simply doing that. That is why I support what the Medicare Commission is beginning to look at seriously. A structure that allows negotiation to be part of the equation makes sense. "Let's see what you and the provider are offering and intend to do, and let's talk about it before we let you get in and start selling the plan to retired Yale professors or anybody else." That's a necessary element of the solution to this problem. And I agree that we need to do that.

Marmor: We are not going to agree in the end, even though Stuart just said that. I am delighted that we agree on the topic. I want to use my last minute to push home one single point, and that is the way in which the language of commentary is distorting our conversation about this topic.

It is simply bizarre to me that anyone believes America's elderly and disabled are interested in shopping around for various kinds of insurance plans. There is not one shred of public opinion evidence or focus group findings to support that. It is, like the Catastrophic Health Insurance Plan of the late 1980s, an idea hatched in Washington that is totally disconnected from the expressed concerns of America's elderly regarding what they care about.

What do they care about? They care about three things for sure. First, they care about the proportion of their income that goes to medical care now, which is near 20 percent on average. Second, they care about losing access to their doctor if things were shifted around. And third, they believe, wrongly, that we can pay for all that through fraud, waste, and abuse control—on that I agree with Stuart.

Anybody who has studied the way by which western industrial societies have aged knows that the only way you make medical care affordable for all within the group or society as a whole is to restrain what you pay for medical services and constrain the volume of those medical services. That can be done fairly or unfairly, but it is a necessary condition and all choice does is shift to health plans that same role. There is no avoiding those constraints.

Moon: As moderator, I will ask each of you to respond to some questions. Stuart, one of the questions asks if we rely on the safety net to provide a minimum guarantee, isn't there a risk that it will become labeled a welfare program and thus be subject to reductions within the budgetary process, leaving many elderly unprotected?

Butler: Yes, that is a legitimate concern, and it is the traditional argument for the politics of a social insurance system. It's what I call the "hostage" approach—try to keep everyone in, in order that people without much power will get a decent deal. The downside of that is, in order to keep one group satisfied, we have had to shortchange the people we really need to help most. We have to face up to that and ask if this is the best way to go forward in the future in terms of helping those who fundamentally need it.

Marmor: Certainly that is a risk. It is the political risk as against the economic risks of the program dramatically changing the actual benefit distribution that takes place.

But there is another point that should be made. Why is Stuart assuming that we can constrain Medicare's costs by the equivalent of a global budget—which is what a voucher times the number of people is—without transforming the plans? It does not follow.

If the problem is the absence of funds in the federal government to expand insurance, you can do that by constraining what is available for the Medicare program either through vouchers or a global budget. It has distributional differences, but we want to separate these two questions, namely, the social effects of changing how it is that people get benefits in Medicare from the affordability of medical care for older, disabled, and poorer people.

Moon: Ted, if one of the problems is that we end up constraining these programs and so then we have essentially a level benefit—or close to a level benefit in the case of Medicare for everyone—will it be too ungenerous for the poor in that way if we spread it as evenly?

Marmor: That might be a problem if, in the course of reforming Medicare appropriately, we jettisoned Medicaid. Nobody is proposing it as far as I know. But it would be a concern.

I see no reason to think people differ ex ante (before they're sick), regarding the range of things they are worried about. They are worried about the probability over their lifetime of a serious medical intervention in the hospital, the possibility of surgery, the possibility they are going to suffer from a long-term ailment, and the affordability of drugs for chronic conditions.

Now, I think Stuart and I may differ a little bit in this area about the facts, not about the values. I think I am the person arguing that in the sphere of medical care there is a more powerful case for egalitarian treatment because the preferences of people with equal capacity to buy would be quite similar.

When people have unequal capacities to buy, they make different decisions. Poor people behave differently from others. But, say you ask, behind the veil of ignorance, what do people care about? I think with respect to medical care the preferences are extraordinarily similar when it comes to security from devastating expenses.

Butler: I would not disagree fundamentally with that at all. I think that is clear in this country and in other countries.

I would say two things, however. One is that when you consider our commitment to a broad set of benefits and assistance to people—I think we need to look at how to ensure that those with low income actually have the better opportunity to obtain care and to afford it. One of the deficiencies of the current system is the political attempt to try to treat everybody equally. That turns out to mean treating the poor worse.

The second thing I'll say is that we should note Ted's suggestion that all we need to do is to look at and do what other countries have done, and simply to constrain the price of medical care. That suggestion lets the cat out of the bag. I will just refer you to our exchange in Health Affairs rather than to elaborate on it. It is the route to hollowed out benefits and to a reduction in quality, where you have an assurance in name only. And if that happens, it will disproportionately hurt those with fewer means, not those with more means who can make up the difference in some way. So we are stuck with this problem, this dilemma, by the politics of social insurance and equality.

The last point I will make is that Ted says that nobody he knows wants to shop around for different plans. He may be right about the people he knows. But that is partly a result of the mythology that has been created by the inadequacy of the debate today. If you tell people they can have everything, they will say: I want everything. Why should I make choices? Why should I set limits? Why don't we take it from foreign aid or something? As long as we tell people they do not have to confront some real choices they will not be inclined to make choices that will be in the interest of achieving long-term improvement in the very benefits they are seeking.

Moon: The next question relates to the issue of private accounts in Social Security. How should the huge administrative costs associated with private accounts be handled? I assume you may want to talk about whether they are huge administrative costs, and that seems to be the distinct pooling advantage of investment.

A related question also asked you to talk about other countries' experience; for example, Chile.

Butler: On administrative costs there are a number of issues associated, and a lot of debate. We could have a long debate over exactly what the numbers are.

But let me make some general points. One is that you do have the problem that the smaller you make those accounts, or the less you allow people to put into them, the bigger proportionately any administrative cost is going to be.

That means that if you take a little bit of the surplus and let people set up little accounts, administrative costs will eat up much of what could be earned in the future. So the scale of the accounts you allow is very important in itself in terms of getting those administrative costs within reason.

The second thing is that those are, in fact, accounts with low administrative cost risks, and small risk, too, would be significantly better than people currently have under Social Security. The Treasury Department, for example, issues Series I bonds that have no management costs, are indexed to inflation, and have a real rate of return that is more than 3 percent. Many people today would be significantly better off than under Social Security with plans containing such bonds.

Marmor: If this were *Crossfire* I'd love to talk about administrative costs for the rest of the session. Stuart concedes that administrative costs of many small accounts are a real topic of concern, and they are. That ought to be stated frontally and honestly. The Chilean experience is God-awful on that question. Why we should be thinking about how to copy the Chilean system of anything I do not know. I am not saying Stuart supports that system. But I have had more dealings with Jose Pinero than I would have ever expected to have in the late twentieth century. It is absurd to be using the experience of Chile. After all, it had a corrupt and collapsing social insurance program. Expensive individual accounts, no doubt, are an improvement on the stability of a corrupt and destroyed system.

The interesting thing about what Stuart said is the remarkable degree to which the advocates of choice end up being the advocates of regulation. Notice—in the name of choice we are going to have to regulate choice; otherwise it cannot serve the social insurance purposes, let alone be at a reasonable cost.

All right. So we are not going to give people a wide range of doing anything, even though that is what they think they are doing when they are controlling their own money, and are deluded into thinking that they, like all the people, will have above average returns.

It is obvious in the case of individual accounts when we use the government's thrift system as a model there is a very restrictive range of choices. The conception provided by Bob Ball, the former commissioner of Social Security, of using the average, high rates of return in the equities as a way of boosting the actuarial balances by increasing revenues involves no choice at all of individual levels of stock selection—no individual choice whatsoever. It leaves individual choice over what to do with one's pension, but not how to create that nest egg.

And I guess I just cannot resist the point that if risk-free Treasury bonds indexed to inflation is the definition of the security we want in Social Insurance, we've already got it.

Moon: In the question of who deals with the issue of risk and choice, there are proposals in which people are talking about protections for people from the downside risks of individual savings accounts. Should there be, for example, protections for certain rates of returns if they are not achieved if we move to personal accounts? I think this is one of the interesting wrinkles that has come up in the debate recently.

Marmor: Well, that is another way of saying we ought to have a guaranteed benefit. It is a way of bringing back in the social insurance contribution and addressing the miasma of individual risk taking.

If you cut off the bottom you can reduce the risk. The return that is appropriate on a risk-bearing basis has changed. It seems to me not to be the right question to be asking.

The right question is: What kind of fundamental platform of economic security, both for retirement and for medical care, do we want and how do we do that? Since this is the last question, I am simply going to end with one other observation about that. The distinction is often drawn by advocates of individual expansion as individual discretion versus government provision of benefits. But the choice is between market-based returns and decisionmaking and government decisionmaking. And *politicization* is the term that is often used to describe the latter.

I want to leave you with one prediction as a political scientist: when you are talking about the health expenses of the elderly, or their retirement, the decision we make will be the object of politicization. There is no avoiding that. If we have regulated choice, then there will be fights about the nature of the choices, and you can see that in the Breaux Commission already. If we have Medicare, we will also have fights about those choices. There is no option in modern democracies to political engagement with the central questions of its citizenry. There is only a question of who wins and who loses by particular arrangements.

Butler: Ted seemed to suggest that when I start talking about any kind of regulation in terms of markets and protecting against downside risk, this suggests that I really do not have my heart in the ability of markets to perform. But in fact, it is the same concession I made at the beginning. That was that he and I agree that a social insurance element is crucial in both of these programs. So I agree that there must be in any kind of market-based reform—in Medicare and particularly in Social Security individual accounts—an element of regulation to ensure that people do, in fact, get minimum returns, and that they are limited in their risk. Thus I have a commitment, like Ted, to a core element of social insurance and the assurance of guaranteed minimum results. In that sense I agree with a minimum defined benefit. I believe that should be the case whether we are talking about vouchers in Medicare or whether we are talking about personal accounts in Social Security.

I do not think the defined benefit should be all of it. Moreover, I think that the way we have conducted the social insurance system has not been effective at achieving the objective that we set ourselves many years ago.

That is really what we are talking about. It is a question of degree as much as anything. In a lot of this debate, people have been wrongly pidgeonholed at one extreme or the other.

That is why I feel that if we really have an honest debate, whether it be in the Medicare Commission or anywhere else, we will find a good deal of common ground, providing we start by talking about the fundamental principles and the central issues. That is why I feel that if people like Ted and me talk enough, and talk at a number of academic sessions, maybe we can encourage other people to do the same thing, and maybe we would have a more elevated discussion of what the options are in the future, rather than the rhetorical, poll-driven discussion that seems to be very much the case today in Washington.

Moon: Thank you both. I think we got what we bargained for, in terms of light and not just heat in this debate.

5

How People
Make Decisions

REFORMS CONTEMPLATED FOR BOTH Social Security and Medicare involve a much greater role for individual decisionmaking, and a responsibility to choose wisely. How do people make decisions about health care and retirement security? What influences those decisions? What kind of information do they use (or not use) in making a choice?

Costs and Benefits of Health- and Retirement-Related Choice
George Loewenstein

FOR MOST PEOPLE, at least some of the time, decisionmaking is both time consuming and painful. We often do not know enough to choose among the options presented to us; we often do not have enough time or motivation to attempt to make good choices; and we rightfully fear that bad decisions will haunt us in the future, tingeing our decisionmaking with feelings of regret. Given all this, it may come as a surprise that most economists and policymakers regard choice as something one cannot have too much of, like clean air or beauty. Choice can be a wonderful thing, as any movie buff who has moved to a city from a small town will verify, but many policymakers, it seems, fail to understand that, while choices bring benefits, they also impose costs. Choices benefit people when they know what they are deciding about and also believe that their decisions are important. However, most of us would prefer

I thank Henry Aaron, Peter Ayton, and Donna, Jean, and Henry Harsch, Mark Peterson, Hannah Riley, and James Thompson for helpful comments and suggestions. I am grateful for financial support from the Center for Integrated Study of the Human Dimensions of Global Change at Carnegie Mellon University, which is funded by NSF grant SBR-9521914.

experts to make decisions for us when we lack relevant expertise. In the absence of such experts, we often accept "default choices" or make other arbitrary decisions that in reality could best be described as "deciding not to decide."

In dealing with the pain of, and time consumed in, decisionmaking, the private sector has much to teach the public sector. As a matter of self-interest, sellers often protect consumers from making decisions that they do not want to make. Car buyers, for example, choose among a real but highly limited range of colors, engine sizes, and other options—all of them alternatives that may enhance their well-being—but they are not asked to choose among differing seat belt mechanisms. They are not given such a choice because they are not competent to evaluate it (and do not wish to invest in obtaining such expertise). Consumers who had to choose between seat belt mechanisms would also worry about the intense regret they would experience if an accident revealed that they had made the wrong choice. Selection of seat belt mechanisms is, therefore, a choice that most people would prefer to leave to engineers. An automobile manufacturer who required consumers to make myriad choices about features that they did not care about would not survive in competition with others who made life easier for them.

Some of the decisions that people face result not from the market, but from government policy. In recent decades, government policies have greatly expanded some types of choices that people face, particularly in the areas of health and saving for retirement. While the market offers at least limited protection against the proliferation of onerous, undesired decisions in the private sector, no such factor constrains decisions spawned by government policies. As a result, rather than expressing latent market demand for a greater variety of alternatives, many new choices linked to government policy reflect, for better or worse, legislative agendas.[1]

Legislation promoting competition in the health sector, for example, has contributed to a proliferation of new health care choices. Whereas previously most employees accepted the single health insurance plan that their company offered, currently many benefit plans offer a bewildering range of options: alternative health maintenance organizations (HMOs) as well as fee-for-service plans with different deductibles, co-payments, payment caps, and monthly costs. Many employers also provide employees with the option of setting up yearly medical expense accounts that are exempt from federal income tax but lost if not used.

Retirees, to an even greater extent than employees, confront a complex and ever-changing array of choices—at a time in their lives when, for many, decisionmaking skills are in decline. Since 1982 a growing number of Medicare enrollees have had the option of joining HMOs. The Balanced Budget Act of 1997 further complicated Medicare beneficiaries' decisionmaking by introducing an array of new add-on Medicare+Choice arrangements, tax-sheltered medical savings accounts, and new types of care providers, known as provider-sponsored organizations (PSOs).

People who get sick also face an expanding range of treatment options and, as mandated by the Patient Self-Determination Act of 1990, are expected to play an active role in deciding what kind of care they receive.[2] People have, of course, always made choices about medical care, but the nature of the choices has changed. Previously, the most important choices were of one's doctor and, perhaps, of hospitals. These two choices have, if anything, been limited by the new trends in insurance, but this reduction in discretion when it comes to doctors and hospitals has been more than offset by the expansion of decisions involving insurance, finances, and treatment.

When saving for retirement, individuals face a similarly bewildering expansion of choices. New investment vehicles proliferate—Individual Retirement Accounts (IRAs), Roth IRAs, 401Ks, and Keogh plans (both defined contribution and defined benefit)—each with their own limitations and tax ramifications. Within each of these options, individuals can exercise discretion over how funds are allocated (for example, among bonds, money market instruments and stocks; and within stocks, among domestic, international, high growth, social choice, and so on). Many of the proposed overhauls of Social Security would extend these choices to part or all of people's social security investments.[3]

Health and retirement decisions are not only distinguished by their provenance in governmental policy; they also are alike in being largely unavoidable. Whereas a consumer who does not want to choose between cable channels can simply not order cable, the choice of one or another health insurance or retirement savings vehicle cannot be evaded. True, many individuals effectively opt out of making these decisions by selecting default options or by following extremely simple rules of thumb, but in doing so they are not avoiding making a decision but simply making the decision in an arbitrary fashion.

Benefits and Costs of Expanding Choice

Do new health- and retirement-related choices more closely resemble picking among a variety of urban movie theaters or sifting through the technical minutiae of auto seat belt mechanisms? Are they beneficial overall or unnecessarily burdensome? The answers to these questions require an explicit analysis of the benefits and costs of expanding choice, and of factors that can change the balance among them.

Benefits

Expanded choice can benefit people in at least two major ways. First, it is beneficial when it allows people to select options that are tailored to their idiosyncratic needs and tastes. Expanding the variety of available rental movies or radio stations is likely to be beneficial because people have heterogeneous tastes for movies and music. By the same token, the benefits conferred by expanded choice options will be smaller when the alternatives that are introduced are relatively indistinguishable or when people have similar needs or preferences. Although some degree of choice may be desirable even for relatively undifferentiated products such as electricity or gasoline, the incremental benefits of increased variety diminish rapidly.

Second, expanded choice can be beneficial when it promotes competition among providers, resulting in improved quality or decreased price.[4] For such a benefit to occur, however, consumers must be reasonably well informed about price and quality and relatively impervious to attempts by providers to obfuscate. If consumers can be misled about price or quality, then competition is likely to focus on marketing rather than price or quality.[5] For example, long distance phone companies spend vast amounts of money to convince consumers that they provide the least expensive service, while most consumers remain bewildered by the competing and seemingly contradictory claims.

Costs

On the cost side, there are at least three major components: (1) *time*—the opportunity costs of investing time in decisionmaking that could be used for other activities; (2) *error*—the tendency to choose badly when overwhelmed by decisions; and (3) *psychic costs*—regret, both anticipated (the anxiety generated by worrying that one has made the wrong decision) and realized (the sinking feeling experienced when one realizes that one could have done better had one made a different choice).

TIME. Like any activity, the more time that is spent on decisionmaking, the less time one has for other pursuits. The cost imposed by time spent on these new decisions, however, can exceed the value of the activities that are displaced. As the demands on time increase, people become increasing anxious about whether they are making the best use of scarce hours and minutes, regretful about tasks left undone, and guilty about relationships that are neglected. As a result they are likely to experience a general decline in enjoyment of even those activities that they continue to find time for. When researching investments on the Internet, for example, one cannot help thinking that not enough time has been spent with the family, but when logged off the computer to devote oneself to the family, it is impossible to protect oneself against the intrusive thought that insufficient attention had been devoted to the investments—a decision of great long-term personal importance.

Expert advice does not offer a simple solution to the problem. Although it may be possible to hire an expert to make some decisions, such advice is typically costly and there is always a risk that a particular expert's interests diverge from one's own. Then there is the problem of choosing between experts, which introduces a new decision when the original goal was to reduce the burdens of decisionmaking. Moreover, experts often disagree among themselves, as revealed by periodic feature articles in financial publications that highlight the lack of consensus when different experts are asked to provide answers to relatively generic questions. This lack of agreement means that choosing between experts can be virtually tantamount to making the decision oneself. It is also a testament to the inherent difficulty of the decisions (as well, perhaps, as the limits on expertise).

ERROR. When choices require extensive time and effort, inevitably many people will not take the time required to inform themselves about the benefits and costs of the options they face. Decision researchers have identified a number of common errors of decisionmaking that are exacerbated by "decision overload." For example, as choice options expand, people evaluate a progressively shrinking number of the options that they are provided with.[6] As the complexity of decisions increases, consumers make decisions using ever-more simplified and suboptimal decision heuristics,[7] such as deciding on the basis of only one attribute.

As decision complexity increases, consumers are also likely to procrastinate on making a decision and to choose arbitrary default options. Thus, for example, purchasers of auto insurance in New Jersey and Pennsylvania were given equivalent choices about whether to pay lower insurance rates in exchange for a reduced right to sue for pain and suffering. In Pennsylvania, the default was the full right to sue, with a rebate for accepting reduced rights; in New Jersey, the default was a limited right to sue with a surcharge to obtain full rights to sue. This relatively subtle difference in the status quo led to a dramatic difference in behavior. In Pennsylvania, approximately 75 percent of drivers retained the full right to sue, whereas only 20 percent did in New Jersey.[8] Although consumers in both states were given a choice, their frequent acceptance of the proffered default suggests that they were mostly deciding not to decide.

An expansion of choices can also be costly in situations in which people are prone to choose badly. One such situation, which is especially relevant to health and retirement-related decisions, is when the consequences of choices are uncertain.[9] Among the pathologies associated with risky decisionmaking, perhaps the most relevant to health and retirement decisions is the propensity to be excessively security prone ("risk averse") when confronting small risks. Unwarranted risk aversion results in part from the tendency to make risky decisions one-at-a-time—to "bracket" decisions narrowly and thus restrict the items that are scrutinized at any one time[10] instead of taking a portfolio perspective that puts individual risks in the perspective of lifetime risks. In one study that illustrates how narrow bracketing leads to extreme risk aversion,[11] researchers offered a group of experimental subjects the option of playing a gamble—a fifty-fifty chance of losing $25 or winning $40—either zero, five, or six times. The great majority chose to play the gamble six times, even though other research shows that they would not have opted to play the gamble only a single time. Another group was first asked whether they would prefer five gambles to none. Most of this group wanted five gambles. Subjects in this group were then asked if they would like to play the gamble one more time, thus rendering their choice into one between five gambles or six (including the five already accepted and one more). Most people refused the sixth gamble when it was isolated in this fashion, even though the other subjects had revealed a preference for playing six rather than five times.

Insurance purchase behavior is one area in which narrow bracketing (as well as other decision anomalies) are in evidence. A trivial but telling example is the widespread purchase by homeowners of insurance to protect themselves against malfunctions in home telephone wiring, a type of insurance that is actuarially extremely cost ineffective (people pay an average of 45 cents each month to insure against an expected loss of 26 cents a month—a 1/200 chance of losing $55). Looked at from a narrow month-by-month framework—that is, when the decision is bracketed narrowly—such risk aversion may seem reasonable (45 cents buys protection against $55 in loss). But from the perspective of risk to lifetime consumption power, the magnitude of the risk these people are facing is minuscule.[12] Insurance, it seems, is not an area of decisionmaking in which people can be counted on to make choices that are consistent with economic logic.

Narrow bracketing of risks has also been implicated in seemingly suboptimal decisionmaking by investors. The "equity premium puzzle" refers to investors' low evaluation of stocks relative to bonds, even after any plausible adjustment for risk, which means that returns to investments in stocks has historically been much higher than investments in bonds. According to Shlomo Bernartzi and Richard Thaler, the cause of the equity premium is that investors dislike stocks because they bracket narrowly—they look at their portfolios frequently, perhaps once a month—even though the average investor is saving for a distant retirement.[13] Over brief periods, stock prices are almost as likely to fall as to rise. For risk-averse investors, the declines will be extremely painful and the rises only mildly enjoyable, so the overall experience might not be worth undertaking. By this logic, if people could resist looking at their portfolios for longer periods—that is, if they bracketed their investment choices more broadly—the likelihood that they would see such losses would diminish, and the clear benefits of stocks would emerge. Supporting this logic,[14] researchers had experimental subjects make investment decisions between stocks and bonds at frequencies that simulated either eight times a year, once a year, or once every five years. Subjects in the two long-term conditions invested the large majority of their funds in stocks, while those in the frequent evaluation condition invested the majority in bonds. It is difficult—not to mention ethically questionable—to shield investors from information about their investments, which means that individuals can reliably be expected to make investment decisions that are too conservative.

Not all investors, it must be acknowledged, are pathologically risk averse. However, the beliefs and behavior of the increasing numbers of investors who risk investing in the stock market provide little assurance about the rationality of even their investment behavior. One survey, for example, found that investors of age fifty-four and younger expected to earn, on average, an annual return of 20 percent on their investments over the next ten years, and many investors seem unshakeable in their belief that they can time the market.[15] One manifestation of this belief is the shockingly high volume of trade—the amount of buying and selling by investors. In 1997, for example, the yearly turnover rate on the New York Stock Exchange was a mind-boggling 69 percent. One recent study that tracked the investment behavior of a large number of private investors found that those who trade the most realize, by far, the worst performance.[16] Moreover, when investors sold one stock and used the proceeds to buy another, the acquired stock, on average, subsequently underperformed divested stock. Investigators also found that men are more overconfident than women about their investment acumen, trade more aggressively, and, as a result, earn an average of about one percentage point less on their investments.[17]

PSYCHIC COSTS. Risk aversion is driven in part by a desire for economic security, but also by the desire to avoid experiencing regret and recrimination. If people generally dislike losing money, they feel even worse about it when they believe they were personally responsible—that is, when they recognize that they could have done better if they had made a different decision.[18] Such feelings of regret and recrimination are exacerbated by what Baruch Fischhoff refers to as "hindsight bias"—the tendency to view outcomes, after the fact, as having been more predictable than they were in prospect.[19] Feelings of regret are an important source of personal misery and thus an added potential cost of expanding choice.

In addition to regrets that are experienced when the consequences of one's decisions are realized, people also often experience anxiety at the time they make decisions. Studies conducted by decision researchers suggest that such anxiety is likely to be particularly acute when people lack expertise in a particular domain.[20] In a typical study, the researchers asked subjects to judge the probability, p, of some future event, such as whether a particular football team would win its next game. They then gave subjects the following choice: (a) bet on the event—for example, if the team wins the next game, you win $10; or (b) bet on a wheel of fortune set to give a p chance of winning $10. Subjects who were knowledgeable in a particular domain (for example, those who knew about football or were familiar with the team in question) generally chose to bet on their knowledge, whereas those who lacked such knowledge preferred to bet on the wheel of fortune (even though the two probabilities were matched for all subjects). This pattern, which Chip Heath and Amos Tversky label the "competence hypothesis," expresses a general rule: people are willing to take risks in domains in which they feel knowledgeable or competent and dislike taking risks when they feel that they lack requisite knowledge or expertise.

Summary

Whether expansion of choice is desirable in a particular domain depends, therefore, on the relative magnitude of these benefits and costs. Expanded choice is generally beneficial when it satisfies two criteria: heterogeneous wants and needs and the expertise to make the correct decision. Expanded choice is inadvisable when it requires expertise that people do not possess. In such situations: (1) the benefits from competition are likely to be minimal; (2) the decisions are likely to take considerable time to make; (3) people are more likely to make bad decisions; and (4) decisionmaking is likely to be a considerable source of anxiety and anticipated regret.

Recent Expansions of Choices

How do health and retirement choices stack up against these twin criteria? On the first criterion—heterogeneous wants and needs—although people have preferences over the new options that are being introduced, it would be an exaggeration to say that they address a powerful latent demand for variety. People who fear catastrophic medical problems, for example, would probably do best to opt for an insurance policy with a high expenditure cap. Whether they do so, however, is dubious, as suggested by the fact that risk-assessment algorithms can explain no more than about 20 percent of the variance in choice of plans.[21] Similarly, although people may, in principle, choose retirement savings plans that are tailored to their own age, anticipated earnings profile, and risk preferences, whether they actually take these factors into account, and the extent of the gains they obtain if they do so, are far from certain.

The second criterion—expertise—similarly does not play out in favor of the expansion of health and retirement choices; the people who are required to make these choices often lack the expertise required to make them quickly, competently, and without experiencing substantial anxiety. An informed choice of retirement plans, for example, requires much more than reading a few fund prospectuses (which is already quite onerous). For some it requires learning a bewildering array of new concepts—stocks, bonds, mutual funds, money market, risk, return, diversification. Thus, a 1995 survey found that a majority of respondents thought that money market funds were riskier than government bonds and felt that their company stock was safer than a diversified portfolio.[22] Also demonstrative of less than perfect rationality on the part of savers was the observation by Bernartzi and Thaler of a striking arbitrariness in people's asset allocation decisions for retirement accounts.[23] They found that investors adopted what they called a "1/n strategy," which entailed dividing their pension contributions evenly across the funds offered in the plan. When this strategy is used, the assets chosen depend greatly on the largely arbitrary makeup of the funds offered in the plan. Informed choice may further require people to think about when they will retire, spending needs during and prior to retirement, and so on. Many, if not most, consumers simply do not have the time or inclination to gain the expertise required to make informed decisions in these domains, which does not prevent them from feeling guilty and anxious about their failure to do so.

The deficiency of expertise is also evident when it comes to health related decisions. Personal observation of family members and friends when they were trying to decide among HMOs and other medical insurance options persuades me that most of the people I know—many with advanced degrees—do not feel competent to make these decisions. They feel that they do not have enough information to make an informed choice and do not want to invest the time and effort that would be required to obtain the information. As a result, they tend to approach these choices with a sense of fatal resignation that whatever plan they select will ultimately prove to have been a regrettable mistake.

Many of the new decisions that have been introduced do not seem to depend as much on one's specific wants or needs as on projections of one's future health or the health of financial markets—neither of which is a prediction that most people feel competent to make. Choice of medical insurance requires a prediction of the types of needs one is likely to face. Choice of medical procedures depends on the success rates of those procedures (including relevant side effects). Determination of a set-aside amount for the year's medical expenses depends on a projection of likely medical-related spending during the year, which in turn depends on medical events that cannot be predicted. Choice of retirement plan depends on projections of one's future income, which will determine when it makes the most sense to pay taxes on the income. Perhaps most dramatically, allocation of investment funds—for example, to stocks versus bonds—should reflect one's projections of inherently unpredictable short- and long-term movements in financial markets.

This plethora of new risky choices, and its dependence on inherently unpredictable future developments, creates numerous opportunities for regret. When there is only one health insurance option available, people may be disappointed if it does not cover a certain type of medication, service, or procedure that they turn out to need, but these feelings are likely to be much less destructive than feelings of regret and self-recrimination that would arise from knowing that a different choice would have avoided the outcome. When there is only one retirement option, retired persons may be disappointed in their postretirement income, but such feelings of privation are likely to be much less personally destructive than the feeling that one's relative poverty is the consequence of having taken excessive financial risks or of having been too risk-averse.

Many of the new decisions that consumers face, moreover, seem to offer the regret-maximizing combination of very little upside, but sizeable downside, potential. Putting money into a set-aside account can at best provide one with the satisfaction of reducing taxes by a small amount, but it subjects one to the hugely regret-inducing outcome of losing money that remained unspent.[24] Likewise, medical care is at best carefree if one has wisely chosen an insurance provider, but it can be a nightmare if one makes the wrong choice. Investment allocation decisions have a significant upside, but even in this situation the emotional downside is substantially greater than the upside because the regret people experience when they make a bad investment decision is much more intense than the elation they experience when they make a good decision.[25]

Conclusion

Margaret Thatcher was caustically referred to as TINA by some of her critics. A relentless advocate of giving people choices where they previously had none, she nevertheless held one exception to the view that more choice is better. When asked whether the changes she was proposing were necessary or even desirable, her response was inevitably, "There Is No Alternative." Contrary to Thatcher's assumption, however, expanded choice—at least that which is the product of legislation—is neither inevitable nor necessarily a good thing. Rational policymaking in this area, as in so many others, requires an analysis of benefits and costs. The analysis just offered has straightforward implications about when choices should *not* be expanded: (1) when they give people new options that they do not care about or for which they do not have well-articulated wants or needs; (2) when people do not have the competence or expertise to decide themselves; (3) when the choices require people to make risky decisions that depend on uncertainties that they have no control over and no expertise in predicting; and (4) when the decisions expose people to substantial downside risk but little upside opportunity. People benefit from decisions when the outcomes matter to them and when they think they know how to tackle them. They procrastinate, rely on fallible "experts," accept default options, or in other ways avoid decisions that do not matter to them or that they do not feel competent to make.

The makers of public policies are at risk for introducing decisions that do not enhance people's well-being because, unlike the case of private sector consumer markets, they do not have to compete against others who have taken these costs into account. Also, new decisions are often introduced in a piece-meal fashion with no attempt to tally the aggregate costs that they impose. Policymakers who contemplate measures that would expand the choices that people face are prone to bracketing the decision narrowly by evaluating each new measure in isolation rather than viewing it as an addition to existing choices that have to be made. When viewed in isolation, each of the new decisions that has been foisted on citizens can appear eminently reasonable. For example, isn't it reasonable for people to choose their own health insurance? Doesn't it make sense for them to invest their retirement funds as they see fit? When decisions cumulate, however, eventually individuals are confronted with a "meta-choice" (a decision about how to approach decisionmaking) between a state of perpetual "decision-triage" or, at the opposite extreme, avoiding decisions to the greatest extent possible, which often means taking the default option where one is offered.[26]

Expanded choice can be a wonderful thing, but it can be onerous when it gives people new options that they do not care about, when it consumes large amounts of scarce time, and when it requires expertise that people do not possess. Are the expanded health and retirement choices that people have been given more analogous to the choice of movie theaters or seat belt mechanisms? In my opinion many are more analogous to seat belt mechanisms. As a result, well-intended health and retirement legislation often produces unintended and unwanted consequences.

Notes

1. Government policies, of course, also often *limit* choices, but my focus is on situations in which choices have been expanded.

2. Edward Guardagnoli and Patricia Ward, "Patient Participation in Decision Making," *Social Science in Medicine,* 47 (1998), pp. 329–39.

3. Government policies have spawned other types of new choices as well. Privatization and deregulation now require an ever-growing number of consumers to decide from whom to buy electric power, gas, and local and long distance telephone service.

4. Increased competition does not always lead to improved market outcomes, even when consumers are well informed. For example, in markets for insurance, if both consumers and providers are well informed about individuals' risks, the market is likely to become highly segmented in a way that reduces risk sharing across individuals. If consumers are informed about their own risks but providers are not, then competition among consumers can lead to a complete breakdown of the market as low-risk consumers opt out of plans that are priced too high relative to the risks they face, thus increasing the riskiness of the remaining pool; this in turn leads to further dropout, and so on.

5. Jules Backman, *Advertising and Competition* (New York University Press, 1967); Julian L. Simon, *Issues in the Economics of Advertising* (University of Illinois Press, 1970).

6. Sheena Sethi-Iyengar and Mark R. Lepper, "When Choice Is Demotivating: Too Much of a Good Thing," working paper, Department of Psychology, Stanford University, 1998.

7. John W. Payne, Eric J. Johnson, and James R. Bettman, *The Adaptive Decision Maker.* (Cambridge University Press, 1993).

8. Eric J. Johnson, John Hershey, Jacqueline Meszaros, and Howard Kunreuther, "Framing, Probability Distortions, and Insurance Decisions," *Journal of Risk and Uncertainty,* 7 (1993), pp. 35–51.

9. Another situation in which people often make suboptimal choices is when they choose between options that offer immediate gratification and long-term gain. In this situation, people display a peculiar combination of temporal myopia and farsightedness. In principle, people want their lives to improve over time; they want to experience increasing income and consumption over their life-course, as well as improving health

and happiness. In practice, they are often driven by short-term temptations and costs. Despite their desire for good teeth, people do not floss. Despite rampant "careerism" among college students, many shy away from challenging math and science courses. Despite a near universal obsession with thinness, obesity is an ever-worsening problem in all age groups. And despite considerable concern about retirement, people procrastinate when it comes to saving money. People often recognize that they have problems with self-control and pay substantial sums (or forego sizeable benefits) for dieting programs, addiction treatment, Christmas clubs, and other programs and devices to aid in their efforts at self-control. The existence of such self-control problems does not in and of itself mitigate against giving people choices, but it does caution against introducing new choice options that offer tempting short-term gratifications but make people worse off in the long run.

10. Daniel Read, George Loewenstein, and Matthew Rabin, "Choice Bracketing," *Journal of Risk and Uncertainty* (forthcoming).

11. Donald A. Redelmeier and Amos Tversky, "On the Framing of Multiple Perspectives," *Psychological Science,* 3 (1992), pp. 191–93.

12. People tend to overinsure not only against trivial risks, but also against risks that evoke dread because they can be vividly imagined, such as cancer (for which people often obtain specific coverage, even when it is already covered by their existing policies), airplane crashes, and loss of one's home due to the death of the family's breadwinner ("home mortgage insurance"). At the same time, insurance experts lament the unpopularity of government-subsidized flood and earthquake insurance, even by those at high risk for one of these calamities. See, for example, H. Kunreuther, R. Ginsberg, L. Miller, P. Sagi, B. Borkan, and N. Katz, *Disaster Insurance Protection: Public Policy Issues* (Wiley, 1978).

13. Shlomo Bernartzi and Richard Thaler, "Myopic Loss-Aversion and the Equity Premium Puzzle," *Quarterly Journal of Economics*, 110 (1995), pp. 75–92.

14. Richard H. Thaler, Amos Tversky, Daniel Kahneman, and Alan Schwartz, "The Effect of Myopia and Loss Aversion on Risk Taking: an Experimental Test," *Quarterly Journal of Economics*, 112 (1997), pp. 647–61.

15. Opinion Research Corporation International, press release.

16. Terrance Odean, "Do Investors Trade Too Much?" working paper, Graduate School of Management, University of California, Davis, 1998.

17. Brad M. Barber and Terrance Odean, "Boys Will Be Boys: Gender, Overconfidence, and Common Stock Investment," working paper, Graduate School of Management, University of California, Davis, 1998.

18. Robert Sugden, "Regret, Recrimination and Rationality," *Theory and Decision*, 19 (1985), pp. 77–99.

19. Baruch Fischhoff, "Hindsight ≠ Foresight: The Effect of Outcome Knowledge on Judgment Under Uncertainty," *Journal of Experimental Psychology: Human Perception and Performance*, 1 (1975), pp. 288–99.

20. Chip Heath and Amos Tversky, "Preference and Belief: Ambiguity and Competence in Choice Under Uncertainty," *Journal of Risk and Uncertainty*, 4 (1991), pp. 5–28.

21. This may be fortunate. If consumers did choose medical insurance based on an accurate projection of their own specific needs, insurance would cease to serve its normal risk-sharing function.

22. John Hancock Financial Services, November 1995; 1995 Gallup Survey of Defined Contribution Plan Participants.

23. Shlomo Bernartzi and Richard Thaler, "Naive Diversification Strategies in Defined Contribution Saving Plans." Working paper. Anderson School at UCLA, 1998.

24. According to a December 25,1998, *New York Times* article (section 1, p.1), the threat of losing unused funds in such accounts propels many people on a mad end-of-the-year dash to spend money on frivolous and unnecessary medical services.

25. Robert Sugden, "Regret, Recrimination and Rationality," pp. 77–99.

26. Given that many people will inevitably choose the latter option, considerable thought should be put into the determination of defaults—of the options that individuals will receive if they fail to make a selection.

Comment by James Lubalin

Choosing Health Insurance

George Loewenstein's excellent article, "Costs and Benefits of Health- and Retirement-Related Choice," focuses on the limitations of human information processing and their implications for the choice of health insurance and retirement plans. Before turning to a review of what we know about how people go about choosing health insurance (which is remarkably consistent with Loewenstein's major themes), it is worth noting that despite some emphasis on increasing choices for consumers in health insurance, many people still lack choice. The issues discussed by Loewenstein and those I will be discussing are only applicable when people have to make a choice among health insurance plans.

From a social policy perspective, the most significant group that lacks choice is the group that lacks insurance entirely. Recent estimates are that roughly 40 million Americans have no access to health insurance.[1] Even many workers who are employed part- or full-time lack any choice of health insurance. For example, more than 90 percent of all employers offer no plans or only one plan to employees.[2] Because large firms are the ones that tend to offer choice, 40 percent of full-time workers have a choice of at least two plans.[3] Only in large companies and in government programs, like Medicare, is choice prevalent.

Choice is already a critical factor in Medicare decisionmaking and will become even more of a factor as the changes wrought by the Balanced Budget Act of 1997 are fully implemented. Until now, Medicare beneficiaries have had a choice of taking traditional fee-for-service coverage or enrolling in a managed care plan. Those opting for traditional Medicare also have had a choice of Medicare Supplemental Insurance plans—simplified in 1986 to ten plan models to help minimize confusion for Medicare beneficiaries. Now there will be more options for basic Medicare coverage—a veritable alphabet soup of choices. For this reason, research on how people make health insurance choices deserves the attention that. Loewenstein and other researchers have focused on it.

My presentation focuses on health care choices and decisions, an area in which my colleagues and I at the Research Triangle Institute (RTI) have been working for some time. Loewenstein's article is consistent with a review that Lauren Harris-Kojetin and I have recently done on the literature on decisionmaking and health care choices.[4] To use his terminology, the focus of what I will be presenting and what we have been studying has to do with the error costs of expanded choice, particularly the costs that occur when information that inevitably goes with those expanded choices is also expanded.

I start from the same place as the Loewenstein by noting that the policy rationale given by those who support expanded choice is that an informed consumer is a better consumer—that giving people more choice and giving them better information about those choices will lead to better decisions. Such an informed consumer model implies that getting more information is better than getting less; that people have the capability to weigh the information and make tradeoffs; that people make tradeoffs based on their own circumstances so that their choices fit them; that consumers will choose the highest quality plans and providers, other things being equal; and that all it takes to assure that consumers make wise decisions is accurate, comparative information. However, as Loewenstein has noted, this rational consumer model does not fit the way people actually behave.

In the first place, it presumes a level of understanding of the health care system and the choices that consumers face that simply does not exist. A review by RTI, Health Economics Research, Inc., and Benova found that consumers are able to describe basic health care options they have in general terms and that they understand that providers can have an impact on quality of care.[5] However, consumers are unclear about the differences between fee-for-service and managed care systems. Regardless of coverage, most do not understand the basics of managed care, such as the role of gatekeepers or the concept of provider networks. So, few had any idea that choice of plan might influence the quality of care they receive. This finding was reiterated in a recent study by Judy Hibbard and her colleagues, for the American Association of Retired Persons (AARP), in which they demonstrated the clear lack of understanding of the existing Medicare options—*particularly among those in managed care plans.*[6] These, presumptively, are people who, though lacking understanding of their choices, followed the heuristic suggested by Loewenstein and chose the cheapest option.

Given this lack of context, it is not surprising that some of the other assumptions of a rational consumer model are violated by the findings of decision research. For example, providing information to consumers will not necessarily improve the quality of their decisions. People are limited in the amount of information they can absorb. Decision researchers tell us that beyond five or six different factors, people's decisions do not improve (because they cannot keep all the information in mind when making choices).[7] There is evidence from our research, and from earlier research done in Oregon, that people are overwhelmed by lengthy health plan report cards and are uncertain about how to use the information.[8] Perhaps the most complex report card yet devised is the one prepared this year for federal workers by the Office of Personnel Management. Through my wife, I am eligible for the Federal Employees Health Benefits Program (FEHBP). So, I had a personal copy of this report to peruse. I was not surprised to hear from an acquaintance that Secretary of Health and Human Services Donna E. Shalala was as bewildered as I with this unintelligible array of data.

Loewenstein noted one simplifying heuristic people use in making choices in the face of uncertainty—selecting based on only one salient dimension. Decision research suggests several others.[9] One is focusing on concrete factors (like cost, benefits, and location) rather than more abstract concepts (like quality of care or accessibility). Another is maintaining one's current choice. Another is relying on someone else's seal of approval (for example, National Committee for Quality Assurance [NCQA] accreditation) rather than looking at factors that are used to arrive at these summary judgments. Since different people would be likely to give different weights to various factors if they actually considered them, relying on the easily understood dimensions, sticking with the familiar, or basing one's choice on the judgments of others can result in suboptimal decisions for individuals making choices.

People's needs for health care are not static. Health status and other circumstances change over time, sometimes dramatically. To make the best choice of health plans, people must anticipate their needs. However, decision research shows that, when faced with unfamiliar information, consumers have difficulty projecting themselves into the situation depicted and anticipating their needs at that time.[10] In general, people tend to be overly optimistic about the future and to focus only on their current situation. That is why focus group participants consistently tell us that the information they most want is about "people like them."[11] Not surprisingly, people who are presented with information about retinal eye exams for diabetics or mammography screening rates for elderly women have a difficult time seeing their relevance to choice of health plan.

One other point that was noted by Loewenstein is that in areas such as health plan choice, people do not have clearly articulated preference structures that they bring to their decisions. In fact, decision research suggests that people actually create their preference structures on the spot, based on the information presented. There is evidence from laboratory research indicating that if you give people information, they will change the attributes they believe should be considered, the importance ratings of individual attributes in the decision process, and actually change their choice of plans.[12] In fact, those who change the attributes they consider are the most likely to change their plan choice. This makes clear that people are potentially educable but, by the same token, it makes clear that people may be vulnerable to manipulation depending on what information they are given and how it is presented.

All said, the informed-consumer model expects too much from consumers. Rather, for those who want to empower consumers (the current trend), the reality exposed by decision research means that they will need to do one of two things. They will need to carefully and parsimoniously provide comparative information and background or contextual information to consumers and provide repeated exposure to such information over time, or they will need to rely on human intermediaries to help consumers interpret comparative information. For Medicare beneficiaries, there is increasing focus on insurance counselors and consumer advocates as potential information intermediaries. However, we must be cautious in our expectations of this second approach because intermediaries are people, too. They are subject to the same information processing limitations we have noted for consumers.[13] Some evidence that intermediaries are likely to use simplifying heuristics in choosing plans includes: (1) employers who keep the same plans over time or select only NCQA-accredited plans; (2) the FEHBP, which includes virtually any plan that wants to serve federal employees; and (3) the vast majority of employers who say nice things about quality but select the plans they offer primarily on cost.

There are a number of organizations, including mine, doing research to find out how to minimize the information and decision burden on consumers by effectively culling information down to a point where it can be understood and used to help inform choice. However, policymakers need to learn that offering more choices is not likely to be helpful if they want consumers to be in a position to make their own decisions. I have been pleased to see insurers venturing slowly into the new Balanced Budget Act Medicare options. They may know, better than their legislative counterparts, that making the choice too complex may drive people back toward what they understand—which is still traditional fee-for-service Medicare.

Notes

1. Agency for Health Care Policy and Research, *MEPS Highlights No. 6, Health Insurance Profile: Race/Ethnicity and Sex–1996,* AHCPR Pub. No. 98–0052 (Rockville, Md.: Agency for Health Care Policy and Research, 1998).

2. National Center for Health Statistics (NCHS), *Employer-Sponsored Health Insurance: State and National Estimates,* DHHS Publication No. (PHS) 98–1017 (Hyattsville, Md.: U.S. Department of Health and Human Services, 1997).

3. NCHS, *Employer-Sponsored Health Insurance.*

4. J. S. Lubalin and L. D. Harris-Kojetin, "What Do Consumers Want and Need to Know in Making Health Care Choices," *Medical Care Research and Review,* 56

(Supplement: The Power of Choice in the Health Care Marketplace and Its Consequences, 1999), 67–102.

5. Research Triangle Institute, Health Economics Research, and Benova, "Information Needs for Consumer Choice Literature Review/Research Design," report submitted to the Health Care Financing Administration, Washington, D.C., 1996.

6. J. Hibbard and J. Jewett, *An Assessment of Medicare Beneficiaries' Understanding of the Differences Between the Traditional Medicare Program and HMOs* (Washington, D.C.: American Association of Retired Persons, 1998).

7. P. Slovic, "Toward Understanding and Improving Decisions," in W. C. Howell and E. A. Fleishman, eds., *Human Performance and Productivity, Volume 2: Information Processing and Decision Making* (Hillsdale, N.J.: Erlbaum, 1982), 157–83.

8. K. L. Carman, P. F. Short, D. O. Farley, J. A. Schnaier, D. B. Elliott, and P. M. Gallagher, "Epilogue: Early Lessons from CAHPS Demonstrations and Evaluations, *Medical Care*, 37 (1999), supplement MS97-MS105; for the Oregon research, see P. Hanes and M. Greenlick, *Oregon Consumer Scorecard Project Final Report* (Portland: Oregon Health Policy Institute, 1996).

9. A. Tversky, S. Sattah, and P. Slovic, "Contingent Weighting in Judgement and Choice," *Psychology Review,* 95 (1988), 371–84.; H. Montgomery and O. Svenson, "A Think-Aloud Study of Dominance Structuring in Decision Processing," in H. Montgomery and O. Svenson, eds., *Process and Structure in Human Decision Making* (Wiley, 1989), 135–50; J. W. Payne, J. R. Bettman, and E. J. Johnson, *The Adaptive Decision Maker* (Cambridge University Press, 1993).

10. J. G. March, "Bounded Rationality, Ambiguity, and the Engineering of Choice," *Bell Journal of Economics*, 9 (1978), 587–608; J. J. Christensen-Szalanski, "Discount Functions and the Measurement of Patients' Values: Women's Decisions during Childbirth," *Medical Decision Making* 4 (1984), 48–58.

11. National Committee for Quality Assurance, "Executive Summary," *NCQA Consumer Information Project: Focus Group Report* (Washington, D.C.: 1995); J. Jewett and J. Hibbard. "Comprehension of Quality Care Indicators: Differences among Privately Insured, Publicly Insured, and Uninsured," *Health Care Financing Review* 18 (1996), 75–94.

12. F. Sainfort and B. Booske, "Role of Information in Consumer Selection of Health Plans," *Health Care Financing Review* 18 (1996): 31–54.

13. J. H. Hibbard, J. J. Jewett, M. W. Legnini, and M. Tusler, "Choosing a Health Plan: Do Large Employers Use the Data?" *Health Affairs* 16 (1997), 172–80.

Comment by Mark J. Warshawsky

Choosing Retirement Plans

I am pleased to discuss George Loewenstein's article, "Costs and Benefits of Health- and Retirement-Related Choice," and to relate it to how people make choices in retirement plans. I will first summarize the main points of Loewenstein's paper and then indicate areas of agreement and disagreement. For the bulk of my remarks, I will discuss the experience of Teachers Insurance and Annuity Association-College Retirement Equities Fund (TIAA-CREF), as reflected in three areas where people in the educational sectors have choices in retirement plans: (1) among pension plan types—that is, between defined benefit and defined contribution plans; (2) among pension plan providers or companies; and (3) among investment accounts.

Loewenstein proposes the key factors that policymakers, both in the private sector and especially in the public sector, should consider in deciding whether and how to offer citizens, taxpayers, retirees, participants, and employees choices among alternative options in health, retirement, insurance, and other economic areas. He lists briefly the benefits of choice; describes in detail the costs of choice (in terms of time, error, and regret); sets forth the criteria for the legitimate expansion of choice; evaluates recent expansions of choice; and concludes that most of these expansions have, on net, been negative. I agree with Loewenstein that whether and how to offer choice should entail a balancing of benefits and costs, that framing alternatives and designing defaults is critical to the success of a choice-based health or retirement program, and that offering choice is more natural in some areas than in others. But I think that he underemphasizes the benefits of choice, particularly over long time periods, and also underestimates people's desire to have alternatives available, even when not utilized.

As Loewenstein indicated, one of the benefits of choice is allowing people to select options tailored to their individual needs and tastes. These benefits may not occur immediately, but as people learn about the availability of options and their usefulness, benefits will accrue over time. For example, in the last decade TIAA-CREF has introduced to participants a wide variety of investment and retirement income options in their pension plans. Not all the options were utilized widely at first, but they are being used increasingly by significant segments of the population. And new options are often demanded by the population, or at least some segments of the population, particularly when they see these options already available to their colleagues, family members, and friends. So far, in the many surveys and focus groups of participants and plan administrators, TIAA-CREF officials have yet to hear in any significant way that the increase in available choices is not worthwhile. Of course, education, framing, and a sensible menu of options help.

I now turn to TIAA-CREF's experience with choice in retirement plans in the education sectors. For the most part, higher education institutions can be divided into three groups with respect to the primary retirement plans offered employees: (1) almost all private institutions have defined contribution plans exclusively, (2) a declining number of public institutions require enrollment in a defined benefit plan sponsored by a state or local government, and (3) many public institutions give employees (sometimes only faculty) a choice of enrolling in a public retirement plan or one of several defined contribution plans approved by the institution. For this latter group, the choice of retirement plan type is very important, because the decision may affect the size of their retirement benefits. The most favorable option will depend on the person's age at employment, the probability of remaining with the current employer until retirement, expected retirement age, risk preferences, the effect of inflation before and after retirement, and other factors that differentially affect the value of defined benefit relative to defined contribution pensions.

Robert L. Clark, Loretta Harper, and M. Melinda Pitts, in a study sponsored by TIAA-CREF, examined the choice of pension type and plan at North Carolina State University (NCState), where newly hired faculty can choose between a defined benefit plan and one of three defined contribution plans.[1] NCState faculty are given thirty days after being hired to make the pension choice; employees who take no action are automatically enrolled in the state plan. The decision between the state plan and one of the defined contribution plans is irrevocable; among the defined contribution plans, shifts and partial selections can be made. Within one year after the introduction of a defined contribution plan in 1971, a majority of new hires enrolled in the defined contribution plan, and this enrollment share has increased over time.

Clark, Harper, and Pitts examined the plan type choices participants made and related those choices to participant socioeconomic characteristics, as well as preferences and opinions expressed in a special survey. They found that faculty hired at older ages, who anticipated remaining at NCState until retirement, were already enrolled in the state plan at a prior job, had lower current salary, or were hired just after the introduction of the defined contribution plan were more likely to choose the defined benefit plan. These are entirely rational and sensible choices consistent with predictions based on economic theory concerning the relative value of pension plans to individuals. Most faculty did not view the choice as a difficult financial decision, and they devoted relatively limited time to making the decision, although 17 percent of the faculty indicated in the survey that, in retrospect, they were "not at all confident" in their decision; most of the people in this latter category had chosen the state-defined benefit plan.

I do not want to leave the impression that I believe that an infinity of choices among plan types, providers, and investment accounts is necessarily and automatically a good thing. Pension plan sponsors have a role in placing some reasonable limits on choice. As an example of what not to do, in the optional retirement plan for higher education institutions in Texas, currently any plan provider can offer an unlimited choice of investment options. As a result, in the pension plans at some community colleges, there are seventy-five to one hundred providers that offer ten or more investment choices each; plan participants at Texas community colleges therefore face more than a thousand investment options! At this scale, there are diminishing—no, negative—returns from choice. Indeed, in recognition of this problem, the University of Texas system within the Texas optional retirement plan has recently reduced the number of approved providers to eight. More generally, I believe the plan sponsor should offer participants sensible investment options, with a range of risk and return opportunities.

I will now look at how TIAA-CREF participants have exercised their investment options. As mentioned earlier, in the last decade TIAA-CREF has expanded the menu of basic asset classes and investment accounts offered to its participants. A majority of participants favor diversification among asset classes. In 1986, 45 percent of total contributions were allocated fifty-fifty to equity and guaranteed investments, and 32 percent of contributions were allocated to a combination of equity and guaranteed classes in other proportions. As of September 1998, 15 percent of premiums were being allocated on a fifty-fifty basis among equity and guaranteed classes, and almost 50 percent of contributions were allocated to other combinations of the various asset classes. There was a distinct increase in allocations to the equity asset group—both through increases in 100 percent allocations to the equity class and in asset combinations that included equity assets and other asset classes as well.

Looking at this experience, the 1995 theory of Shlomo Bernartzi and Richard Thaler, as cited by Loewenstein, even if it was true at some time, is no longer the case.[2] TIAA-CREF participants, as shown by their asset allocation choices, do not seem fearful of the riskiness of equity investments. Evidence on contribution flows in other defined contribution plans is consistent with the TIAA-CREF experience on this score. I would also note that although TIAA-CREF participants have embraced the new investment accounts and asset classes, there is little evidence from TIAA-CREF in support of the 1998 Bernartzi and Thaler theory cited by Loewenstein.[3] Only a handful of our participants divide their contributions evenly across the investment accounts or asset classes.

In a study I conducted with my TIAA-CREF colleagues, John Ameriks and Frank King, we looked at the asset allocation behavior of TIAA-CREF participants by age, gender, and size of account.[4] We found that younger segments of the population contributed more to equity and fixed-income asset classes compared to the guaranteed asset class than older participants. We also noted that men contributed more to equity than women, although the differences were not large and were shrinking over time. Finally, we found that participants with the smallest account sizes—generally newer, younger participants—had the most allocated to equity. These patterns of investment behavior do not seem unreasonable.

In conclusion, although policymakers surely have to weigh the benefits and costs of providing options in various health, retirement, and insurance programs, when carefully designed, efficiently administered, and built upon a solid public-defined benefit program, choice-based defined contribution retirement programs improve the welfare of the affected populations.

Note

1. Robert L. Clark, Loretta Harper, and M. Melinda Pitts, "Faculty Pension Choices in a Public Institution: Defined Benefit and Defined Contribution Plans," *TIAA-CREF Research Dialogues,* 50 (March 1997).

2. Shlomo Bernartzi and Richard Thaler, "Myopic Loss-Aversion and the Equity Premium Puzzle," *Quarterly Journal of Economics,* 110 (1995), pp. 75–92.

3. Shlomo Bernartzi and Richard Thaler, "Naive Diversification Strategies in Defined Contribution Saving Plans." Working paper. Anderson School at UCLA, 1998.

4. John Ameriks, Frank King, and Mark Warshawsky, "Premium Allocations and Accumulations in TIAA-CREF—Trends in Participants' Choices among Asset Classes and Investment Accounts," *TIAA-CREF Research Dialogues,* 51 (July 1997).

Comment by Fredda Vladeck

Learning from Workers and Retirees

I have been a social worker for the last twenty-seven years, so I bring that perspective to this discussion. For the last seven years I have been working exclusively in the world of labor unions—an interesting choice for a social worker. Social workers are trained to help people deal with the consequences of the decisions they have made. When I moved to Washington, D.C., from New York City, I found myself at the International Brotherhood of Teamsters hearing the problems Teamster retirees (about 500,000 strong) were having as a consequence of decisions they made, either overtly or passively, at contract time or at the time of their retirement.

Known for having some of the highest pensions in organized labor, Teamsters were shocked to learn that about 12 percent of their retired members were living at or below the poverty level. Not surprisingly, the older they were, the more likely they were to be part of that 12 percent.

In fact, retirees from different eras faced different problems. One group was made up of those who retired in the mid-1970s to early 1980s who were just making it. As employers went out of business, those nearing retirement were faced with either moving to where there was work or retiring earlier than expected and getting a reduced pension. By the mid-1980s this group was seeing the effects of pensions with no inflation adjuster.

In the late 1980s, pensions for new retirees began rising steadily. Before the ink was dry on some contracts, members put in their retirement papers—without making sure the increases were retroactive; without making sure their papers were in order and their monthly benefits reflected the years of service they thought they had; without understanding that, except in a few local unions, any retiree health coverage they might have had would end when they became Medicare eligible. This group was the most vocal about the need for cost-of-living adjustments (COLAs), as pensions for new retirees increased most dramatically during the 1990s.

There was a perception among Teamsters, both active and retired, that with the new pension benefits negotiated in the early 1990s—some as high as $3,000 a month—that those who were going out under the latest contracts had it made in the shade. Whether or not, at age fifty, they took a twenty-five-and-out option—with or without the joint spousal option—the perception was that the pension benefit combined with the monthly Social Security check was going to see these guys through.

With the freight contract in 1994, the Teamsters saw the strong probability that history was going to repeat itself if they did not do something to educate their members about the consequences, at age seventy-nine, of the decisions they were making at age fifty. The Teamsters leadership committed itself to undertaking a nationwide retirement planning and education program. Premised on the four-legged stool model, the Teamsters quickly realized that they needed to establish a national 401(k) program so that their members could access a tax-deferred savings vehicle that did not sock it to them on commissions and fees and that did not have them relying on the "brother-in-law" for investment advice.

With the national 401(k) in place, they set about developing the planning and education program. Now a social worker is taught to always start where the client is, and where the client is, I would suggest, depends on where you sit. If you are an investment firm, selling retirement planning services and investment strategies, your approach is going to be investment oriented because "Social Security may not be there when you need it."

If you are the union leadership, with a belief in the importance of social insurance for working men and women, and you are trying to help your union members plan for a secure retirement, you first need to find out what it is they do and do not know. You also need to understand the context in which they make their decisions.

The others have spoken about decisionmaking theories, the information people need to have, and how to get that information to people. Fortunately, I do not have to repeat all that.

The Teamsters found out that their members lacked basic information and understanding about the myriad programs and benefits on which they were basing their retirement decisions. The intergenerational war over Social Security and Medicare was just heating up and the members were truly confused by all the soundbites bombarding them. Once again, the members, at age fifty, were being asked to make decisions (this time political) without the information they needed to have about what that would mean to them when they were seventy-nine.

The Teamsters needed to go back and do the basic education about how Social Security worked, how Medicare worked, and how their pension plans worked. With more than 180 different pension plans in the Teamster system, members needed some basic information in order to make informed decisions—no matter what pension plan they were under. They needed basic education about how pension plans worked, what the rules were, how to learn the rules of their specific plans, the specific individual information they needed

to make their own plan, and from whom—besides their buddy next to them—
to get the information—all the things under discussion at this conference.

So, in 1995, the Teamsters began the education process. Armed with a core
group of trained staff and a guidebook written for the members that included
worksheets at the end of each chapter, Teamster officials like myself started
doing seminars at local unions around the country. Spouses were required to
attend the intensive workshops for members who were within five years of
retiring. Shop stewards were trained on how to make sure their members took
responsibility, from point of entry to the time they decided to leave, for the
basic steps they needed to take throughout their working careers to make sure
they were ready to retire.

I'm not going to discuss how successful we were. I think that experiment is
still going on. But some common themes were heard as we went across the
country talking to literally thousands of members. The most common thing was
the question, "How much money do I need?"

It is a pretty basic question to which the answer is: "It depends." How can we
tell people what the rate of inflation will be or what their risks will be over the
next thirty or more years? How do we help them? They are the ones who will
have to make the decisions. They could put it in this fund or that fund. But how
much money will they need?

This was a common refrain. I am not sure there is anyone who would be
willing to tell them exactly how much money they are going to need. What we
learned is that advisers need to be careful and understand what decisions they
are asking people to make and what information they provide them to make
those decisions.

A whole industry has sprung up around this new field of consumer information. Even I partake in some of it through the Health Care Financing
Administration's National Medicare Education Partnership. (Increasingly, this
seems to be how Congress tries to sell managed care to Medicare beneficiaries,
whether they want it or not.) Thousands upon thousands of jobs have been
created in this new service industry through benefit consulting firms, marketing firms, etc. All are trying to figure out what the information is that people
need and how to sell it to them.

Foundations are spending millions upon millions of dollars doing surveys,
public opinion polls, and the like on what kind of information people want. We
are spending millions determining the best method for getting information to
consumers and making sure it is in usable form, with the right kind of
information. Meanwhile, with all these millions spent on information and its
packaging, the number of uninsured in this country now stands at 44 million
and is growing. I am not sure who we think will be left to utilize this stuff.

Let me conclude with this insight. As I have traveled across this country talking with working men and women about their anxieties about retirement, and as the few members of the National Bipartisan Commission on the Future of Medicare who were brave enough to hold public field hearings heard from beneficiaries and users of the various programs, I am not sure any of us has heard people asking for more "choices" and endless bits of information. What people are asking for is more security. I would suggest that we need to go back to social work basics and start where the clients are.

6

Regulating Reforms

T HE ARTICLES in this chapter discuss the regulation that
would be necessary to make markets work if Medicare
reform goes in the direction of market-based choices and Social Security
reform adds mandatory retirement savings accounts. They explore the regulation that would be needed to structure markets, assure competition, and protect
consumers. Issues related to the regulation of the Social Security trust fund
investment in the market are discussed, as well as the question of the extent to
which consumers should be protected from making bad choices.

View from the Securities and
Exchange Commission
Paul R. Carey

IN JANUARY 1999 President Clinton unveiled his plan to
reform Social Security. Others have put forth different proposals, and the
debate was quickly under way. I want to stress that the Securities and Exchange
Commission (SEC) neither endorses nor opposes any particular Social Security reform proposal. Given that the SEC's mandate is to protect the interest of
investors, we are concerned about investor protection.

While Social Security reform has not been a traditional area of expertise for
the SEC, many of the issues that arise, such as investor education; financial
literacy; corporate governance; disclosure of material information, including
expense information; and sales practices have long been concerns for us.

At Chairman Arthur Levitt's request, I am leading the commission's efforts
to provide advice to policymakers on how best to address the investor protec-

The views expressed in this chapter are mine and not the views of the commission.

115

tion issues that arise under various reform proposals. I would like to outline some of the efforts that the commission staff is undertaking to better enable us to provide such advice. I will raise many questions that we are working to resolve, and that we think should be addressed in the reform effort. While the reform proposals thus far cover a wide range of topics, almost every reform proposal involves some type of market investment. I will use what I think of as the two benchmarks of the reform debate to illustrate the types of investor protection issues that we are concerned with.

At one end of the spectrum are plans where some of an individual's payroll or contributions would be invested in an individual private account. On the other end are plans where the government would invest some or all of the Social Security trust fund into the market. Regardless of which path Social Security reform takes, policymakers will need to make decisions about how to resolve basic investor protection issues.

First, I would like to discuss the types of issues that we are analyzing in the event that Congress adopts a reform plan that includes individual accounts. Clearly, investor education should be a key component of any individual account program. An individual account system could involve the creation of some 140,000,000 individual accounts, one for each American worker. While many of these workers already invest in the market—indeed, recent statistics show that one of every three households now owns mutual funds—many would be new investors. To maximize the success of this type of program, we need to ensure that all investors understand the relationship between risk and return. Investors must understand the rationale behind diversified portfolio strategies. In addition, investors need to understand that years to retirement should be a factor in determining the appropriate level of risk.

Investors should also understand that the administrative costs of investing in the market will diminish returns. While a 1 percent administrative fee may sound modest at the time of investment, investors need to realize that this 1 percent fee would reduce an ending account balance by 17 percent over a twenty-year period.

At the SEC, we have been working with the mutual fund industry to ensure that fees are adequately disclosed to investors. We have much investor education work left to do, however. Recent surveys indicate that approximately 8 percent of investors fully understand the fees that funds charge. Under any system of individual accounts, however, account expenses must be clearly disclosed. Investors must be able to understand the disclosure so that they can easily compare expenses between investing options. They also need to recognize that switching investments may entail additional expense, thereby diminishing returns.

Other issues deserve careful consideration. Policymakers need to decide who should be managing workers' money. For example, would the management of individual accounts be open to all broker-dealers and investment advisers? Or, should criteria be developed to determine who could manage individual accounts? Would limiting the pool of eligible money managers decrease the possibility of sales practice abuses?

Similarly, policymakers will need to decide what investment choices will be permitted. Should an unlimited number of investment choices, ranging from individual stocks, options, bonds, and private placements to mutual funds, be permitted? Or, would it make more sense, from an administrative and investor protection standpoint, for the government to designate a finite number of choices, as it does in the federal Thrift Savings Plan? If the answer is yes, should the finite number of choices be limited to investments, such as index funds and money market funds?

We can learn much from the experiences of other countries who have embarked upon privatization. We can look to countries like Chile and Great Britain to learn about some of the benefits that a system of individual accounts can provide. But we also need to educate our workers so that they do not fall prey to the mis-selling experience that occurred in Great Britain or the excessive switching problem occurring in Chile.

In hopes of avoiding the investor losses that resulted from the mis-selling and switching problems in these countries, we should also carefully consider issues such as how fees should be structured and how often investors should be permitted to switch investments. Should front-end loads be permitted or would an annual flat fee be a better option? It is important to consider whether a fee structure might unintentionally reward money managers who convince workers to make frequent investment switches. For that matter, should switches be permitted at any time during the year or perhaps only quarterly or annually? Decreasing the number of times investment switches would be permitted may curb excessive switching, but it would also limit investors' flexibility. An appropriate balance should be struck between permitting flexibility, but discouraging excessive switching. Similarly, permitting greater flexibility could have the unintended effect of encouraging investors to try to take advantage of short-term market fluctuations rather than manage their account with a view to the longer term.

Small accounts present a unique set of issues. Many plans propose diverting 2 percent of a worker's salary to an individual account. There are roughly 40,000,000 workers in this country earning less than $8,500 a year. Under the 2 percent plans, each of these workers would annually contribute $170 or less to an individual account. Would an individual account of this size make economic sense for both the worker and the money manager? Or, would it make more sense for these workers to invest in a program like the federal Thrift Savings Plan until their accounts increase in value?

Let me now turn to some of the issues that we are analyzing in the event that Congress adopts a reform plan that includes government investment of some portion of the trust fund into the market. Proponents of this approach point out that administrative costs would be lower and market risk would be spread more broadly than under a system of individual accounts. However, this option has served as a lightning rod for criticism. Federal Reserve Chairman Alan Greenspan has expressed concerns that the investment decisions for the portion of the trust fund invested in the market might be influenced by political pressures. Many wonder who would decide what to buy and whether there would be political pressure on the government to invest only in companies that produce socially responsible products. Critics also have asked how the government shares would be voted. Some plans envision the government retaining an investment adviser to serve as portfolio manager for the portion of the trust fund assets to be invested in the market.

With respect to voting, several arrangements come to mind. The portfolio manager, like portfolio managers of mutual funds, could vote the shares held by the trust fund consistent with the fiduciary duties, or, in other words, the portfolio manager could vote the shares in a manner that is in the best interest of its shareholders, without any interference in the process by government. Other voting arrangements are also possible. For example, the portfolio manager could mirror the votes of the other shareholders. In simpler terms, the portfolio manager would cast votes in the same proportion as the votes cast by the other shareholders of the issuer. These and other types of voting arrangements are useful to explore and may serve to lessen the potential for misuse of voting powers.

With respect to investment choices, some of the concerns raised may be lessened if the trust fund assets were invested in accordance with an already existing index. Or, investment choices could be made pursuant to preestablished investment criteria. Of course, the selection of the portfolio manager and the creation of the investment criteria raise other issues about how these things would be accomplished.

Critics have also raised other important issues. Some worry that government investment of the trust fund assets could provide an incentive for the government to try to control market fluctuations. If the fund invests in individual securities, as opposed to an index, should the investments be diversified? Would sufficient quality investments be available given the large amount of money to be invested? We also need to consider whether the massive influx of capital into the market will have an effect on other market activities, like capital formation or the rate of return on investment.

More issues still deserve consideration. Should the trust fund be subject to protections similar to those of mutual funds, which are subject to regulation under the Investment Company Act of 1940? For example, mutual fund portfolio managers must comply with restrictions on their ability to enter into affiliated transactions with the funds they manage and must comply with shareholder voting rights provisions. From an investor protection standpoint, we need to consider whether it makes sense for these types of provisions to apply to a trust fund portfolio manager. Similarly, we should think about what qualifications the portfolio manager should possess.

These are challenging and compelling issues. As we all know, there are no easy answers to these questions. But we continue to believe that any solution should be guided by the two tenets of investor protection and investor education. While Congress wrestles with the difficult policy issues, weighs the competing interests, and strikes the appropriate balances, we are working to ensure that we are prepared to frame the pertinent investor protection issues and propose adequate solutions. We look forward to providing assistance in an appropriate fashion. And regardless of which path the reform takes, we remain committed to our mandate to protect investors. William O. Douglas, the Supreme Court justice and the commission's second chairman, said it best when he said of the SEC: "We are the investors' advocate."

Comment by William A. Niskanen

Regulatory Implications

Let us start from some first principles. No regulation of private markets, other than the common provisions of commercial law, is necessary when people are informed, when they face a range of choices, and when they bear the marginal benefits and costs of their own choices. Some type and amount of regulation, thus, may be appropriate when people are not or cannot be adequately informed, their choices are restricted, or some of the marginal benefits and costs of their choices are borne by other people.

Even in these conditions, however, regulation may not be the optimal policy response. A superior response, for example, may be to change one or more of the underlying conditions of the social insurance plan so that markets work better without increased regulation. And, in some cases, especially for those who value freedom, the best policy is to do nothing when the acknowledged costs of an imperfect market are lower than the costs of any possible policy response.

Above all, it is important not to assume that no good thing could happen without the government's direction or approval. With this framework in mind, let me first address the easy issue: the regulation of private retirement accounts financed from part of the payroll tax. In this case, I suggest, the only rationale for regulation is that our government will almost surely provide some safety net for those who, for whatever reason, do not accumulate a socially adequate retirement annuity.

Absent regulation, the higher the safety net, the more willing people would be to make riskier investments. This pattern of behavior can impose severe cost on taxpayers. For the same reason, for example, many of the savings and loan (S&L) bank managers made more risky investments after deposit insurance was formally increased to $100,000 per account and effectively extended to all accounts. And the taxpayers ended up with a bill of about $150 billion for the S&L bailout.

One should not be as surprised that all the proposals for increasing dependence upon prefunded private retirement accounts as a substitute for Social Security include both a government-financed safety net and some regulation of the private accounts.

The appropriate regulation of the private retirement accounts, from my perspective, seems quite simple: the government would certify any number of broad-based stock and bond funds that meet some specified risk criteria. Individuals, in turn, would be allowed to invest in any one or more of these approved funds, possibly subject to a constraint that each portfolio include a share of bonds that increases maybe 1 or 2 percent a year with age.

At such time that an individual has purchased an annuity larger than the government-financed safety net, there would be no further regulation on incremental investments. In other words, once they have beat the safety net, then there is no longer any obvious rationale for regulating the portfolios, and they can make any investments.

There are no apparent reasons to regulate the information on these approved portfolios, other than the usual penalties on fraud. I receive quarterly reports on my private pension accounts and more unsolicited financial advice than I need.

In contrast, in some forty years of work experience, I have never received any information on my Social Security account. And the information available on request, I am told, is quite misleading.

Finally, I am unimpressed with the argument that American workers could not make an intelligent choice among these approved funds in their own interests. Chilean workers have made just this type of choice for eighteen years to their great benefit.

The issues bearing on the regulation of Medicare suppliers are much more complex for, in this case, the customers are poorly informed, have few choices, and pay little for the services they receive. The current structure of Medicare is an invitation to increasingly ineffective regulation. The cost of current benefits continues to escalate, since neither the suppliers nor the patients have much incentive to control costs.

Among the reasons for these conditions are the following: The limit on balance billing has transformed the Medicare reimbursement rates into price controls, inducing the suppliers to reduce the quality of services and the patients to demand more services. A one-size-fits-all benefit package increases the political demands to add specific benefits. No type or amount of regulation can be as effective in disciplining waste, fraud, and abuse as informed consumers who face real choices and pay at least some of the costs of the services they use.

In this case, I suggest the focus of the policy debate should be on the structure of Medicare, rather than on the proliferation of regulations, such as the Patient's Bill of Rights now being considered, in the vain hope of offsetting the biased incentives inherent in the current structure.

Now, as you should expect by this time, I suggest the structure of Medicare should be changed to increase the information, choice, and incentives of both the suppliers and the consumers. In my own proposal for a three-part payment structure, the Medicare-eligible population would pay nothing for the cost of a standard annual physical.[1] They would then pay the full price for incremental services up to an income-tested deductible. They would also pay a copayment for services above the deductible, equal to the difference between the provider fee and a Medicare reimbursement rate equal to the rate charged by the lowest cost provider for that service in the region.

The primary effects of this payment structure would be to encourage an annual physical, reduce the amount of routine medical services demanded (especially by those with higher income), and reduce the use of the highest price medical services for expenditures above the deductible. The amount by which Medicare payments would be reduced would be a function, thus, of both income and the relative use of the higher-priced services.

Eliminating the restrictions on balance billing is necessary to ensure a continued supply of medical services to the Medicare-eligible population. And the reduction of medical services demanded by this group would also reduce the relative inflation of medical services to all groups.

Medicare would then be transferred from a comprehensive health insurance plan into a catastrophic plan for which the deductible is proportional to income. By improving choice and incentives, this proposal would require little or no Medicare-specific regulation.

In conclusion, a consumer-friendly social insurance system requires very little specific regulation.

Note

1. Niskanen, William A., and Marilyn Moon, "Should Eligibility for Medicare Be Means-Tested? A Debate" in Andrew E. Scharlach and Lenard W. Kaye, eds., *Controversial Issues in Aging* (Allyn and Bacon 1997), pp. 13–21.

Comment by Kathleen Sebelius

State Insurance Perspective

I do not differ substantially from the premise that was laid out by William Niskanen. Where I do differ is that virtually none of the elements that he describes in the marketplace exists right now. While I think you could have that scenario if you moved into a very different system, the system we have right now does not lend itself very well.

My comments are directed toward the health insurance arena—especially Medicare. In terms of Medicare, we do not have a real market right now, so you cannot apply free market principles. We do not have uniform regulation. Health insurance has a dual regulatory system. Right now, in Kansas, as in most states, the market looks like a 30-30-30-10 split: about 30 percent of the people are fully insured under state regulation; 30 percent of the people are in self-insured ERISA plans, both employees and retirees; 30 percent are in some kind of government insurance, again under a federal umbrella, either Medicaid or Medicare; and 10 percent are uninsured. Kansas has a relatively low uninsurance rate.

I am the Kansas state insurance commissioner. My agency regulates only 30 percent of the market. There really is no counterpart at the federal level, so we have a lot of consumers who have some form of insurance without a direct access to consumer information, problem solving, or complaint handling—and that is one of the difficulties with the current system.

Not only that, there is little real competition. Again, using my state as an example, the encouragement of seniors to consider moving to Medicare health maintenance organizations (HMOs) is difficult, because we only have two areas of the state that even offer HMOs as an option. The rest is fee-for-service. You cannot drive people toward the lower-cost managed care option when they have no choice to opt into that option. You cannot set a price system based on making cost-value choices if you do not have a choice to make in the marketplace. It does not work very well.

Also, I think we have a series of ideas that have been promulgated both by Congress and by federal agencies that frankly I am not sure are true. I know in our experience that the seniors who have chosen managed care as an option, in the two parts of the state that they can have that option, are typically not healthier than the general population. They did not select the HMO option because they love managed care and are thrilled about this new system. They wanted to get low- or no-cost prescription drugs and to move into a zero-premium plan.

So it is an adverse selection. We do not have a healthier population in HMOs. In many cases, we have a poorer and sicker population. So I am not sure that it is correct to assume that somehow we are going to be able to shave money off the HMOs because they are dealing with a healthier population. This premise is certainly not true in Kansas.

We just had a sort of mini-crisis around the country, which, I think, is a pretty good indication of how government practices and regulatory policies do not necessarily fit. The Balanced Budget Act of 1997 led to Medicare+Choice, with its emphasis on moving people into Medicare managed care, shaving money off HMOs, and putting risk adjustment in place. This continued and, I think, amplified some of the real discriminatory factors of the rural versus urban split. We had thousands of managed care companies leave the marketplace. This left half a million seniors, who had opted into managed care and were happily in that system for five years, without an insurance plan to chose from. In a short period of time they had to get back into a system where they once again picked up a premium and had to purchase Medicare supplemental insurance. There was a great disconnection between the government policy and what was actually happening to seniors.

Luckily, we in Kansas were not terribly affected because we do not have a lot of managed care options, and the two areas of the state where they operate continued in operation. But I think we are going to see more such problems in the next few years. Regulators cannot fix government practices that do not work. Market players will not play in a system where they cannot make money. A lot of the for-profit HMOs looked at the new budget numbers, at the system, and said, "We're gone." They left on October 1, 1998, because of the Balanced Budget Act. They left the marketplace. That is not a productive way to conduct public policy.

Other potential crises are on the horizon. The possibility now exists for provider-sponsored organizations to begin to operate, not by state guidelines or state solvency standards, but by new federal standards. But at the end of three years, their federal license expires, and they come back under state jurisdiction. Frankly, if that occurs, we will be forced to put them out of business, because our laws require a solvency standard that is different from the federal solvency standard. It does not make a lot of sense to me that I will be faced with telling seniors who are getting their health care delivered by one system that we are going to have to move them to another.

I disagree with Niskanen in terms of the value of a fixed benefits package. Having different benefits package automatically causes adverse selection. Take out drugs. Take out treatment for chronic illness. Raise the out-of-pocket expense. You automatically create a selection process so healthier and wealthier seniors opt into this plan. Because they have more cash to pay out of pocket, they do not need the prescription drug plan as much as less healthy seniors. I think this might produce a splintered market that is not cost-effective and shifts expenses to those who can least afford to pay. We would do well to have fixed benefits that really meet the needs of seniors and then allow companies to actually compete with one another—what a novel thought! Companies would have to come into the market, bid for the service, and advertise what they are bidding, all in a very informed way. Seniors cannot deal just with printed information. And while there may be a whole lot of great information on the Internet, by and large Medicare beneficiaries do not use the Internet. Less than 10 percent have access or interest in the Internet. We are dealing with a population in which 60 percent of Medicare seniors have below a high school education; 25 percent have below an eighth-grade education. What we need are counselors in local communities, meeting one-on-one with live human beings—not a computerized phone system where someone may answer the phone who knows something about what you need to know somewhere down the line.

To get to the *informed consumer*, which is a favorite term, there are a lot of steps that must be taken. There needs to be a competitive market. We need reasonable regulations over that market. Consumers need real choices; they should not desperately choose plans because they need the benefits, but select a fixed benefit package. That forces companies to compete on service and price. That is a regulatory system that would pull government out of the operation, would make sense, and would give people choices. Frankly, that would be a system that we do not have now and there are a lot of steps between where we are and where we are going.

7

Policy Implementation, Predictions, and Expectations

THE ARTICLES THAT FOLLOW feature some of the key players from two high-profile policy discussions—the White House Conference on Social Security and the National Bipartisan Commission on the Future of Medicare. These participants offer their views on Social Security and Medicare reform.

Preserve, Protect, and Improve—Not Dismantle
Edward M. Kennedy

SOCIAL SECURITY AND MEDICARE are our two most important and successful social insurance programs, and major proposals affecting them are already a central topic of discussion in the 106th Congress. Social Security and Medicare represent America at its best. They reflect a commitment to every worker that disability and retirement will not mean poverty and untreated illness. They are a compact between the federal government and its citizens that says: work hard and contribute to the system when you are young and we will guarantee basic security when you are old.

It is said that the measure of a society is how well it takes care of its most vulnerable citizens—the very young and the very old. And by that standard, Social Security and Medicare are among the finest achievements in our history.

Medicare and Social Security are entitlements, but they are earned entitlements. They are not welfare. They are not charity. They carry no stigma. They are true social insurance.

All of us know that both Medicare and Social Security have redistributive aspects. But we also know that the American people know as well that, at the most basic level, they are programs to which everyone contributes and from which everyone benefits.

The immense success of Social Security and Medicare does not mean that they do not require adjustments, modernization, and improvement. But the right approach is to address these needs without undermining the basic guarantees. We need to keep the security in Social Security, and keep the promise of good medical care in Medicare.

For the decades that Social Security and Medicare have been in place, our government has said, "They will be there when you retire." The quality of retirement and the quality of health care should not depend on the ups and downs of the stock market and the whims of private insurance companies. Our goal is to preserve the ironclad guarantee of health security and financial security in the all-important retirement years. We do not have to destroy Social Security and Medicare in order to save them.

Social Security

On Social Security, all sides can agree that it is the most successful program ever designed to lift the elderly out of poverty and to guarantee their financial security. For two-thirds of American senior citizens, Social Security retirement benefits provide more than half their annual income. For 42 percent of them, it is more than three-quarters of their income.

Social Security enables millions of elderly Americans to spend their retirement years in dignity. Without it, half the nation's elderly would be living in poverty.

But it is much more than a retirement program. Approximately 30 percent of its benefits support disabled persons of all ages, and their families, and surviving dependents of breadwinners who have died prematurely. Each year Social Security benefits keep more than one million children out of poverty. It is a comprehensive insurance policy, protecting vast numbers of Americans from catastrophic loss of earning power.

Like Mark Twain, the obituaries for Social Security are premature. The program is fundamentally sound. It has significant resources to fully fund current benefits for thirty years. Beyond 2030, as the population ages, the shortfall will begin and continue to worsen if nothing is done.

If we plan for the future by addressing this problem now, the shortfall can be eliminated with relatively minor adjustments. The benefit expectations of future recipients can be preserved, and the solvency of Social Security guaranteed for at least the next seventy-five years.

Unfortunately, the magnitude of the long-term financial problem is being exaggerated by those whose goal is to privatize a major portion of the current system. As a recent editorial in *Business Week* magazine said:

There are two simple truths about the Social Security crisis. A modest long-term problem is being hyped into an impending catastrophe. And the battle lines drawn in Washington over Social Security have less to do with pragmatic solutions than with liberal-conservative wars dating back to the Roosevelt administration.

Instead of saving Social Security, plans to divert a portion of its revenues into private accounts would undermine the guaranteed benefits that senior citizens rely on. Private accounts would be fine as a supplement to Social Security, but they are no substitute for it. The guaranteed benefits of Social Security are the only firm foundation on which to build a secure retirement.

The concept of creating private retirement accounts with payroll tax dollars taken from the trust fund is incompatible with the fundamental principle of social insurance at the heart of Social Security. Every dollar shifted to these private accounts will be one dollar less for the guarantee of financial security. To do so would put the risk on each individual instead of spreading the risk across the workforce.

Those who argue for individual accounts make their case based on "average returns." But life is not lived "on average." For every worker whose private account produces above-average retirement benefits, another worker will be left with inadequate resources for retirement.

A recent Brookings Institution study vividly illustrates the wide variation in retirement savings that workers who invest the same amount of money in the same stocks over a forty-year period will have, depending on when they reach retirement age.

A worker who retired in 1975 would have received less than half the real retirement income of a worker investing the same amount of money in the same stocks who retired in 1969.

A worker who retired on October 20, 1987, and purchased an annuity would receive a monthly payment 18 percent less than a worker who retired in September of the same year.

A worker who retired on August 31, 1998, and purchased an annuity would receive 21 percent less than a worker who retired just two months earlier.

These variations demonstrate the substantial risks to retirees that can result from substituting individual investment accounts for part of Social Security's guaranteed benefits. Suppose a worker who has spent forty years in physically strenuous jobs reaches retirement age during a bear market. What will we tell him or her—"You have to keep working until the bulls return to Wall Street"?

Shifting payroll tax dollars from Social Security to private accounts would undermine social insurance principles in another way. The goal of Social

Security is to provide elderly citizens with financial security in old age, regardless of their salary in their working years. That is why Social Security has always had a progressive benefits structure. Low-income workers receive a higher return on their payroll tax payments than other workers.

The reason is obvious. Without a progressive benefits structure, employees who spent their working years in low-wage jobs would never be able to retire. Their payroll tax contributions could not possibly finance a secure retirement. Americans paid at the minimum wage work every bit as hard—often harder—than those who receive far more. They have earned the right to retire with dignity and security. The progressive structure particularly helps women, who generally earn less and live longer than men. Privatization, by its very nature, eliminates progressivity in benefits. It would harm those seniors the most whose need is greatest. It would push millions into poverty.

The plan announced by President Clinton in his 1999 State of the Union address would allocate nearly two-thirds of the budget surplus to the Social Security trust fund, thereby closing the shortfall without raising taxes or significantly reducing benefits. Much of the shortfall can be closed by merely broadening the investments made by the trust fund. This step would increase the annual rate of return in a manner that the foremost experts on Social Security consider safe. Similar investments are routinely made by most state and municipal public pension funds. There would be absolutely no risk to individual beneficiaries. The overwhelming majority of today's workers would be unaffected by these changes. Current and future beneficiaries would be protected.

I believe there is a role for private accounts, as long as they are a supplement to Social Security, not a substitute. So, I embrace the president's dual strategy—to protect Social Security's guaranteed benefits and create greater opportunities for Americans to save more for their retirement through the proposed "USA accounts." It is the right way to save Social Security and make it even stronger for the future.

Medicare

Medicare is just as critical for the elderly as Social Security, and it faces three great, related challenges. Its benefit package is outdated and inadequate. It does not do enough to give senior citizens the highest quality health care possible. The trust fund continues to be precarious, and it will be exhausted at some point early in the next century.

Because of gaps in Medicare, the growing cost of the Part B premium, and the high cost of supplemental private insurance, Medicare now pays only 50 percent of the medical costs of the elderly. On average senior citizens pay 19 percent of their income to purchase the health care they need—three times as much as younger citizens and almost as much as they paid before Medicare was enacted.

The greatest gap in Medicare—and the greatest anachronism—is its failure to cover prescription drugs. Ninety-nine percent of all employer-based plans— 99 percent—cover prescription drugs today. But Medicare is still stuck in the thirty-five years ago past, when private plans did not provide the coverage.

Prescription drugs are the single largest out-of-pocket cost to the elderly for health services. The average senior citizen fills an average of eighteen prescriptions a year and takes four to six prescriptions daily. Many face monthly bills of $100 or $200 or more.

The lack of prescription drug coverage is not just a financial burden to the elderly. It condemns too many senior citizens to second-class medicine. Prescription drugs are essential for effective medical care. And they will be even more so in the years ahead, since so many of the miracle cures of the future will be based on pharmaceutical products.

President Clinton has correctly identified prescription drug coverage as one of the highest priorities in Medicare reform. Action is long overdue, and Congress should act in 1999 to address it. There could be no better or more appropriate way to finance this new benefit than recovering, through legislation or through the lawsuit the president has announced, the exorbitant cost that smoking imposes on Medicare and our society as a whole.

We must solve the other problems of Medicare, too. Misuse of prescription drugs results in avoidable illnesses that cost Medicare as much as $16 billion annually, while imposing vast misery on senior citizens.

Illness due to pneumonia and influenza costs Medicare $3 billion a year. But 86 percent of the elderly are not vaccinated against pneumonia, and only half receive the recommended flu shots.

Stroke attacks 3 million Americans a year—a high proportion on Medicare—at a cost of $30 billion a year. Victims receiving the new clot-dissolving drugs in the first hours after a stroke recover more fully and quickly than other patients. But timely use of this new therapy is rare.

Beta blockers taken after a heart attack should be standard treatment to reduce the likelihood of future attacks. But only a fraction of the elderly receive them.

Only 15 percent of elderly women receive timely pap smears and mammograms, with tragic results and unnecessary costs to Medicare as well.

The largest challenge that Medicare faces is financing the baby boom generation. This is the challenge that has received the most attention in the press and in Congress. It is an important debate—but it is also a debate that is filled with misinterpretation.

Understanding certain facts helps us put the long-term financing issue in perspective. President Clinton's proposal to use 15 percent of the surplus to fund Medicare will keep it healthy until at least 2020. This the longest projected period of solvency that Medicare has had in its entire history. In addition, long-term projections in a field as dynamic as modern medicine are of little value. Twenty years ago, who would have imagined the outpouring of new scientific findings that offer hope for curing the diseases that afflict millions of our fellow citizens?

Who would have predicted that so many procedures that routinely required long hospital stays would be successfully performed on an outpatient basis or require only a few days of hospital care, thereby saving large sums for Medicare?

The new biology of the next century means that no one can say with certainty that heart disease or cancer will even be treated in a hospital.

Unlike Social Security, any approach that calls for steps now to keep Medicare solvent for the next thirty to fifty years is doomed to failure.

These basic facts about Medicare are ample reason to avoid solutions based on harsh benefit cuts or large tax increases. But they are not an excuse for inaction. The 106th Congress can set Medicare on a course that will result in reduced costs and better care in the future, even if we cannot predict their long-term impact today. Numerous corrections and adjustments have been made in Medicare since it was first enacted in 1965—and there will be many more in the future. Our job is not the impossible one of foreseeing every twenty-first century contingency or accounting for every projected shortfall. We can set a wise direction for the future today without pretending to solve every problem we will encounter in the next century.

That direction for the future should include coverage of prescription drugs and other benefit improvements to assure that Medicare provides the continuing financial protection and access to care that are its fundamental promise to the elderly. When senior citizens do not fill the prescriptions they need to treat their illness or try to do so by taking half as many pills as the doctor prescribes, they are injuring their health—and creating unnecessary costs for Medicare.

Reform must also include a new effort to improve the health of the elderly. The gaps between the best medical practice and actual practice must be narrowed. Every senior citizen deserves the most appropriate therapy after a heart attack. No senior citizen who goes to an emergency room with a stroke should be denied the immediate access to medically appropriate clot-busting drugs.

Senior citizens care greatly about doing the right things to protect and improve their health, but they need information and help. We can do more to encourage lifestyle changes that promote health and prevent disease. We can do more to encourage preventive services. And we can make a greater commitment to buy medical research—the engine of improved medical care for senior citizens and for all of us.

Improving the health of the elderly is worth doing for its own sake, but it is also one of the most important ways to keep Medicare affordable as the population ages. A recent study at Duke and Princeton found that by slightly accelerating the current decline in disability among senior citizens, we can reap potentially immense savings for Medicare. Every senior citizen saved from disability saves Medicare $10,000 to $15,000 annually. Savings through better health far outweigh the cost associated with increased age. The common-sense notion that healthier seniors need fewer health services adds up to major savings for Medicare.

In addition, Medicare needs more tools to manage its benefits—not by denying freedom of choice to beneficiaries, but by offering cost-effective options and economical services. In the 1980s Medicare led the way in prudent purchasing of health care services by adopting the prospective payment system for hospital patients and fee schedules for physician services. In the twenty-first century Medicare can lead the way in offering senior citizens better services at lower cost.

Finally, since the creation of the health maintenance organization (HMO) option in 1985, conventional Medicare has had private sector alternatives and private sector competition. These choices were expanded, with appropriate safeguards, in the Balanced Budget Act of 1997. But under the current payment structure, none of the savings from the private sector efficiencies result in lower Medicare expenditures. And that problem will grow as private options expand.

The combination of better benefits, better health care, greater opportunity for Medicare to purchase services at lower cost, and fairer accounting for private sector alternatives will set the program on the right course. It will mean lower costs, greater peace of mind for the elderly, and sounder fiscal footing for Medicare.

With so many positive alternatives available to strengthen Medicare, it would be a mistake to weaken it by taking steps that would unfairly penalize the oldest and sickest senior citizens, that could force the elderly to give up their family physicians and the right to see the specialists of their choice, and that would undermine the fundamental social insurance principle. That is the essence of Medicare's success.

This course was decisively rejected by President Clinton, by Democrats in Congress, and by the American people when the Republican Congress tried to undermine Medicare in 1995 and 1996. Unfortunately, we may have to fight those battles again.

It makes no sense to reduce existing benefits by means testing premiums, by raising the eligibility age, or by charging new copayments for services. At a time when countless Medicare beneficiaries are already straining to pay the cost of health care on limited incomes, these cutbacks in Medicare are unwise, unnecessary, and unacceptable.

I also oppose steps to link Medicare premiums to the cost of private sector premiums. Under this so-called premium support concept, HMOs and other private plans could underbid conventional Medicare because their quality of care is lower or their choice of doctors is restricted, or because their market is manipulated to attract only the healthy. As a result, premiums would rise steeply for those who stay in conventional Medicare. Too often, they would be the oldest and sickest beneficiaries, who value most the right to chose their family doctor.

By 2025, according to the scenario developed by a respected member of this academy, Dr. Marilyn Moon, beneficiaries could pay an extra premium of more than $1,200 a year, just to remain in Medicare. And this projection does not even take into account the extra upward spiral in premiums that could result as the healthy and wealthy bail out, leaving the oldest, poorest, and sickest behind.

Senior citizens and their children and grandchildren deserve an improved and strengthened Medicare that can meet the challenges of the twenty-first century. And I believe the American people can be counted on to reject any steps to undermine Medicare by privatizing it.

Social Security was the proudest accomplishment of President Roosevelt's New Deal. President John Kennedy took a special pride in his sponsorship of Medicare in the Senate. He campaigned for it as a presidential candidate and fought for it as president—and he would be proud of it today.

Those great achievements are now six decades in the past in the case of Social Security and three decades in the case of Medicare. But the fundamental truth that guided those programs to extraordinary success in the twentieth century are alive and well as we enter the twenty-first century.

Every worker deserves financial and health security in retirement after a lifetime of work. Every family deserves protection against the disability or death of a breadwinner. Let us rededicate ourselves to protecting, preserving, and improving Social Security and Medicare, so that these truths will be as self-evident to every American in the new century as they are to us today.

Searching for Solutions
John Breaux

I AM DELIGHTED to speak about the work of the National Bipartisan Commission on the Future of Medicare, of which I am chairman. There are eight Republican and eight Democratic appointees on the Medicare Commission. The commission has members who participated in writing the first program in 1965 (John Dingell), as well as members who have run the program (Bruce Vladeck). The commission includes people who have written dissertations on this subject and doctors who have practiced under the program. The members have very strong opinions about the problems and solutions regarding Medicare. While it will be a challenge for this commission of experts to achieve a supermajority of eleven votes, we are all committed to working together, so I remain optimistic.

Let me share with you some of the newspaper reports of our last meeting, which I have found to be truly fascinating. These reports reflect various interpretations from people who sat in the same meeting and listened to the session that we had for the better part of one morning.

The headline in the *Washington Post* read "Medicare Reform Panel Split: Discord Centers on Which Benefits to Guarantee." The headline in the *New York Times*, another reputable publication, read "Commission Nears a Consensus on Redesigning Medicare." Then I looked at the *Los Angeles Times* and the headline was "Medicare Reformers Fear Deadlock."

I was confused, so I thought the proper place I should look for an accurate description of what we did was *Congress Daily*, which is really in tune with the daily activities of Congress. *Congress Daily* said "Medicare Panel Debates Extending the March First Deadline." That was the biggest thing they got out of the whole meeting.

The point is, do not believe everything you read about what we are doing.

Let me share with you what we are trying to do on the Medicare Commission and why we are attempting to do it, at least from my perspective. The statute creating the Medicare Commission charged us with making recommendations regarding a comprehensive approach to preserve the Medicare program and analyzing potential solutions to the problems identified as threatening the financial integrity of the program. The focus on Medicare's solvency is obviously important, but Medicare is facing challenges well beyond its bottom line. As Bob Reischauer has said, Medicare faces the four "i" problems: insolvency, inadequacy, inefficiency, and inequity.

In terms of facing *insolvency*, Medicare will grow from 12 percent of the federal budget to 28 percent in 2030. Medicare's Hospital Insurance Trust

Fund, which is funded primarily with payroll taxes, will be insolvent beginning in 2008. The program is *inadequate* insofar as its benefits package does not reflect what most Americans with employer-sponsored coverage receive. As I've said many times, prescription drugs are as important today as a hospital bed was in 1965, and Medicare's current benefit package does not cover them. In addition, Medicare covers only about half of the current health care costs of today's beneficiaries, with seniors paying an average of $2,000 out-of-pocket each year on health care. It entitles beneficiaries to health benefits that are not as good as most people get through employer-sponsored health care.

The system of government-administered pricing and congressional micromanagement causes *inefficiencies* in the way health care services are delivered to seniors. We cannot continue to manage a health program for 40 million beneficiaries from Washington, D.C.

Lastly, the current program is *inequitable* in that there is no geographically uniform or constant set of benefits. If beneficiaries live in southern California or Florida, Medicare will pay for prescription drugs or dental benefits if they join a health maintenance organization. If beneficiaries live in rural Nebraska, they get nothing approaching such benefits.

Medicare has been one of the greatest social achievements of this century. It has lifted millions of our nation's elderly out of poverty and given them the security of knowing that their health care would be taken care of when they grow old. Before Medicare, less than half of all seniors had health insurance. Major illnesses often wiped out a lifetime of savings and imposed huge financial burdens on seniors and their families. Today, 99 percent of seniors have health insurance. The poverty rate among seniors has dropped from 35 percent to 12 percent. Today, the United States has the ninth highest life expectancy in the world. But for the over sixty-five population, life expectancy is the highest in the world. This is further evidence that Medicare has been a huge success. Unfortunately, the debate over Medicare is often dominated by the politics of entitlement.

I have been asked why I support structural changes to Medicare based on a premium support model and why we should not tinker with the current system by cutting payments to providers or raising more revenues. People ask me why I would touch the real "third rail" of American politics and suggest reforming a program that enjoys so much public support. My goal in putting forth this premium support model is to improve health care delivery for our nation's seniors. We simply cannot expect our 1965 model to work in the twenty-first century—and simply putting more gas into the 1965 model does not do anything to make it run better.

Medicare's most remarkable achievement—universal health care coverage for older and disabled Americans—should not be tarnished by politics and distrust. However, political pressures to protect the status quo should not prevent this commission from making recommendations to make Medicare a better program. I have heard from many members of Congress who have asked me whether they can tell beneficiaries in their state or district that they will get a package as good and at least as affordable as they have today. In terms of the benefits package beneficiaries have today, I would argue that it is not as comprehensive as it should be and it is becoming increasingly less affordable.

To those who would say we are only interested in maintaining and defending the status quo, I would say we should be looking at ways to improve the status quo since the current program does not meet the goals many would like it to. I am committed to finding a way to meet those goals.

Former senator Harris Wofford (D-Pa.) was an advocate of giving every citizen in this country access to the same health care system their representative or senator have. Medicare beneficiaries do not come close to having as good a system as I or any other federal employee have. Their system, I would argue, is not as good as anyone who works for a state government. It is not as good as anyone who works for a local government. And it is not as good for them as most employer-sponsored plans purchased by individual citizens in this country. It is not as good as it should be, it is not as good as it can be, and it is not as good as it must be.

Medicare is a much more complicated problem to solve than Social Security, which is basically a question of how you get x number of dollars to pay x number of dollars in benefits for x number of beneficiaries. With Medicare we are talking about finding a way to reform a national health care delivery system for 40 million Americans, whose ranks will soon increase by an additional 77 million baby boomers. That is a much more difficult and urgent problem than the one facing Social Security.

What I have tried to do with the plan that we have out there is to take the best features of what I have as a federal employee and try to adapt the features of the Federal Employees Health Benefit Program (FEHBP) to the Medicare program.

This proposal starts by creating a Medicare Board to run the program. There are many important details that need to be worked out, but essentially the Medicare Board will be entrusted with ensuring quality standards and negotiating on behalf of the 40 million seniors for the best premiums they can possibly get. In this respect, the board would operate much like the Office of Personnel Management, which negotiates on behalf of the 9 million federal workers and dependents for the right to serve these enrollees.

The Medicare Board would have authority to approve a minimum benefit package and ensure that plans do not design benefits packages that would lead to adverse selection. For example, plans would not be allowed to offer a benefit package with just five home health visits, while offering a generous health club membership. They would be required to make sure that beneficiaries are accurately informed each year about what the plans are offering and what their benefits and cost-sharing responsibilities are. Beneficiaries would be able to change plans on an annual basis and move to the plan that best fits their health care needs.

I am impressed with some of the experts who have testified. Federal Reserve Chairman Alan Greenspan recently testified before the House Ways and Means Committee, headed by Representative Bill Thomas (R-Calif.), talking about how this concept would better adapt to the rapidly changing world of twenty-first-century health care.

I, as a member of Congress, do not want to have to be involved in micromanaging by body parts—deciding what benefits should be covered and how much each one is going to be paid from the federal treasury. I am not qualified to do that. I would dare say that neither are 95 percent of the members of the Congress. We become the pawns of special interest every time they want to increase the amount paid for a particular service or add a particular service to the Medicare package. That is not good science. That is not good medicine. That is not even good politics because we all suffer as a result of a system that is micromanaged out of Washington in a way that is not efficient, not effective, and certainly not adequate.

The next and perhaps most important question is: What does the package contain?

I want to be clear on this point: the proposal I have put forward with Representative Thomas would guarantee a defined set of benefits that will be written into law. This proposal preserves Medicare as an entitlement, so opponents of this concept who try to characterize it as a voucher or strictly defined contribution system do not understand what we are doing.

The revised statute would be clear that beneficiaries are still entitled to the same benefits they have today. By that I mean inpatient hospital care, doctor services, other medical and health services, skilled nursing facility care, home health care, hospice care, and specified preventive services, just to name a few.

The next question is how to decide what the government's share of the premium would be. Let me emphasize that the current Medicare program for seniors does not cover 47 percent of the cost of a beneficiary's health care and beneficiaries spend an average of $2,000 out of pocket every year on services Medicare does not cover.

The current government entitlement is a guarantee to pay all Part A costs and 75 percent of Part B costs. Under current law, all of Part A and 75 percent of Part B would equal 88 percent of Parts A and B combined once the home health transfer enacted in 1997 was completed. Since 88 percent of Medicare spending is paid by the federal government, this proposal says the federal government would continue to pay 88 percent of any premium for plans at the national weighted average. The beneficiary would pay 12 percent. This premium support concept, therefore, guarantees as an entitlement that the government will pay 88 percent of a premium reflecting all the benefits in Parts A and B.

The goal of this proposal is to begin to coordinate all the different sources of health care coverage currently utilized by beneficiaries and then add to that coverage. Under the proposal I have put forward with Representative Thomas, all entities would submit their plans to the Medicare Board. Then the Board would calculate the national weighted average of all these plans.

Now, if you choose to enroll in a plan that is right at the national average of $5,700, for example, then you would pay 12 percent of that as a premium (approximately $708). If beneficiaries want to pick a plan whose premium is higher than the national weighted average, they would pay the full incremental cost of choosing that plan. They would have the right to do that if they want to, but that would be their choice. This would give beneficiaries an incentive to choose an efficient plan that best suits their health care needs.

The next question is what do you do with traditional fee-for-service programs that about 83 percent of beneficiaries still participate in. Under current estimates, nearly half of all Medicare beneficiaries will be enrolled in fee-for-service program in 2030 so it is critical that fee-for-service care remains a viable, affordable option for all beneficiaries who want it.

I support creating essentially a "new and improved fee-for-service Medicare" that would give the Health Care Financing Administration (HCFA) the administrative tools it has long sought to offer a more competitive plan.

Beneficiaries would still have the option to stay in the fee-for-service program, but they would also have this whole new world of options, where plans would compete on market prices—not reimbursement rates administratively set in Washington.

With regard to the eligibility age, we are recommending that eligibility should be set along the same lines as Social Security. We should not change it tomorrow to age sixty-seven, but change it over the next twenty-four years at an average rate of one month per year. This would not affect anyone who is in the program today. Clearly, we need to consider some kind of buy-in or new eligibility standard for people who cannot continue to work past sixty-five and whose eligibility would be otherwise delayed. We are working on incorporating a provision like that in our proposal.

Finally, there is the question of what to do with prescription drugs and how to address the issue of financing. Prescription drugs, I have said, are as important today as a hospital bed was in 1965. Maybe even more so because people are treated better, more efficiently, and often times more cost-effectively with prescription drugs than through invasive surgery or a lengthy hospital stay. How do we handle that? I think everyone would like to give prescription drugs to every senior who needs them. The question is: How do we pay for them? There is not enough money with what the president has proposed. There has got to be some other ways to look at this and find some savings somewhere to allow us to include a drug package that makes sense in the premium support system. This leads to the issue of financing. Clearly, additional revenue will be needed as the baby boom generation ages into the program.

I do not want to talk about raising the payroll tax. It is obscenely high now for most people. But we need to look beyond the current definition of solvency that is limited to the status of the Part A trust fund. We need to redefine solvency to recognize the fact that an increasing share of Medicare spending is being paid out of general revenue due to increased Part B spending. These are very difficult issues the commission is grappling with, but I am hopeful that we will be able to achieve bipartisan consensus.

Legislating Reforms for Social Security and Medicare
Bill Thomas

THE IDEA OF THE THEME of this program, "Social Security and Medicare: Individual versus Collective Risk and Responsibility," is one that can be examined on a number of different levels—obviously, risk and responsibility in terms of the individual, and the social responsibility for the program itself. But it can be looked at on a number of other levels, given the various participants—who they are and how they focus on the subject matter.

It is an amazing time in which to discuss these issues because five years ago the speech would have begun: Social Security or Medicare, interchangeable, is the third rail of American politics. Touch it and you die.

My real fear is that this has been turned into some version of a nineteenth-century quack medicine shock machine in which if you grab hold of it and, if you are demagogic enough (that is, if you can urge that we do not sell seniors down the river by not modernizing the Health Care Financing Administration (HCFA) and Medicare, but that we demand that every senior have a government-provided, taxpayer-funded prescription drug program) that shock therapy just might be a prescription that somebody can move from a minority to a majority party position.

Neither of the approaches—leave it alone because it will kill you politically or use it for narrow partisan purposes—really addresses anything that needs to be done. Neither is a structure that gets us anywhere, because, as I see it, what we have to do in as cooperative a climate as we can create, is to figure out how to fairly balance those individual and collective resources to provide an adequate health care policy for our seniors that not only incorporates today's technology in health care delivery changes but creates a mechanism in which tomorrow's technology and health care delivery structures can be integrated in a timely and a cost-effective manner. And that is really the crux of it, and frankly it is an extremely difficult thing to do.

However, it is not a difficult thing for me to stand here and praise Senator John Breaux (D-La.). I think he deserves an accommodation, and if anybody knows me well, I do not do this freely.

That does not mean that I expect a price for what I am going to say. It means that my level of requiring someone to be praised is relatively high. I spent more than a decade in the classroom and I believe you earned the grades you got. Sitting there does not get you a "C"; being a normal productive individual got you a C. Exceeding that significantly got you a B, and bringing yourself to my attention in a surprising and unique way got you an A.

In this particular endeavor Senator Breaux has brought to my attention in a unique and singularly unusual way courage and the willingness to be someone on point, especially considering that he is a member of the minority party in the House and the Senate, and given where the president and the administration are going and why.

Senator Breaux has offered some concrete proposals to address those shared goals I think all of us hold. But for these proposals to get firmed up and to, in fact, produce our minimum goal, which is eleven votes in the commission, will be very difficult. You need those eleven plus votes to create a climate in the House and the Senate to act legislatively on those proposals.

The problem I have is that most of the time when people are criticizing some of the proposals that the senator put on the table, they are criticizing proposals that are clearly to meet tomorrow's needs in today's conceptual context. In looking at the issues, one of the ones I especially like is today's seniors debating the age-eligibility question in which anybody under forty if they really wanted to be a fair participant in the debate—ought to stay in the room and anybody over forty ought to leave, to discuss what tomorrow is going to look like in terms of it directly affecting you. But obviously, that does not occur.

One of the things that has been most perplexing is that the current retirees in both Social Security and Medicare have been the recipients of the greatest transfer of intergenerational wealth in the history of the world. That is a dramatic way of putting it. The way Federal Reserve Chairman Alan Greenspan put it in front of the Ways and Means Committee last week was that these current retirees are enjoying a return on their investments at greater than market value—something on the order of two- or three-fold. And that admirable achievement simply cannot be sustained because of the demographic situation in which we find ourselves. So, if we cannot sustain it, we need to figure out how we overhaul Medicare.

Let us focus narrowly on Medicare. Does Medicare need an overhaul? Of course it does. Does HCFA need to be modernized? Of course it does. But if you are going to provide competitive tools for a modern HCFA, then those competitive tools have to be exercised by HCFA in a competitive environment. I mean, providing those competitive tools to the current structure makes no sense at all if you really want to achieve what we were talking about, and that is an effective integration of today's and tomorrow's technology in health care delivery systems in a timely and cost-efficient manner. If that is our goal, then you have to modernize HCFA, understanding it has to be placed in more of a competitive model structure.

Do we need prescription drugs for all seniors? Of course we do. But the question is not, do seniors have drugs now? No. Do we need to put it in today's HCFA? Yes. And that is the political battle, and some want to do it and some do not. If that is the environment in which this discussion takes place, we will all have failed seniors.

That is why I was a little bothered at a recent White House conference in which the president began his discussion on Medicare before throwing it over to Uwe Reinhardt, who was then able to utilize economic terms like *sinful* and other terms that allowed us to place it in a neutral context.

The president discussed the need for seniors to have prescription drugs using an anecdote in which he related the story of a couple in New Hampshire who were forced to trade food for medicine. Would it surprise you that in today's health affairs, if you have not looked at it, that the latest data—from 1995—puts this discussion of prescription drugs for seniors in the context of 65 percent of all seniors having some form of drug supplemental payment. And as managed care continues a modest increase of penetration, it is almost universal that you get some prescription drug structure under that, so the numbers would have gone up.

If you examine it carefully, if government was as efficient as it should have been in getting those people who are currently eligible for the government subsidy programs for seniors into those subsidy programs, then the number of seniors covered by some prescription drug benefit plan would be 80 percent. And yet the context we are supposed to discuss asks how we deal with making sure *all* seniors—especially near-poor seniors who cannot play either the government subsidy game or the current out-of-pocket or employer-subsidy game for prescriptions—are the ones who are protected from really losing out in this system. How do we engage in a meaningful discussion if the context is, "Americans do not have prescription drugs and they are trading food for medicine"? If it is an anecdotal discussion, it is going to be extremely difficult to get to a responsible conclusion.

The commission has limited time in which to put together concrete proposals. I am ready to look at any concrete proposals by any responsible member of the Medicare Commission to adjust or modify the proposal that has been laid on the table. Senator Breaux's plan is not a voucher plan. It is not a defined benefit. It is not a Cajun gumbo that people will choke on. It is a proposal that has broad support, but when you get into the details, you always have difficulty in fleshing them out. There has been way too much criticism and not enough concrete proposals as to how to make adjustments to arrive at eleven members. We need eleven plus members with the courage to agree to a plan that sets the context in the right way; that is, a climate of accommodation and compromise, handing this solution off to the House and the Senate so that it can be negotiated. I'm very concerned about this approach of using Medicare as a nineteenth-century shock prescription to elevate some folks into the majority.

Although Republicans are now in the majority, I spent sixteen years in the minority. The reason I came to Washington was to help pass laws when in the minority. I very rarely had an opportunity to participate at the level that I would have liked to have participated.

Since I have been a chairman, and part of the majority, there have been some pleasurable moments. The one that stands out was the fact that after an acrimonious 1995 and 1996 campaign over the future of Medicare in which some folks utilized that nineteenth-century shock treatment, hopefully for their advantage, and failed, we sat down and worked out an arrangement of accommodation and compromise. I have to give great credit to Representative Ben Cardin (D-Md.), my friend and colleague on the Health subcommittee. We crafted a proposal using preventive care as a core, very modest in its overall scope and direction; it was a stopgap measure. But it was an 11 to 0 subcommittee vote; a 33 to 1 Ways and Means Committee vote. It passed the House, it passed the Senate, and it became law. It was filled with imperfections, but at least it was a modest step in what most of us thought was the right direction.

To bring about that same climate for what we consider to be our last real opportunity to make the kinds of changes that will make Medicare flexible and effective, we need your help to focus on providing solid, structural suggestions to the chairman, to myself, and to the members of the Medicare Commission, using the senator's basic model. If we can do this we can share in that very warm feeling of putting together legislative packages in difficult environments and watching them pass. But the most important factor is that this changes the lives of all Americans—seniors today, others tomorrow—in a positive and effective way. And that is what we are supposed to be about.

Creating a Solid Framework for Retirement Security
Kenneth Apfel

IT IS AN HONOR to discuss an issue that is so important not only to the National Academy of Social Insurance (NASI), but to all Americans.

For some time now, I have viewed the first decade of the next century as a major crossroads for this nation. Years ago, I saw what appeared to be insurmountable challenges. With $300 billion a year budget deficits, would we as a nation be prepared to deal with our future challenges? Would we have the will to deal with the demographic challenges that loomed on the horizon?

Through some very hard work by President Clinton, by Congress, and by the American people, the path ahead is not as steep as it once appeared. I believe we are in a particular moment in time in which we can deal with this issue, for the sake of the future. The need for action, in my opinion, has never been clearer.

The aging of America is an issue we simply must face as a nation. NASI understands that because of the number of older Americans nearly doubling thirty years from now, we have to find a way to provide for their retirement without unduly burdening future generations. We must, as the president has said, save Social Security for the twenty-first century.

Social Security has been the solid, dependable foundation for retirement security for more than sixty years. It is not only the most successful domestic program in history, I believe that it is one of the great achievements of America's twentieth century.

Both policymakers and the American public recognize Social Security as our most important antipoverty program. Today, about 11 percent of older Americans live in poverty, but that number would have risen to more than 50 percent if not for the Social Security system.

The program also represents a financial safety net for millions of working-age Americans. One-third of our beneficiaries are not retirees, but are severely disabled Americans or the surviving family members of workers.

Social Security has, in truth and in fact, become part of the social fabric of this country. It is the jewel in the crown of American social policy. I believe this program is absolutely irreplaceable. In the president's 1999 State of the Union Address, he proposed a long-range strategy for strengthening Social Security well into the twenty-first century.

I want to talk about the president's proposals, which I strongly support, and briefly discuss four critical points: (1) the opportunity that the federal budget surplus provides us, (2) the need for more advanced funding of Social Security, (3) the advantages of the president's proposals over some of the alternatives, and (4) the need for increased retirement savings, above and beyond Social Security.

Let me reiterate that today there really is a remarkable window of opportunity, an opportunity that many of us could not have imagined just a few short years ago, to address this long-term generational issue. For the first time in a generation, we not only enjoy federal budget surpluses, but we foresee federal budget surpluses for a generation into the future.

Our fiscal discipline has given us an opportunity now to help provide for those future retirement needs. As the president said at the White House Conference on Social Security, "the current prosperity was created not by rash actions in Washington, but by getting the deficit down, by getting the budget balanced. We also should face the challenge of the aging of America in the same way."

So, how can we remedy this situation? The president believes, and I wholeheartedly agree, that we should use this window of opportunity presented by the budget surpluses to pay down the debt and advance fund more of the Social Security system.

Historically, Social Security was purposely established as an intergenerational transfer of resources, so that there could be immediate help for older citizens in a Depression-era economy. We could not wait for a generation or two to establish an advanced-funded system. It was not then needed since tax flow adequately supported the intergenerational transfer system. In any one year, revenues collected were more than enough to pay benefits.

In 1983, as a result of legislation to improve long-range program funding, we moved from purely pay-as-you-go to the start of a partial reserve financing system. And today, at the center of the debate, I believe, are the advanced funding issues, and the questions of whether the government can set aside resources to meet future liabilities. Do we, as a democratic society, have the will to set aside resources and resist the temptation to use those resources for other activities?

The president says, yes, we do. He has proposed that we use federal budget surpluses to pay down the debt and partially advance fund more of the Social Security system, investing a portion of the surplus in the private sector. These proposals would extend the life of the trust funds an additional twenty-three years.

Specifically, the president has proposed that 62 percent of the federal budget surplus over the next fifteen years be transferred to Social Security. This represents a commitment of an added $2.8 trillion to the Social Security trust funds. In this era of prosperity, there could be no better use for this historic surplus than for ensuring retirement security for future generations.

The president's proposal to invest a small part of the surpluses in the private market has generated some controversy. But it is actually a modest proposal. Under current law, trust fund reserves may only be invested in U.S. government securities. These securities are the safest investments available, but they have a relatively low rate of return. Stocks, over time, have returned about 7 percent annually after inflation, while bonds have yielded about half that.

Diversifying the trust fund portfolio to include a modest portion of stocks would produce added "investment income" and reduce the potential shortfall for Social Security. It would provide a higher rate of return with minimal risk.

Social Security's investments would represent only about 4 percent of the stock market. By comparison, state and local pensions now represent about 10 percent of the market. If state and local pensions had not, years ago, diversified their portfolios, then states and localities would be faced with difficult choices. They would have to raise taxes significantly or curtail pensions significantly.

In terms of the Social Security financing issue, the question is this: Do we want modest equity investments or, say, a lower benefit structure? I think the choice is clear.

Secretary Robert E. Rubin characterized this approach as a "prudent balance between achieving some additional yield and, at the same time, not exposing the Social Security trust funds to imprudent levels of risk." The secretary further noted that "if, in fact, the stock market does go down, beneficiaries would not be at risk, because the federal government stands behind the Social Security benefits."

The administration recognizes that appropriate safeguards are needed to avoid politicizing the investment process. Under the president's proposal, the administration and Congress, working together, would craft a plan that ensures independent management without political interference. Funds would be invested by private money managers, not by the government.

I believe these are the best first steps toward ensuring long-range Social Security solvency. Others have contended over the past year that we should use payroll tax reduction for the creation of individual accounts, which workers could invest as they wish. The proposal has attracted considerable interest because it offers freedom of choice and control of investments. This proposal taps into strong American values. But it is also fraught with problems. I believe it would move us in the wrong direction.

Under these proposals, usually referred to within the Washington beltway as "carve outs," the guaranteed economic security provided by Social Security would be reduced. Rather than providing the advanced funding that can help ensure a foundation of benefit payments to retirees in the coming century, carve-out proposals would take tax dollars from the Social Security trust fund reserves. As President Clinton noted in his State of the Union Address, we should "not drain resources from Social Security in the name of saving it."

The bottom line is that the carve-out approach digs a deeper hole. At the same time, individuals would be exposed to fluctuations in the market. And while, over time, the stock market has outperformed any other investment vehicle, individual workers would have to hope that providence provides the timing for them to retire in a bull market and not a bear market.

This does not always happen. In Chile, for example, the defined-benefit pension system was converted largely to a private savings plan in 1981. The old Chilean system did need dramatic reform. And for many years a strong market allowed their private pension system to surpass their targeted rates of return. The Chilean market is now in a period of downturn and individual investors must bear the burden of that added risk. Recently, the head of the Chilean Social Security system asked workers considering retirement to delay their decisions until the value of their private investments stabilized.

As the commissioner of Social Security, I would never want to be put in that position. We need to maintain a program that will provide a solid foundation for retirement, while also recognizing that responsibility for retirement security rests not only with Social Security. We must also strengthen retirement savings.

The president's proposals would use part of the surplus to help Americans create wealth for their retirement years through Universal Savings Accounts (USAs). But let me make a distinction here. The USAs provide individuals with added resources and individual choices in saving for their retirement. The USAs do not carve out a portion of the current payroll tax; they do not take money designated to the trust funds; they do not require a reduction in the defined-benefit portion of the Social Security system; and they do not make the solvency problem worse.

In conclusion, let me say that I believe the president's proposals represent a solid framework for ensuring retirement security through the first half of the next century. But the president also said that we need a basis for achieving bipartisan reform for at least the next seventy-five years, while also strengthening economic security for older women, particularly widows. Of course, there are still some hard-nosed choices that we must face—and we ought to do that now.

The president has put forward what I believe to be a bold but prudent approach to Social Security reform. It uses the budget surpluses—the first the nation has enjoyed in a generation—to help preserve a program that is of overriding importance to this country. It uses this window of opportunity that we now have to provide for the advanced funding that will move us closer to a financially secure system. It melds the safety of the current Social Security trust fund reserves with private investments to realize greater returns in the private market. It calls on us to work together to make the tough choices to strengthen Social Security for at least seventy-five years. And, as the president said, it helps us meet our historic responsibilities for the twenty-first century.

The participants in this conference understand what is at stake. The vast majority of American workers will be able to enjoy a comfortable retirement and the rewards of a life of labor only if the nation's Social Security system is secure. Social Security must be part of the retirement plan for my generation and for my children's generation. Social Security must be there for those whose lives did not turn out exactly as planned and need disability and survivors benefits.

Social insurance principles remain a proven mechanism for dealing with the variety of economic risks that all Americans face.

As I said earlier, we stand at a crossroads. But, thankfully, now all the paths do not lead up Mt. Everest. We can do this. We should do this. I believe the American people are counting on us. Let us get to work and get the job done.

Keeping Medicare Strong for the Next Generation
Nancy Ann DeParle

MEDICARE AND SOCIAL SECURITY are two of the most important and successful social insurance programs of this century. And both are at a crossroads. As we survey the results of the implementation of the Balanced Budget Act and look toward the report of the Medicare Commission, I think it is appropriate to pause and think about what Medicare means in this country.

For more than thirty years, Medicare has provided millions of elderly and disabled Americans with health insurance coverage. Before Medicare, the elderly were disproportionally poor compared to the rest of the population. In 1959, 35 percent of those sixty-five and older were below the poverty line.

Since Medicare, the poverty rate for the elderly population has dropped to 13 percent, although 70 percent of the elderly are still in households with incomes below $25,000. Before Medicare, 50 percent of the elderly had no health insurance. What I hear continually as I meet and visit with seniors is, "Thank you for Medicare. My parents didn't have anything, and I have Medicare to rely on."

Since the implementation of Medicare in 1966, one of the most important accomplishments is that life expectancy at birth for men and women has increased by approximately six years. It seems clear that Medicare has changed what it means to grow old in America, and what it means to be disabled in America.

But our aging society presents a demographic challenge unlike any that we have witnessed in this century. Current and future beneficiaries rely on Medicare's entitlement to benefits. They expect the government to provide it. Without it, seniors and the disabled would lose the security and the peace of mind that Medicare has provided for the last thirty-five years.

The Balanced Budget Act was an important first step to strengthening and protecting the Medicare program by extending the life of the trust fund for ten years. And, as I think you know, the growth rate in Medicare spending last year was close to the lowest ever. Our actuaries attribute the slowdown in the growth of spending to the reforms in the Balanced Budget Act, as well as to the initiatives that have been undertaken in the past few years to combat waste, fraud, and abuse and strengthen program integrity in Medicare.

We have been very busy at the Health Care Financing Administration (HCFA), to say the least, implementing the more than three hundred provisions that were in the Balanced Budget Act legislation, including new payment systems, program integrity safeguards, and a host of other changes. We are also implementing the new Medicare+Choice program, which allows Medicare beneficiaries to choose from a broader range of health plans and options.

This requires a massive new beneficiary education campaign. This program provides beneficiaries with the kind of information they need to understand what Medicare covers and what their health plan choices are.

The Balanced Budget Act also included new protections for beneficiaries and for providers, as well as creating the National Bipartisan Commission on the Future of Medicare, whose mission is to examine changes to the program that may be needed to preserve solvency.

I know you have heard from Senator John Breaux (D-La.) and Representative Bill Thomas (R-Calif.), who are the cochairs of that effort, so I will not spend a lot of time on the details of their premium support model. But I will say that I think it is appropriate for us to pause and think about just what it is that we are trying to fix.

Medicare, after all, is one of the largest undertakings any government has ever attempted. We now have more than 39 million beneficiaries. We process close to a billion claims annually. We expect to pay $241 billion in claims this year. We deal with approximately 1.3 million Medicare providers. It goes without saying that we play a huge role in the national economy. Medicare is the largest single source of revenue for the nation's hospitals, physicians, home health care agencies, clinical laboratories, durable medical equipment suppliers, physical and occupational therapists, and just about every other sort of health care provider you can name. So, what affects Medicare affects the nation.

The Balanced Budget Act cut reimbursements to virtually everyone on that list. And I sometimes think that I have met with just about all those 1.3 million providers over the past year.

It is important that as we look at the work of the commission, and at the options that they are examining to strengthen and protect Medicare, to also recognize that what we are trying to do is an enormously complicated job. In fact, it is not a huge bureaucracy that is doing it.

There are 4,000 people who work at the HCFA. They are managing Medicare. They are also working with the states to manage the Medicaid program. We are launching and running the new children's health insurance program and a host of other activities.

They make coverage decisions. They implement our policy. They have an enormous job to do, and I am the first to admit it is enormous. *I am also one of the first to say that the HCFA can make improvements in the way it conducts its work.* Some of the conversations about reducing the role of the HCFA or cutting back the government role reminds me a little of what Sir Winston Churchill had to say about democracy. He said that "no one pretends that it is perfect. But it is, in fact, the worst form of government other than anything else anybody has ever come up with."

I believe that the way we administer the Medicare program can fall into that category. There is, in fact, a lot of evidence to suggest that reducing the government's role here is not the right approach. Yes, we need more administrative resources to do the job. And yes, we need more management flexibility. But we should not do anything that erodes the government's role, which is a critical role, in overseeing such a massive program that is funded by the taxpayers and provides important protections for beneficiaries.

As we consider ways to improve the Medicare program and extend its solvency, there are some fundamental principles that should guide our thinking. We need to be clear about what we hope to achieve. And again, I would say that is a strengthened and improved Medicare program.

To achieve that, we first have to ensure a guaranteed benefit package that includes prescription drug coverage. Prescription drugs have become not just an important, but also a critical weapon in the arsenal of treatments for illness and disability. Just as hospital and physician services were the staples of health care delivery in 1965, prescription drugs are essential for good medicine today. And right now, more than one-third of Medicare beneficiaries do not have any insurance protection for these drug expenditures. And for those beneficiaries with coverage, it is not always comprehensive.

Second, we need to modernize the fee-for-service Medicare program so that it can compete successfully and remain an affordable choice for all beneficiaries. There have been a number of proposals discussed over the past few years. We want to work toward getting more of those tools so that the HCFA can be more flexible and respond more to a market-oriented system that is dedicated to the good of its customers, the beneficiaries.

Third, we have to ensure clear and adequate support for low-income beneficiaries so that they are able to have the same choices that are available to other beneficiaries. We cannot do anything that erodes the support for this population.

Finally, we have to ensure a stable and adequate level of financial support. In his 1999 State of the Union Address, the president proposed some steps to provide the stable financing the program needs to assure the solvency of the Medicare trust fund through 2020.

The president's framework would reserve 15 percent of the projected surpluses, around $650 billion to $700 billion over the next fifteen years for the Medicare Trust Fund. These funds would be prohibited from being used for any other purpose, so they will ensure that the money goes to helping meet the health care needs of older and disabled Americans and extending the solvency of the trust fund. The president believes that the Medicare Commission, and Congress, should use these new dedicated dollars as part of broader bipartisan reforms, including the drug benefit that I mentioned, which are essential to providing efficient health care to beneficiaries into the twenty-first century.

Medicare has changed what it means to grow old in America. As we move into the new century, we have the challenge and the responsibility to strengthen and protect the Medicare program and ensure that it will be there for the next generation. I want to thank the National Academy of Social Insurance for the far-reaching and unrelenting work being done to help us think about these issues and the administration of the program—especially as we try to figure out how to ensure that Medicare will be there and will be strong for the next generation.

Comment by Sharon Canner

Bipartisan Reform

1999 is a year of opportunity. The stars seem to be in alignment. We have a budget surplus. We have growing bipartisan leadership. And the American people, judging from the polls, have said that Medicare and Social Security reform should be at the top of the domestic agenda.

One year ago, Warren Batts, the chairman of the National Association of Manufacturers (NAM), talked to this organization about Social Security reform. The National Academy of Social Insurance should be commended for continuing to focus on this issue. We should not be discouraged that we have not solved this problem one year later. Rather, it is a positive that entitlement reform has moved so much higher in the national conscience.

On a personal note, I joined NAM in the fall of 1982 as a health care lobbyist—or so I thought. I was dumbfounded when I was also assigned Social Security. The good news, said my boss, was that the issue would be solved in six months and I would never have to bother with it again. Proposed reforms were touted as a seventy-five-year fix. I found the issue totally boring and uninteresting, just a bunch of numbers. Interestingly enough some seventeen years later, I am covering Social Security once again. I have a lot more interest today. Perhaps, it is because I am closer to retirement!

Yes, we are beginning to climb the Mt. Everest of reform, as Ken Afpel has noted. And President Clinton deserves praise for dedicating part of the surplus to Social Security. The president has also said that the current system, as currently structured, is not doable and it must be fixed for it to survive for future generations.

If the budget surpluses do not materialize, however, then what? We need to do more. The president has stated that savings accounts for retirement are doable and feasible. And on that, we agree with him.

The president's version of savings accounts, called Universal Savings Accounts (USAs), is in addition to current Social Security. USAs are an add-on to the system. His plan makes no structural change to Social Security. Absent structural reform, the system will continue to go in the red, beginning in 2013. By 2030, Social Security will be able to pay only 75 percent of promised benefits.

In addition to USAs, the president has recommended government investment of the Social Security trust funds in the private equities market. Much has already been said by other authors on the problems created by this approach. Even Alicia Munnell, a former member of the president's Council of Economic

Advisers, has raised concerns about government investing. In a 1995 study by Congress's Joint Committee on Taxation, Munnell and others noted that government investment of private pension funds would result in lower returns for beneficiaries—an estimated $30 trillion less over a thirty-year period. Government investing has a lot of political risks as well, as mentioned earlier.

On a more positive note, there is growing bipartisan leadership for reform. In 1998 a bipartisan group of House and Senate members, as well as financial, benefits, and actuarial experts and employer representatives came together as the National Commission on Retirement Policy and produced a proposal later introduced as legislation. The commission was cochaired by Senators John Breaux (D-La.) and Judd Gregg (R-N.H.) and Representatives Jim Kolbe (R-Ariz.) and Charles Stenholm (D-Texas).

The commission proposal features personal retirement accounts that would permit workers to invest a portion of their Social Security payroll tax in the private market. This is in contrast to government investing as proposed by the president. Since these individually controlled funds would be invested in pooled stocks over the long term, the risk would be significantly reduced. In fact this is far less risky than depending on the Social Security trust fund that is scheduled to soon incur red ink. The power of compound interest will help grow a nest egg for retirement. As an example of the advantage of equities, consider the fact that the Standard and Poor's Index over the last five years returned 146 percent and over ten years it returned 362 percent.

Consider one more example. When President Clinton came into office in 1993, the Dow Jones average was 3,200. And even last August, after the great market tumble, the Dow was still more than double its 1993 reading.

Contrast these returns with someone born in 1960. When this person retires and begins collecting Social Security benefits, he or she will receive only about a 1 to 2 percent return on the taxes paid. For some minorities with a short life expectancy, the return could be negative. And any portion of the personal retirement account not used by the retiree would pass to survivors and heirs. The current Social Security program has no such feature. In addition to personal retirement accounts, the commission plan and the NAM believe we must retain a safety net, a basic level of benefits for all.

On a final note, I want to clarify the mischaracterization of the term *privatization* of Social Security. The government will never abandon Social Security to be run by the private sector. No politician worth his or her salt would let the system go unregulated. There will always be government regulation.

In summary, I urge you to do your homework. Evaluate the proposals. Do not necessarily believe what you have heard. Trust yourself. Read the facts and form your own opinions. I think that is critical as we move forward to what I hope are solutions for Social Security.

On Medicare, the president has offered to reserve 15 percent of the surplus, which is a good start. More money, however, will not fix the problems of a thirty-year-old program. The president has wisely left the task to the Medicare Commission led by Senator Breaux and Congressman Bill Thomas (R-Calif.). For his part, Senator Breaux has shown great courage in advancing the premium support plan. Much work remains with a host of controversial issues, such as age. The commission would raise that eligibility age to sixty-seven to be compatible with Social Security. A word of caution here. The many employers who provide retiree health care and tie their plans to Medicare would see a major increase in costs. This would likely discourage employer retiree coverage that is already in decline.

Senator Breaux's premium support plan deserves careful study. Rather than micromanage the many details of this proposal, the commissioners could better serve the cause by endorsing the broad outlines of the proposal, leaving Congress to debate the details.

Taken together, we can have a bipartisan effort to reform both Medicare and Social Security. But I submit that Social Security is probably first in line for reform. After all, the program is just a matter of numbers as opposed to the more emotional issue of health care.

Comment by John Rother

Preparing for the Long Term

We baby boomers are an optimistic crew, but we want to be reassured about our future. As this conference comes to a close, we stand within forty-eight weeks of the end of the twentieth century. It is time to get moving on this agenda. We have seen the number of older people in this country double since 1960. We have made some accommodations as a society to absorb that. Surely, we can make further accommodations to absorb yet another doubling when we ourselves retire.

We can stay optimistic as long as we are prudent. President Clinton deserves some credit for getting this debate started in the name of prudence. He has, in a way that is quite dramatic, transformed the framework of the debate. Two weeks ago we would be having an entirely different discussion, and that is after all the study panels and all the cost-benefit tradeoffs. I would like to make a few key points about where the American Association of Retired Persons (AARP) stands on what has already happened.

First, I think it is important to say that we need immediate action to strengthen Social Security. If we are going to reassure younger people about their futures, which is the point here, then we need to act. Even with the use of future surpluses, I would second what the president has said about finishing the job.

As I understand it, the remaining deficit is about 1 percent of payroll. We can take a collection of fairly modest changes in revenues and benefits together to do that. What is interesting about what the president has put out there is that he is not only looking at solvency. He is really looking at how Social Security fits in a total scheme to strengthen the economy so that when we get to 2020 or 2030 we will have a stronger base out of which to finance our own retirement. The idea of buying down the public debt and lowering the debt load for the future is quite creative and deserves more attention than it has gotten.

Sure, there are some accounting questions, but if it is true that the alternative is immediate spending and immediate consumption, then surely we as a group could agree that, in the name of prudence, in the name of reassurance, it might make sense to think about longer term strategies for strengthening the economy by reducing the debt load.

Another idea that deserves more attention is something that Representative John Kasich (R-Ohio), Senator William Roth (R-Del.), and other Republicans have put forward, which is a focus on the more serious problem in our famous three-legged stool, and that is the fact that half of Americans do not have a pension and more than half are not saving adequately for retirement. This is the big challenge.

Whether it is called a Universal Savings Account or something else, a mechanism that would let more ordinary Americans, particularly those of moderate low income, start to put together real retirement savings on top of Social Security is an important step that we should not let slip from our grasp. It is extremely crucial, I think, to the future well-being of that boomer generation, not just to say that they can count on Social Security but that we give them a real mechanism to start saving every week for their own future.

Finally, on the question of stock market investment, the president has made an intriguing proposal. In political terms, the issue is whether we can really insulate it from political manipulation. If members do not see all kinds of protections from political interference there, they are not going to be comfortable with it.

Assuming that we can put together a mechanism that does, indeed, insulate investment decisions, then the question may be: What are we looking at in terms of alternatives? As Ken Apfel mentioned, the alternatives to not doing this might be deeper benefit cuts or higher revenues, and I think then the question is an open question as to where the American public might be on the idea of investment. But the first thing is to make real the promise of insulation from any possibility of political manipulation.

Just a quick comment on what Senator Breaux and Representative Thomas said on premium support. To me, it is premature to offer judgment on a plan that right now is mostly a label, but it is not premature to ask some questions. And I think the first question you have to ask is what problem are we trying to solve here?

To the extent that this whole Medicare debate has for years been primarily in the context of a budget framework, and the issue of Medicare has been framed in terms of solvency, then what the president did was actually quite helpful, in effect saying let us let the budget surplus take care of the solvency issue and now let us start to focus on really fixing up Medicare as a health care program. Let us look at inadequacy, at inefficiency, and at the equities of it. I think that is a tremendous opportunity.

This gives us an opening that we did not have before to free ourselves of budget-based health care policy. Certainly, Medicare, the traditional program, needs modernization. The Health Care Financing Administration needs flexibility and resources. But the key questions to ask here are, what will this proposal do for beneficiaries and for out-of-pocket costs, which are already rising and will continue to rise fairly dramatically? What evidence is there that competition itself can really deliver improvements? I think it is a mixed record to date. What kinds of regulatory mechanisms would be necessary to ensure that this competition would be fair? If we are going to rely on a Medicare board, who is that board accountable to? Is there a fiduciary duty to the beneficiaries or is the board charged with bringing the program in under an arbitrary budget bottom line?

Finally, the key question really is: How can we move this whole system to take more seriously the challenge of delivering health care and keeping the population healthy into the twenty-first century? We will need the new tools. We will certainly need prescription drugs. We need to think more creatively about how to pay health plans so that they do the right thing.

In closing, let me repeat: we boomers are an optimistic group, and we have a big opportunity here if we only take advantage of it to plan and prepare for the long term. I hope we take advantage of it.

Comment by David Smith

Dealing with the Big Questions

I think the policy debate has been framed extraordinarily well, and that bodes well for a resolution that protects and strengthens our current system. I would like to make a few observations about where we are in this discussion and what I think that means for how this debate unfolds and what it means for the country.

First, I want to underscore something that everybody has noted: none of us thought half a decade ago that we would be sitting on the edge of the millennium with a real shot at assuring the security, integrity, and vitality of the Social Security and Medicare programs without radical benefit cuts or jolting tax increases.

We have that opportunity now. It is an opportunity that was earned by an enormous amount of hard work. It would be a huge failure if we were to squander that moment and failed to act.

I do not know if that means we must act immediately or even in 2000, but it does mean that we need to be very careful about how we deal with the surplus and that we should not make rash judgments that preclude, take away, or diminish our ability to use the surplus to address the two questions that are before us.

Second, I was struck by how clearly these issues are being drawn. It is clear to me that the discussion about the difference between individual and collective accounts in Social Security and a defined benefit and—despite the terminology objection by Senator John Breaux (D-La.)—a voucher in Medicare presents two versions of the same debate. This is a discussion about whether we will undo the century's most important social achievement: putting these two gigantic, efficient, enormously important social programs in place. Those who want to take Social Security apart, who want to substitute individual accounts, do not want, as Sharon Canner has suggested, simply to earn a slightly better rate of return. They want to transform a defined benefit system into a defined contribution system. They want to shift the risk from all to each of us. As do those who propose changing Medicare to a fixed-rate voucher program.

Assume for the moment that Ken Apfel, who is almost my age and has a similar work history, and I retired six months apart from each other. Imagine one of us retired April 1, 1998, and the other retired in October, six months later, and that we were obliged to annuitize the value of our private accounts on those two dates. I did that calculation, pretending that I was retiring in both cases. The value of my annuity was down by 21 percent in October, not because

I was dopier or was not as lucky as someone else, but because my birthday was on the wrong date.

If you get the stock market wrong, through bad judgment or bad luck or an unfortunate astrological sign, and you have an individual account, you are at its mercy. That is a huge difference. We ought not to pretend that it is the kind of trivial difference that people sometimes suggest.

The other issue that is before us is the president's proposal. The proposal did us an enormous service. It clearly framed two important issues. I have already mentioned one: Will we replace the social insurance system with an individual account system? The president's answer to that question is squarely, no. That does not end the discussion. There is a range of proposals still out there that would do just that, but the president's contribution to this discussion and his clear answer, that we want to preserve and protect the system, is a great starting place.

The president also addressed equally squarely the other important question before us. We have been told that we either need to find new revenues or cut benefits. The president acknowledged that. The commitment of $2.7 trillion— cited as $2.8 trillion–or 62 percent of the anticipated surpluses is an enormously important step in the right direction. It does not get us all the way home. As Apfel said, it gets us about halfway home. That leaves a big chunk of work to be done and poses the second important question: Will we fill that other half of the shortfall with benefit cuts or find additional revenues? It will come as no surprise that the AFL-CIO believes the answer for the second-half shortfall should be the same answer that the president found for the first half, and for reasons that Apfel made clear.

This program is the bedrock of retirement security for working Americans. It is not part of it. It is not a little bit of retirement savings here, a little bit of Social Security there, and a little bit of private pensions there. It is the bulk of retirement income for today's retirees. As we face the future, that system and its benefit levels need to be protected. As we seek to find the other half of the pot, we ought to continue to look for new revenues and the place to start is with the earnings cap and possible adjustments to it.

One brief comment on Medicare. Senator Breaux referred to Bob Reischauer's "i" list: insolvency, inadequacy, inefficiency, and inequity. Nancy Ann DeParle listed four goals that we ought to have in mind as we think about Medicare. And Senator Breaux also talked about three big questions that have to be answered. What we now know about premium support and the level of specification of those ideas suggests that it does not meet any of the proposed tests. It does not answer the questions that DeParle asked. It does not answer the questions that Senator Breaux himself asked. And it does not solve any of the problems that Reischauer raised. We need to devote more work and more time to this issue. The commission's work does not lay the basis to get this one right yet.

8

International Perspectives on Health Policy Reform

IN THIS CHAPTER Uwe Reinhardt offers an international view of health care. A critic of the chaos and administrative waste in the U.S. health care system, Reinhardt compares U.S. and European cultural values regarding health care and discusses the almost universal dissatisfaction across the globe with the prevailing health systems. While all systems involve trade-offs, he contends that the trade-offs in the United States operate to the detriment of the needy and that social ethics are imbedded in the financing of health care. The text is drawn from an after-dinner presentation.

Thoughts on the Political Economy of Sharing
Uwe Reinhardt

DURING THE PAST several years my wife, Cheng Tsung-mei, has joined me at conferences on "health reform" in the United States, Austria, Canada, China, Hong Kong, Singapore, Taiwan, Japan, Poland, France, England, Germany, and Israel. Ultimately, there has emerged from that experience Cheng Tsung-mei's Cosmic Law of Health Care:

People will be unhappy with their health system regardless of how much their nation spends on that system.

From this cosmic law she quickly deduced two cosmic corollaries on health reform:

There will always be health reform, everywhere on the globe.

and

Health reform will always fail, everywhere on the globe.

If Cheng Tsung-mei is right, and she rarely is not, one may pick any year in the next millennium and safely predict that the National Academy of Social Insurance will be busy making inputs into the major health reform initiative then before the nation. That initiative will be expected to resolve once and for all the global dual problems of *cost* and *quality*. In the United States, the reform will be expected also to solve the uniquely American problem of access to appropriate care for the then X million uninsured Americans (up from Y million a decade earlier, which in turn was up from Z million the decade before that). Then as now American policymakers and their advisers will be reluctant to learn from the experience of foreign health systems that "ration" health care; then as now there will be the hope that the United States can avoid rationing health care by relying on "the market."

Reasons for the Perennial Health Care Malaise

Cheng Tsung-mei's cosmic health care law rests on several factors and beliefs, some of which are unique to health care. They warrant repeating from time to time, if only to remind ourselves why health reform initiatives will forever be akin to the search for the Holy Grail.

The Lack of Economic Legitimacy

First and foremost, by its very nature the typical health care transaction lacks economic legitimacy. That is so, because health care transactions are not based on the personal cost-benefit analysis that the purchasers of ordinary commodities routinely make in the marketplace. The idea that perfect competition within a capitalist order will automatically maximize social welfare rests crucially on this personal cost-benefit calculus. At the very least, that calculus makes sure that every transaction between those who pay for a thing and those who sell it is mutually beneficial.

The proponents of medical savings accounts (MSAs) believe that this fundamental cost-benefit calculus could be made to work also for most health care transactions, if only the recipients could be made to feel personally the cost of the care they receive, at the time they receive it. As someone who, like most members of this audience, has "consumed" sundry health care from time to time, I wonder where I would get the technical know-how to judge the clinical merits of the tests and procedures that might be recommended to me by physicians, even if I were forced to bear the full fiscal brunt of those recommendations. Furthermore, among every large random sample of health care "consumers," about 10 to 15 percent account for 70 to 80 percent of that cohort's entire annual health spending. Even under a regime of MSAs, then, a large fraction of annual health spending would be likely to be covered by third-party payments, which would spare patients the required cost-benefit calculus.

In short, I remain persuaded that, by and large, the personal cost-benefit calculus posited for the competitive market in textbooks of economics cannot ever be made to work properly in the context of personal health care. Absent that foundation, however, the distant third-party payers who are likely to write the final checks for the bulk of health care costs will always harbor the suspicion that they are being forced by both patients and their physicians to pay in part for waste and abuse, if not for outright fraud. On that same suspicion, many American politicians routinely announce that they cannot in good conscience vote for an expansion of health insurance coverage unless waste, fraud, and abuse are first excised from our health system. Finally, on that same suspicion, many other politicians announce that they could easily finance broader health insurance coverage simply by eliminating the waste, fraud, and abuse allegedly rampant in our health system. And so it goes.

It is understandable that widespread waste, fraud, and abuse might be suspected in the American health system, which spends so much more on health care than any other nation (in 1997, 13.6 percent of the U.S. gross domestic product [GDP] went to health care, or $ 4,090 per capita). Remarkably, however, waste, fraud, and abuse are viewed as untapped economic reservoirs also in neighboring Canada (which spent 9.3 percent of its GDP on health care in 1997), in Germany (which spent 10.4 percent), the United Kingdom (which spent 6.7 percent), and in virtually any other nation. That suspicion is driven by the knowledge that the typical health care transaction lacks economic legitimacy. Because that legitimacy will always be lacking in health care, the suspicion of waste, fraud, and abuse in health care will always be present, as will be the mutual rancor among payers and providers that such a suspicion begets. Since we cannot avoid it, we might as well get used to it.

The Just Price Doctrine

A second reason for perennial, universal unhappiness over health care is that those who render health care typically chafe under budgets that they consider too tight. They loudly air that sentiment at every conceivable occasion. Their conviction in this regard is strengthened further by the (thoughtless) mantra that health and life are priceless, which is taken to mean that any enhancement of either is ipso facto justified. And everywhere there remains so much more health to be enhanced and life to be expanded!

Physicians in particular tend to consider themselves permanently under-paid. This is so regardless of the actual level of their income relative to average employee compensation in the rest of society. Even American physicians, who often describe themselves as professional entrepreneurs and just as often pay lip service to the virtue of the free market, believe that their own income should be exempt from the harsh laws of supply and demand. Instead, they subscribe to something akin to the medieval doctrine of just price. That theory holds that people should be paid according to their status in society (a doctrine, inciden-tally, advocated for physicians by no less an authority than Adam Smith, the father of modern economics).[1] Physicians everywhere echo this medieval doctrine whenever they despair over the meager financial returns to their long training and daily industry, and when they deplore the high incomes earned in ordinary commerce and in sports by persons of presumably lesser social stature. The lesson here is that, however generously a nation may actually compensate its physicians (and by international standards Americans are really quite generous on this score), physicians will never be content with their reward.

The Growing Reluctance to Share

A third major reason for the perennial, universal unhappiness over health care is rooted in the ethical precepts that most modern societies seek to impose on their health systems, with varying degrees of success. That ethic almost everywhere forces the well-to-do to subsidize with their taxes the health care received by poor people. In health care, any reluctance to being one's poor brothers' and sisters' keeper is reinforced further by the inexorable spreading of the income distribution in high-tech economies; this serves increasingly to estrange the well-to-do from the poor.

A natural reluctance to share economic resources is further fueled by the confluence of three beliefs. First, there is the growing belief among the well-to-do that poverty is a form of free occupational choice, rather than merely the product of misfortune. Second, many of the healthy believe that most illness in modern societies is the product of personal life style, rather than heredity or chance. That belief makes illness the personal fault and financial responsibility of the afflicted. It also feeds the hypothesis that universal health insurance coverage would not noticeably enhance the health status of the poor, in part because the poor would not manage their own health properly and also because so much of the health care rendered by modern health systems is thought wasteful if not outright useless.

For these reasons alone, the idea of sharing has become rather unfashionable among the well-to-do, certainly in the United States. The growing reluctance to share is legitimized further by the belief among Americans that they are overtaxed—although as a percent of GDP Americans pay less taxes overall than do citizens in any other nation in the Organization for Economic Cooperation and Development (OECD). The macroeconomic theory that social solidarity itself is a major impediment to economic growth also fuels the reluctance to share. The assumption is that social solidarity blunts the individual's incentive to work hard, to save, and to take risks in entrepreneurship. Often it also embodies the hypothesis that taxation diverts resources from capital formation into consumption.

To illustrate, in 1997 I had raised in the pages of the *Journal of the American Medical Association* the following question:

> To the extent that the health-care system could make it possible, and as a matter of national policy, should the child of poor Americans have the same chance of avoiding preventable illness or of being cured from a given illness as does the child of a rich American family?[2]

All the letters to the editor triggered by that question expressed anger at my having raised the question at all. All but one of the letter writers followed this nation's traditional cultural pattern of delicately skirting the question itself. To his credit, the author of the remaining letter, University of Chicago Distinguished Law Professor Richard Epstein, author of *Mortal Peril: Our Inalienable Right to Health Care?*[3] had the courage and courtesy of answering the question forthrightly. He responded with a vehement "No!" He had explained his reasoning earlier, in a letter to the *New York Times*. That letter had protested passage by Congress of the Children's Health Insurance Program (CHIP). In the letter, Epstein defended his proposal to ration health care by family income, even for children, as follows:

> Allowing wealth to matter [in the allocation of health care] is likely to do far better in the long run than any policy that insists on allocating health care without regard to ability to pay. To repeat, any effort to redistribute from rich to poor in the present generation necessarily entails the redistribution from the future to the present generation.[4]

In positing this macroeconomic growth theory, Epstein undoubtedly drew inspiration from his colleague Nobel Laureate economist Milton Friedman.

During the health reform debate of the early 1990s, Friedman had advocated the complete abolition of the Medicare and Medicaid programs. He proposed that instead every American family should have only catastrophic health insurance coverage "with a deductible of $20,000 a year or 30 percent of the [family] units' income during the prior two years, whichever is lower."[5] Clearly, such a policy envisages rationing health care by income class.

At the moment, the sundry misgivings over health care enumerated above channel themselves into two distinct aims for health reform: (1) better accountability for the resources used by the health sector, and (2) a reallocation of the financial burden of ill health from the collective budget of society as a whole to the individual patient. To be sure, few policy analysts and certainly fewer politicians would ever articulate the second aim quite so bluntly. More commonly, that aim is couched in code words, such as *consumer empowerment* or *market efficiency*. As I have argued at length elsewhere, however, the word *efficiency* actually is meaningless in the absence of a clearly articulated social goal that is to be efficiently reached.[6] The distributive ethic to be observed by the health system surely is one important dimension of the social goal it is to pursue. For example, to argue that the government-controlled health systems of Canada and Europe are less efficient than the market-driven American system would be utter nonsense. These health systems espouse different social goals than seem to be posited for the American health system. More often than not, advocacy of a market-driven health care system for the sake of greater "efficiency" should be understood to embody the idea to ration health care at least to some extent by income class. That idea is not yet accepted by policymakers in many other nations. I will return to this important point further on.

Accountability for Resource Use

Throughout the industrialized world, the percentage of the population aged sixty-five or older is rising inexorably. One could tell one of two quite different stories about this prospect, depending upon the folklore one would wish to feed.

If one sought to stoke the alarm that this prospect seems to stir in many souls, one would begin the story with a bar graph that shows on the vertical axis the average per capita health spending for different age groups in the United States—from infants at the left of the horizontal axis to the very old at the right. The shape of that display is well known to this audience. It shows that average per capita health spending starts to rise significantly after age fifty-five. Depending on the nation being discussed, spending on seventy-five-year olds will be three to five times as high as spending on, say, thirty-five-year-olds. Next, one would point out that the populations of all industrialized nations will drift ever more rapidly into the right side of this graph—into the tall per capita spending bars. The story could be dramatized further by presenting a second graph, which would show the percentage of the population aged sixty-five and over on the vertical axis and the next two to four decades on the horizontal time axis. Now, if the vertical axis were properly scaled from 0 to 100 percent, then the aging of the population actually would manifest itself as only a very slight rise in the line. Even the much feared retirement of the huge U.S. baby boom generation after the year 2010 would show up as merely a ripple. To heighten the audience's alarm one would scale the vertical axis from, say, 10 percent to 25 percent. That rescaling would project for the United States a veritable baby-boom tsunami that threatens to drown us all. Coupled with the earlier display on age-specific health spending, the projected tsunami and the story one would build upon it could not fail but to whip up the desired paranoia. Peter G. Petersen, former U.S. secretary of commerce, and Richard Lamm, former governor of Colorado, would lose yet more nights of sleep over the graying of America.

On the other hand, if one sought to calm tempers and redirect attention away from the aging of the population per se to more important variables that might be amenable to policy intervention, then one would tell quite a different story. That story would begin with regression analyses or simulations designed to isolate solely the effect of the aging of the population on average per capita health spending. For example, if one regressed average per capita health spending in U.S. counties in some year on the percentage of the county's population that is over age sixty-five, one would be likely to get a very low regression. In fact, the coefficient on the "aging" variable may or may not be statistically different from zero. The same low explanatory power of the aging variable has been found in other countries as well, even if that variable is broken down further in a multivariate regression. Alternatively, if one held the national average per capita health spending for different age-sex cohorts constant at some base-year level and then used only the changes in the demographic structure of the U.S. population to explain the secular growth in average national per capita health spending over the past two or three decades, one would find that the demographic change explains only a small fraction of the total secular growth in per capita health spending. The same, of course, would be found in any other nation.

One concludes from this second set of exercises and the story it begets that the aging of the population should be the least of our worries about the future. That story also recommends extreme caution in the interpretation of projections of future health spending for the elderly. In the hands of properly "incented" analysts, these simulations can be made to conjure up any number of scenarios, depending upon the policy responses one seeks to trigger. Far better than worrying about such conjectures about the future would be paying more attention to the question why the aging variable by itself explains so little of the current crossnational or intranational variation in health spending.

Crossnational Variations in Health Spending

Health services researchers have been struck for decades by the high variation of health spending per capita across nations, without visible effects on measurable health indicators (see table 8-1).[7] Close to 80 percent of the variation in per capita health spending across nations in the OECD can be explained simply by the corresponding variation in per capita income. But even after adjusting the spending data for per capita income, the United States still spends about $1,000 more per capita on health care than would be predicted by its per capita income. It is legitimate, therefore, to inquire just what additional benefits Americans actually purchase with these added outlays. So far the research on this issue has been remarkably thin, perhaps because neither the Congress, nor American employers, nor most foundations that fund health services research—and certainly not the providers of health care in this country—have ever shown any curiosity on this point.

Inter- and intranational comparisons of resource use in health care tend to be based on comparative health spending. As illustrated in figure 8-1, however, these comparisons ought to distinguish between two distinct costs on the rest of society. These are (1) the opportunity cost of the real resources (human labor, structures, equipment, and supplies) that are used up in the process of health care rather than in another economic activity, and (2) the financial resources (money) that are transferred from the rest of society to the providers of these real resources, per unit of real resource (for example, per physician hour). These money transfers are generalized claims on goods and services and are paid the providers as a reward for surrendering their real resources to health care. We usually express the totality of these monetary transfers arbitrarily as a percentage of our GDP. Thus, when we say that the United States in 1997 devoted 13.5 percent of its GDP on health care, we mean that the providers of health care (and those who indirectly support them with supplies, equipment, and services, collectively) were rewarded with monetary claims with which they could have bought 13.5 percent of the American GDP, had they wanted to. In fact, they may have recycled part of that American health spending not into the American economy but into countries supplying Americans with imported goods.

Table 8-1.   *Health Spending and the Aged in Selected Countries, 1997*

Country	Health Spending		Population Aged 65 +	
	Per-Capita (US$)	*Percent of GDP*	*Percent*	*U.S =1.00*
United States	3,925	13.5	12.7	1.00
Germany	2,339	10.4	15.6	1.23
Canada	2,095	9.0	12.0	0.94
France	2,051	9.6	15.4	1.21
Australia	1,805	8.4	12.0	0.94
Japan	1,741	7.3	14.6	1.15
Sweden	1,728	8.6	17.4	1.37
United Kingdom	1,347	6.7	15.6	1.23

Source: Gerard F. Andersen and Jean-Pierre Pouillier, "Health Spending, Access and Outcomes: Trends in Industralized Countries," *Health Affairs* (May/June 1999), exhibits 1 and 6.

In a paper with the tongue-in-cheek title "Resource Allocation in Health Care: The Allocation of Life Styles to Providers," I sought long ago to draw attention to the crucial difference between these two distinct resource flows, because they are so frequently confused in the debate on health policy.[8] For example, spokespersons for health care providers routinely pretend that any reduction in the flow of financial resources to them will lead to a reduction in the real resource flow to patients. That may be so, but it need not be so. It is entirely possible that of two nations, A and B, nation A allocates fewer real resources to health care than does nation B, and yet cedes to the providers of these real resources a higher share of its GDP than does nation B. In his empirical analysis of this issue, Mark Pauly concluded that the United States appears to fit the case of nation A.[9] The U.S. health system seems to burn fewer

Figure 8-1.   *The Two "Cost Flows in Modern Health Care: Real Resource Costs versus Health Spending*

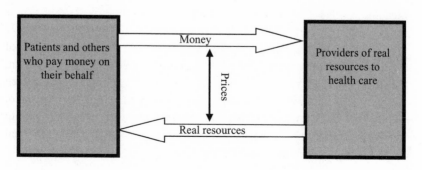

real resources per capita on health care than do most other nations in the OECD. On the other hand, we transfer much more money per unit of real resource to the providers of these resources (including, one should add, to health service researchers who devote their time to the health sector).

A more recent study by McKinsey & Company dramatically illustrates this conclusion.[10] In late 1996 that well-known management-consulting firm published the product of a multiyear study of the health systems of the United States, the United Kingdom, and Germany, conducted by about twenty of the firm's employees. They worked under the tutelage of an outside advisory board of distinguished clinicians and economists, among them Nobel Laureate Kenneth Arrow. The study sought to explain the observed crossnational health spending per capita of the three nations included in the study by exploring differences in productivity at the microeconomic level of managing four common diseases. Table 8-2 presents the gist of the comparison between Germany and the United States.

According to the methodology used by the McKinsey team, in 1990 per capita health spending in the United States exceeded Germany's by close to $1,000 (U.S.) in purchasing power parity, although, as noted, Germany's population then was older than that of the United States. The McKinsey research team reports that Germany's clinical productivity is actually lower than that in the United States. According to their calculation, if the American health system had been identical to Germany's except for the differential in clinical productivity, then the United States would actually have spent $390 (or 26.5 percent) less per capita on health care than did Germany. On the other hand, the prices of health services were much higher in the United States than they were in Germany. According to the McKinsey study, had the American health system been identical to Germany's in all respects except the prices paid for health care, then the United States would have spent $737 (or 50 percent) more on health care than did Germany. The remainder of the numbers in the table should be analogously interpreted. Overall, according to the report, the net effect of all differences combined made American per capita health spending in 1990 exceed Germany's by 65.6 percent.

It is puzzling why the McKinsey team sees in these findings reasons to urge upon Germany the type of health reforms that the United States and the United Kingdom had initiated during the first half of the 1990s. In fact, neither the McKinsey team nor two members of its external advisory board who subsequently published a paper based on the report refer explicitly to *clinical* productivity, to distinguish it from *total system's* productivity.[11] They simply conclude that the American health system is more "productively efficient" than either Germany's or the United Kingdom's. In fact, the McKinsey team

Table 8-2. *Decomposition of Differential Health Spending in Germany and the United States, 1990*

Spending	Amount[a]	Percent
Per capita spending in Germany	1,473	100.0
Per capita spending in the United States	2,439	165.6
Reasons behind higher costs in the United States		
Use of real medical inputs	(390)	−26.5
Higher prices	737	+50.0
Higher administrative costs	360	+24.4
"Other" higher costs	259	+17.6
Total additional costs per capita	966	+65.6

a. U.S. dollars in purchasing power parity.
Source: Martin N. Baily and Alan M. Garber, "Health Care Productivity," in Martin N. Baily, Peter C. Reiss, and Clifford Winston, eds., *Brookings Papers on Economic Activity: Microeconomics* (Brookings, 1997), figure 10.

confidently predicted in 1996 that "Germany's productivity gap with the U.S. . . . is widening," which would imply a narrowing of the per capita spending gap. The McKinsey team might be astonished to learn that during the 1990s the spending gap actually widened.[12] According to the most recently published OECD data, by 1997 Germany spent $2,339 per capita on health care and the United States spent $3,925, or 68 percent more.[13]

As David Cutler properly notes in his commentary on the report, the McKinsey team may well have exaggerated the alleged gap in clinical productivity.[14] That could be so because the higher productivity attributed to the United States reflects mainly this country's lower average length of hospital stays. As is well known, the marginal (avoidable) costs of the last, or convalescent, days saved in a hospital stay are much lower than the average-cost figure used in the report. These average costs include fixed costs that are not avoided through shorter hospital stays.

Even if one takes the McKinsey numbers at face value, one is struck by the fact that more than the entire cost saving attributable to the allegedly superior American clinical productivity ($390) is absorbed by the American system's much higher administrative costs ($360) and whatever items hide in the catchall category "other" ($259). The administrative costs estimated by the McKinsey team do not even include the cost of the countless hours American patients spend choosing among health insurance plans and claims processing, nor the considerable costs employers must absorb into payroll expense to provide health insurance coverage for their employees. The latter costs reportedly range anywhere from 6 to 15 percent of total premium paid, depending upon the type of insurance product.[15] Neither cost is counted, as they should be, in the published national health spending data used in the McKinsey study.

To pretend that there is no connection between administrative overhead and clinical productivity would be bold. There is bound to be a trade-off between the two and an optimal point on that trade-off frontier. In the present case, one may well ask whether overall social well-being in Germany (or the United States, for that matter) would be enhanced by wringing ever more clinical productivity out of the health care delivery system—to the point of severely demoralizing the health work force along with patients—only to fritter away the achieved savings in added administrative and other overhead. The McKinsey team, in this instance, and health-policy analysts, in general, pay insufficient attention to this trade-off.

As noted in table 8-3, the McKinsey team estimated that about half of the difference in per capita health spending in Germany and the United States reflects higher money transfers per unit of real resource to the providers of these real resources. In contemplating the reform of Medicare, and of the American health system in general, an important question is whether the relatively higher money transfers that Americans now make to their providers of health care are absolutely necessary to attract sufficient quantities of real resources into the health system, or whether these money transfers still include what economists call "economic rents." Economic rent is the fraction of the price that is not needed to attract a given real resource to a particular enterprise. One is driven to raise that delicate issue by the repeated mention in the debate on health policy of a pervasive surplus of physicians and of excess capacity all around. In theory, the surplus of a thing implies that the price of that thing is set too high for market clearance and that it could be lowered without causing a shortage of the thing. It is one of the more fundamental laws of economics.

Intranational Variations in Health Spending

American eyes tend to glaze over whenever they behold data from other nations' health systems, perhaps because these foreign systems are deemed inferior and hence irrelevant to the American experience. It is therefore imperative always to legitimize crossnational comparisons of health systems with intra-American data on health spending to drive home the point that the intra-U.S. variation in health spending per capita also raises questions about the manner in which our health system uses financial and real resources. At the risk of belaboring the well known, table 8-3 reminds the audience of the Wennberg variations, published regularly by John Wennberg and his associates in their *Dartmouth Atlas of Health Care*.[16]

John Wennberg and his associates have presented similar data to the U.S. Congress for almost two decades. One should think that legislative representa-

Table 8-3.   *Total Medicare Reimbursement per Enrollee, 1996*[a]

State	Reimbursement	Percent
Florida		
Miami	$7,783	100
Tampa	$5,658	73
Tallahassee	$4,958	64
Louisiana		
Baton Rouge	$7,700	99
New Orleans	$7,317	94
Shreveport	$3,923	50
New York		
New York City	$6,055	78
Buffalo	$4,199	54
Albany	$4,026	52
Minnesota		
Rochester	$4,148	53
Duluth	$3,760	48
Minneapolis	$3,700	48
Oregon		
Bend	$4,231	54
Portland	$3,923	50
Eugene	$3,506	45

Source: The Dartmouth Atlas of Health Care 1999 (American Hospital Association Health Forum, 1999), table of chapter 1.

a. Adjusted for differences in age, sex, race, illness, and the cost of practice.

tives who usually profess such solicitude for the taxpayers' money would have felt the moral obligation to explain to American taxpayers why their government forces them to pay twice as much in taxes to provide adequate health care for the American elderly in such high-cost regions as New York or Florida than they need to pay to procure presumably equally adequate care for similar elderly Americans in Oregon, Minnesota, and other low-cost regions. Furthermore, one should think that a Congress that is inclined to stage elaborate public hearings at the slightest hint of wrongdoing in so many areas would have staged at least one public hearing at which representatives of organized medicine in the various regions would be asked to explain to the American people, and to one another, why these differential tax payments are necessary to provide for America's elderly. In my view, that justification should precede any attempt by Congress to visit greater sacrifices on elderly Americans—especially on the low-income elderly—in any contemplated Medicare reform.

The lack of accountability on the part of Congress has moved this policy analyst to behold the entire American debate on the aging baby boom generation with detached amusement. It has also led me to make light of that issue in testimony before the Congress, at the risk of invoking the ire of some members of Congress. There really is something vaguely amusing about a nation that wrings its hands in despair over the much feared tsunami of the aging baby boom generation, when that nation so far has shown so little interest in learning from the experience abroad and, indeed, in learning from the rich and varied American experience itself. After all, if over the next decade or so all American physicians could be taught to practice the more economic style of medicine that is customary in Oregon and Minnesota, health care for the aging baby boomers would be one of the nation's more trivial problems.

A good start in that direction could have been made, for example, if in 1992 Congress had seen fit to impose volume performance standards not only on Medicare payments to physicians but also on Medicare payments to all health care providers. Furthermore, the volume-performance standards should have been imposed on each state separately, or possibly on even smaller geographic units. It is not too late to contemplate such a policy now, and there are good reasons to do so. As long as the traditional Medicare program is allowed to perpetuate these regional variations in health spending, then the managed care industry will insist, and rightly so, that the premiums it is paid by government should parallel these variations. Furthermore, the longer these huge regional variations in per capita Medicare spending are allowed to persist, the more difficult it will be to restructure the Medicare program along the lines favored by Senator John Breaux (D-La.) and Congressman Bill Thomas (R-Calif.). They would base a risk-adjusted, defined per capita contribution payable by Medicare to the elderly on a national average of premiums bid competitively by private insurance carriers for a defined benefit package.

Social Ethics and Health Policy

Much of the current debate on Medicare reform is not over the total amount of health spending per elderly American, but merely over the fraction of total per capita spending that is to be tax financed. In plain English, the debate is over the proper allocation of the financial burden of illness to (a) the collectivity of taxpayers and (b) the elderly individual.

In fact, the idea that the Medicare reforms now being contemplated will reduce overall per capita health spending on the elderly seems dubious. The traditional Medicare spends only about 2 percent of the funds it collects on administration. Any system of managed competition among private health plans is apt to spend anywhere between 15–20 percent of premiums paid on administration, marketing, and profits. Furthermore, it is not clear that private health plans will be able to obtain from the providers of health care the relatively low prices Medicare has paid. For both reasons, a safer assumption would be that privatizing the cost- and quality-control of the Medicare program through managed competition among private health insurance plans is likely to drive up total health spending per elderly American. On the other hand, as part of the contemplated reforms Congress may, of course, succeed in lowering the taxpayer's share of the higher total. Congress may even succeed in reducing even the absolute levels of future public spending on the elderly below currently projected levels.

Unfortunately, as noted, American policymakers are extremely reluctant to broach this delicate subject head-on. It would be fascinating, for example, to observe a politician respond to the question of whether or not health care properly ought to be rationed among America's elderly on basis of price and the individual elderly's ability to pay. It would be equally fascinating to observe the reaction to this question by policy analysts. Although the ideological spectrum on the proper distributive justice for any given type of health care good or service varies infinitely, the schools of thought on the matter can be grouped into roughly three distinct categories: pure egalitarian; quasi–two-tiered; and multi-tiered, income-based.

Pure Egalitarianism

One end of the spectrum is occupied by the pure egalitarians. They believe that health care should be available to all members of society on roughly equal terms (certainly within a locality), regardless of the individual's ability to pay for that care. This ethic implies a one-tier health system. The Canadian health system has been constructed explicitly on that ethic, which is openly recited in Canada whenever health policy is debated. In practice, even the Canadian health system is two tiered. Well-to-do Canadians who find themselves dissatisfied with the availability of desired health care in Canada always have the option of obtaining care in the United States, on terms not affordable to all Canadians. The magnitude of that export of American health care to Canada has been poorly researched and, therefore, remains anyone's guess. But there undoubtedly is such an export. There also is an import of primary care services from Canada to the United States. It occurs when low-income and poorly insured Americans living near the Canadian border travel to Canada for relatively cheaper (or free) primary care, including low-cost obstetrical care.

Quasi-Two-Tiered Health Care

In practice, a purely egalitarian health system probably is not sustainable because it requires more regulation and more denials to members of the upper-income strata than are politically tolerable. Most of the European nations have long accepted the idea that the concept of social solidarity must be coupled with a safety valve that allows the well-to-do to buy out of the general social contract, or at least to top it off. In these countries, the well-to-do can purchase private insurance that enables them to obtain health care on somewhat better terms than those available to the rest of society. Usually, however, these better terms do not noticeably affect survival or cure rates, with the possible exception of the United Kingdom. Instead, one may think of these systems as the analogue of an aircraft with two or three classes. Although first- and business-class passengers travel on slightly more comfortable terms than do coach passengers, all passengers lift off and land at the same time and under exactly the same conditions of safety.[17] Such a system probably is the most egalitarian version of health care ever to be tolerated in the United States or, for that matter, anywhere in the world.

Multi-Tiered, Income-Based Health Care

Finally, toward the other extreme of the ideological spectrum is the view that health care is not different from other basic commodities, such as food, clothing, and shelter. Of these necessities, everyone is guaranteed a basic minimum quantity and quality, but their quantity and quality is allowed to vary by income class. It can be said that this concept of health care now serves as the tacitly accepted ethical foundation for American health policy in general. It is likely to guide American health policy deep into the next millennium. The fundamental question this development raises for Americans is: Will a multi-tiered future health system ration only the amenities surrounding health care by income class and not contributions to health status and survival probabilities? Will it also ration by income class those medical services that could make a difference in health status and in longevity?

The so-called Jackson Hole model of managed competition advocated by Paul Ellwood, Alain Enthoven, and others is ideally suited to construct a multi-tiered, income-based health system.[18] In that model, the collective financing of health care is confined to a defined contribution large enough to guarantee everyone an agreed-upon basic minimum quantity and quality of health care. But the model also allows individual households to supplement that defined contribution with their own funds. That escape valve allows individual families to procure health insurance and health care on preferred terms and at higher desired quantities and quality. Depending upon the temper of the times, such a model could effect a relatively egalitarian or relatively nonegalitarian distribution of health care. In an era in which sharing in health care is becoming unfashionable, the Jackson Hole model would be likely to evolve into a system that features, at one extreme, health plans with tightly rationed health care, reserved mainly for low-income households and, at the other extreme, health plans with open-ended, nonrationed, luxurious health care, reserved for the upper-income classes. The multi-tiered Jackson Hole model probably remains the politically most viable structure for our health care system in the foreseeable future.

The Medicare+Choice option added to the Medicare program as part of the Balanced Budget Act of 1997, and many current proposals to "privatize" Medicare further, all tend to build upon the Jackson Hole model. As such, they probably would sanction the rationing of health care by income class as a permanent feature of our health system for our elderly. Although few proponents of the approach—least of all the politicians who favor it—would be likely to say so openly, they need not be reticent on this point. After all, as Marilyn Moon has reminded us with her research over the years, the benefit package of the traditional Medicare program has always been so limited in breadth and depth that it effectively has confronted the elderly with a multi-tiered, income-based health system all along.[19] At issue, then, is not whether further privatization of Medicare would create afresh a multi-tier health system for the elderly. At issue is the question whether the income-based tiering that future Medicare reforms might engender would be more or less pronounced than the income-based tiering that we have tolerated in that program.

It is a peculiar American habit to impute to the word *competition* the idea that it must be based on price. Dictionaries define competition simply as rivalry. As the world of sports amply demonstrates, rivalries can occur over many dimensions other than price. Canadian and German physicians, for example, bill third-party carriers on uniform fee schedules and therefore cannot compete for patients on the basis of price. They compete vigorously nevertheless, on those dimensions that patients perceive as "quality." Similarly, health plans could be made to compete for enrollees not on the basis of the premiums they charge enrollees but strictly on the basis of the quality of a defined benefit package that they offer their enrollees. Herman Somers and Anne Somers had proposed such a managed-competition model for the United States as early as 1972.[20] Under their model, the competing private health plans would have had to accept a tax-financed defined contribution as payment in full for a comprehensive benefit package specified in the law. The approach was intended to graft a roughly egalitarian distributive ethic upon a model of what the Somerses called "regulated competition." That term is more candid than "managed competition" about the extensive set of government regulations that is implied by any model based on competing private health insurers.

It is difficult to imagine that an egalitarian model such as the Somers's would have resonance in today's social, economic, and political climate. It is mentioned here only in passing, for the sake of analytic completeness.

Conclusion

The central theme of this discussion has been that the current worldwide quest for health reform is only in part about accountability, efficiency, the share of the GDP allocated to health care, and economic growth. Embedded in the debate over these seemingly technical terms lies the deeper problem of sharing the more amazing benefits of modern health care among members of society. Unlike other nations that openly discuss the distributive ethic that should drive their health systems, Americans have steadfastly refused to make this the central subject of forthright debate. Instead, we let our ethic emerge haphazardly from endless legislative skirmishes that tend to be conducted in technical code words.

When health care was simple and cheap, and when family income was clustered more narrowly than it is now about its mean, a more or less egalitarian sharing of health care seemed feasible. It also made sense to a generation that had shared the economic upheaval of the Great Depression and that had jointly surrounded the mortal roulette wheel of World War II. Both events taught Americans that one's position in the nation's income distribution is more the product of luck than providence. In the decades following World War II it became politically correct to proclaim for health care an egalitarian distributive ethic, even in the United States.

In the meantime, the income distribution throughout the industrialized world has been spreading apart. The more fortunate members of the generations born after World War II seem less impressed with the role that luck has played in determining their position in the nation's income distribution. Many fortunate members of these younger generations have only the vaguest notions about life at the other end of the income distribution. In the meantime, health care has become complex and costly. Sharing, say, coronary bypasses or liver transplants on an egalitarian basis now means bestowing the monetary equivalent of fully loaded BMWs or diamond solitaires on unknown persons whose earlier life styles might be suspected of having forfeited a warrant for such generous gifts. Under those circumstances, sharing the ever more remarkable and ever more expensive blessings of our health system becomes a major political challenge.

If one had to force the moral choices before us into one crisp picture, it might look something like the graph in figure 8-2. Even the Clinton health reform

Figure 8-2.   *The Trade-Off We Face in Health Care*

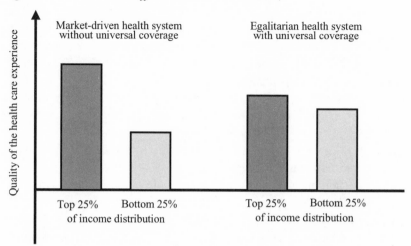

plan, which was at least ostensibly intended as a gesture toward egalitarianism, probably would have moved the American health system more permanently toward panel A—the market-driven health system without universal coverage.[21] The U.S. Congress and many health analysts who advise policymakers appear to have officially embraced the distributive ethic embedded in panel A since its demise. Because, as noted, even the traditional Medicare program has never been able to bestow upon the elderly a truly egalitarian distribution of health care, it seems natural to view panel A also as the likely habitat of Medicare in the future. Certainly, if Medicare paid the elderly a defined contribution set at X percent of some national average premium, and if Medicare allowed health plans to charge additional premiums on top of that defined contribution, then the distributive ethic espoused with such a policy would be that underlying panel A.

Panels A and B are alternative moral visions for the good society. Both are legitimate, and both merit respect. What does not warrant respect, in my view, is debating health reform without putting before the general public as clearly as possible the moral choices implied by the proposed reforms. A common lament among policymakers in Washington, D.C., is that any formal reference to distributive ethics conjures up images of "class warfare" and unduly "politicizes" a debate that should, presumably, be conducted strictly among experts and on technical terms. That is an amazing proposition from the people who preside over a democracy. Is one to think of the United States as the modern version of Plato's Republic, in which a small group of periodically elected high priests and their hired sages (policy wonks) define behind closed doors the "good society" and then cram their vision down the throats of the plebs, without the benefit of forthright public debate? An alternative vision of our democracy, one I had to study to become a naturalized American citizen and one taught to our American children in American high schools, is that the views of the plebs do matter crucially in this regard. With that view, it is entirely proper to politicize Medicare reform, to make social ethics the core of the debate on that reform, and to make the debate itself an integral part of major election campaigns—say, the presidential and congressional elections in the year 2000.

An allied theme in this discussion has been that, distributive ethics aside, policymakers have a moral obligation to make sure that a sloppily run health system does not inadvertently price kindness out of the nation's soul. In an earlier paper I had sought to make this idea graphic with a display originally presented to a first-year class in economics (see figure 8-2).[22] The idea is that the well-to-do in civilized societies will seek to purchase in the marketplace kind acts for the less fortunate members of society, but that their demand for such kind acts is price-elastic. The higher the price per kind act is, the fewer kind acts the well-to-do demand and finance on behalf of the poor. With this theory, one cannot infer the kindness of a people from what they actually do—say, from the use rates QUS and QOECD in figure 8-3. One can infer these noble sentiments only from what nations would do at alternative prices for kind acts—that is, from the shape and position of the entire demand-curve for kind acts. What a nation actually does in this regard depends not only on this demand curve, but also on its supply of kind acts (see figure 8-3).

A theme running through this presentation has been that the American supply-curve for kind acts in health care sits needlessly high in this scheme. One reason it sits high is that, relative to other countries, the contributors of real resources to health care in the United States are quite generously paid. During the 1990s, managed care in the private sector, along with Medicare and Medicaid, has sought to drive down the kindness-supply curve mainly by reducing this generosity. It appears that this "managed-price" strategy has by now run its full course.

A second reason for the high position of our kindness-supply curve is that there just have to be major inefficiencies in the use of real resources used in health care. One infers as much from the Wennberg variations. One infers it also from the findings of panels of distinguished experts that American health care is rife with "overuse, underuse and misuse."[23]

Finally, a third reason why the American supply-of-kindness curve in health care sits so high is the extraordinarily expensive administrative overlay that needs to be financed with our so-called health care spending. It is remarkable

Figure 8-3.   *Pricing Kindness out of a Kind Nation's Soul*

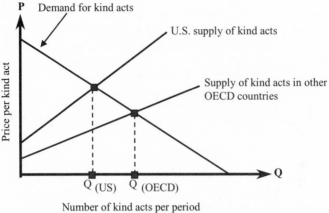

Number of kind acts per period

that, as the nation has begun to hound its clinicians and patients alike to manage the production of health care ever more efficiently, so little attention has been paid to this facet of our health system. It is even more remarkable how many economists, who should know better, eclipse administrative costs from their concept of the "productive efficiency" of a health system. It would be unwise, and downright immoral, to abstract from these high transactions cost as we grapple with one of the more daunting challenges of the new millennium: the political economy of sharing health care within nations that are ever wealthier overall but that have widening income distributions.

Notes

1. Adam Smith, *An Inquiry into the Nature and Causes of the Wealth of Nations* (New York: Modern Library, 1937), chapter X, p. 105.

2. Uwe E. Reinhardt, "Wanted: A Clearly Articulated Social Ethic for American Health Care," *Journal of the American Medical Association* (November 5, 1997), pp. 1446–67.

3. Richard A. Epstein, *Mortal Peril: Our Inalienable Right to Health Care?* (Addison-Wesley, 1997).

4. Richard A. Epstein, letter to the editors, *New York Times* (August 10, 1997), p. 14.

5. Milton Friedman, "Gammon's Law Points to Health Care Solution," *Wall Street Journal* (November 12, 1991), p. A21.

6. Uwe E. Reinhardt, "Abstracting from Distributional Effects, This Policy is Efficient," in Morris L. Barer, Thomas E. Getzen, and Greg L. Stoddard, eds., *Health, Health Care and Health Economics* (John Wiley, 1997), p. 153.

7. Gerard F. Andersen and Jean-Pierre Pouillier, "Health Spending, Access and Outcomes: Trends in Industrialized Countries," *Health Affairs* (May/June 1999), exhibit 6.

8. Uwe E. Reinhardt, "Resource Allocation in Health Care: The Allocation of Life Styles to Providers," *Milbank Memorial Quarterly*, 65, no. 2 (1987): 153–76.

9. Mark V. Pauly, "U.S. Health Care Costs: The Untold True Story," *Health Affairs* (Fall 1995), p. 152–59.

10. McKinsey Global Institute, *Health Care Productivity* (McKinsey, October 1996).

11. Martin N. Baily and Alan M. Garber, "Health Care Productivity" (including comments by Ernst R. Berndt and David M. Cutler), in Martin N. Baily, Peter C. Reiss, and Clifford Winston, eds., *Brookings Papers on Economic Activity: Microeconomics* (Brookings, 1997), p. 143–214.

12. McKinsey Global Institute, *Health Care Productivity,* pp. 6, 8–10.

13. Andersen and Pouillier, "Health Spending, Access, and Outcomes," exhibit 1.

14. McKinsey Global Institute, *Health Care Productivity*, pp. 209–14.

15. Data reported by Towers Perrin, cited in "Vital Signs," *Ob. Gyn. News* (August 15, 1999), p. 1.

16. The latest version is John H. Wennberg and Megan M. Cooper, *The Quality of Medical Care in the United States: A Report on the Medicare Program* (American Hospital Association Health Forum, 1999). A related website is http://www.dartmouth.edu/~atlas/.

17. I first heard Karen Davis of the Commonwealth Fund offer this useful analogy.

18. Paul M. Ellwood, Alain C. Enthoven, and Lynn Etheredge, "The Jackson Hole Initiatives for a Twenty-First Century American Health System," *Health Economics* 1 (1992), pp. 149–68.

19. Marilyn Moon, *Medicare Now and in the Future*, 2nd. ed. (Urban Institute Press, 1996), table 1, p. 11.

20. Herman M. Somers and Anne R. Somers, "Major Issues in Health Insurance," *Milbank Memorial Fund Quarterly* (April 1972), pp. 177–210.

21. Because the Clinton plan was based on an employer-mandate, whose cost would have been shifted backwards to employees, its financing probably would have been regressive. Furthermore, because the plan relied on the Jackson Hole model of cost and quality control, it would be unlikely to have distributed health care on an egalitarian basis.

22. Uwe E. Reinhardt, "Employer-Based Health Insurance: R.I.P.," in Stuart H. Altman, Uwe E. Reinhardt, and Alexandra E. Shields, eds., *The Future U.S. Healthcare System: Who Will Care for the Uninsured?* (Chicago: Health Administration Press, 1997), pp. 325–52.

23. Mark R. Chassin, "Assessing Strategies for Quality Improvements," *Health Affairs* (May/June 1997), pp. 151–61.

9

How Public Opinion
Affects Reform

THIS CHAPTER DISCUSSES the influence of public opinion in policymaking for Social Security and Medicare. The authors explore how the public reaches judgment, the stability of such judgments, and the use and misuse of polls in the policy process. Noting that public knowledge and support for Social Security is strong, they discuss the extent to which polls shed light on the kinds of policy choices and tradeoffs the public and politicians will support. Special attention is given to assessing public understanding and evaluation of proposals that would substitute compulsory individual responsibility for government risk-pooling in the Social Security program.

Is Social Security Reform Ready
for the American Public?
Benjamin I. Page

WHY MIGHT POLICY EXPERTS and decision makers want to know something about public opinion concerning the reform of Medicare and Social Security? One obvious answer is that public opinion can affect what is politically feasible. If experts' favorite reform proposals should turn out to be

Several conference participants and editors of this volume, including Beth Kobliner, William Spriggs, Bill Gradison, Carolyn Lukensmeyer, and Eric Kingson, offered helpful comments and suggestions. In addition, I am grateful to Bob Shapiro, Jason Barabas, Larry Jacobs, and Fay Cook for commenting on an earlier draft and providing a number of useful materials. The excellent 1998 National Academy of Social Insurance paper by Jacobs and Shapiro, with its exhaustive compilation and analysis of Social Security survey questions through 1997, provided much of the foundation for this review.

utterly unacceptable to the American public, if efforts to enact them would provoke anger and outrage and the electoral defeat of officeholders who embraced them, then they are not politically feasible and might as well be set aside.

In order to assess the political feasibility of various reform proposals we need to assess not only how acceptable or unacceptable to the public they appear to be at the present moment, but whether and to what extent public opinion might be expected to change—in response to changing events, new information, or the deliberative process—so that reform proposals may become more or less feasible in the future.

I take it that a concern with political feasibility lies behind the question I was asked to address: "Is the public ready for reform of Medicare and Social Security?" I will do my best to answer that question, with the focus on Social Security. At the same time, I suggest that we should also be interested in looking at public opinion from a different point of view. I hope we will ask not only how public opinion affects what is politically feasible, but also how, in a democracy, the policy preferences of ordinary citizens might constitute a proper input into collective decisions on what we *ought* to do about Social Security and Medicare. These programs, after all, affect many millions of Americans in vital ways. It seems possible that ordinary Americans have ideas and opinions and preferences that should be taken into account. Policymakers may want to ask not just "what can we get away with?"—what is not totally unacceptable to the public—but also "what should we do?" in light of what the public wants done.

For this reason I have taken the liberty of turning the focus of my discussion upside down, asking, "Is Social Security reform ready for the American Public?" That is, are policymakers willing to reflect the true preferences of ordinary Americans in the reform process? How well do the most prominent reform proposals mesh with what the American public would prefer to do?

The argument for taking public opinion as a positive input into decisionmaking, rather than just a constraint on decisions, is—it seems to me—strongest to the extent that we can assess what deliberative, fully informed public opinion wants, or will want, or would want. Again, we must look beyond what the polls say right now and must ask whether opinions will change—or would change—if and when full information was supplied to the public and careful deliberation occurred. Absent effective crystal balls, this might seem to be a matter of pure speculation, but it turns out that scientific methods and available polling data can be helpful in assessing the future and even the hypothetical as well as the current state of public opinion.

A number of incorrect or misleading ideas about public opinion seem to have found their way into the mass media and political discourse. Before proceeding into the specifics of entitlement reform, therefore, I need to say something about the general theoretical and methodological framework within which I analyze public opinion.

A Perspective on Public Opinion

Robert Y. Shapiro of Columbia University and I have set forth a perspective on public opinion based on our analysis of several thousand survey questions that have been asked of samples of the American public over a fifty-year period.[1] Our perspective is not universally accepted, but I think it has come to prevail in recent years among those interested in relationships between public opinion and public policy. It should be particularly relevant to highly salient policy issues like those concerning Social Security and Medicare. Let me give a brief summary of our main points.

In looking at patterns and trends over time in what we call the collective policy preferences of the American public (as measured by the marginal frequencies of responses to survey questions—that is, by the percentages of Americans saying they favor or oppose particular policies), we found that these collective policy preferences have a number of properties that are quite different from the properties of individuals' opinions.

Numerous studies have shown that most Americans are only sporadically interested in politics and are poorly informed about political matters, even matters that we may consider quite basic.[2] Most people's expressed attitudes fail to line up coherently along the standard liberal/conservative ideological dimension (although they may have different structures of their own), and some survey responses fluctuate with such apparent randomness over time that Philip Converse argued that they reflect "non-attitudes."[3] But collective public opinion, based on the aggregation of individual preferences, looks quite different. Statistical aggregation tends to eliminate a lot of the random noise found in individuals' survey responses. Moreover, collective deliberation—involving division of labor among ordinary citizens, experts, communicators, and opinion leaders—enables even the poorly informed to come to sensible political opinions based on cues from those they trust.[4]

Shapiro and I found that Americans' collective policy preferences—as measured by percentages of the population responding one way or another to questions about public policy—are generally quite stable; they rarely fluctuate at all, except in response to major relevant events (for example, in foreign policy.) If one graphs collective policy preferences over time they generally form flat or gently sloped lines, with small to moderate bumps but few high hills or deep valleys, over the course of years and even decades. The widespread idea that collective policy preferences are "changeable" or "fickle" is incorrect.[5]

Moreover, we found that when collective policy preferences change they tend to do so in regular, predictable ways. Some changes reflect gradual, long-term social changes in values, behavior, or population demographics; others reflect new events or new information that is conveyed to the public. It is possible to predict short-term changes in public opinion with great accuracy simply by counting what views are conveyed through the mass media and who expresses them. Nonpartisan experts and commentators have a particularly strong impact on public opinion.[6]

In our judgment, most changes in collective policy preferences also tend to be sensible changes. That is, when public opinion changes, it usually does so in ways that a well-informed observer would find reasonable in the light of new information and new events, as that information and those events are conveyed to the public through the mass media. In other words, we believe that the public generally makes good use of new information and changes its opinions in sensible ways.

Further, we found that Americans' collective policy preferences are generally consistent with each other. The notion that the public holds wildly inconsistent, mutually incompatible opinions is not correct.[7] Collective preferences about different aspects of policy generally fall into coherent patterns, which reflect basic underlying beliefs and values as well as the specific and unique details of particular policy issues. The public is capable of making clear distinctions among alternative policies.[8]

In short, our examination of thousands of survey questions asked over a period of five decades has convinced us that the American public, as a collectivity, has real and serious opinions about many matters of public policy—opinions that can be measured accurately and reliably through survey research.

Understanding Polls

To be sure, in designing and analyzing opinion surveys certain pitfalls can trap the unwary. The most hazardous pitfalls involve question wording, because the precise way in which a question is formulated can profoundly affect how people respond to it. A strongly biased question—for example, one with a prologue that presents powerful arguments in favor of a particular policy alternative and weak arguments against it—can sometimes bludgeon a number of people to go along with what the pollster wants to hear. A confused or ambiguous question is likely to elicit confused or ambiguous answers. A highly specific question may reveal views on highly specific matters without necessarily supporting any grand generalization about the shape of public opinion.

The point here is not that the average American is nit-picking, stupid, or suggestible, but rather that the meaning of survey responses is highly dependent upon the exact meaning of survey questions. The meaning of questions depends in turn upon the precise wording of those questions—and indeed sometimes upon the context of the whole survey and the interview situation. Two recent survey questions, for example, gave quite different (but both probably misleading) impressions concerning how people feel about privatizing Social Security, by endowing hypothetical candidates "Smith" and "Jones" with wordy positions on the issue that sounded innovative or stodgy, sound or risky.[9]

Fortunately the science and art of survey research is now well advanced. Skillful people design hundreds of policy-related questions for scores of national surveys every year, and competition helps keep them honest. TV- and newspaper-sponsored polls, as well as academic surveys, are now generally of high quality; indeed the former are often more useful to policymakers than the latter because media polls tend to be more timely and more closely linked to specific policy alternatives. In this context, even poorly worded or blatantly biased questions can be useful to the careful interpreter because they can help reveal just how firm or mushy opinion is and how far it can be pushed. Thus abundant data often exist to illuminate what Americans think about major issues of public policy. Social Security, for example, has been the subject over the years of a great many useful survey questions—probably hundreds of them.

In interpreting the mass of survey data on a topic like Social Security, which will be my focus here (coherence and feasibility are best served by focusing on one issue, but many of the main points will apply to Medicare as well), the most important methodological guideline is to pay attention to the precise wording of questions. This means taking seriously what each question says and looking for patterns in the responses to many different questions. It also means avoiding excessive generalization from any one survey result and avoiding any statements at all about opinion "trends" or changes unless they are based on repetitions over time of identical survey questions.

Americans' Opinions about Social Security

In certain respects public opinion concerning Social Security resembles public opinion about other policies. For one thing, there are limits to the amount of information that the average American has about the program, its problems, or proposed reforms. For example, a Princeton Survey Research Associates (PSRA) survey for Americans Discuss Social Security (ADSS) in the spring of 1998 found that most people did not have a clear idea of how big a share of the federal budget Social Security takes up, and few claimed to have heard much about a series of current reform proposals.[10]

At the same time, the analysis of scores of different surveys from recent years indicates that on Social Security, as on other major issues, Americans have collective policy preferences that are very real. Collective preferences about many aspects of Social Security are quite stable; when identical questions are repeated over time they produce trend lines that shift slowly if at all. These opinions are generally consistent with each other and form coherent patterns that reflect Americans' basic beliefs and values. The public makes sharp distinctions among policy alternatives. In short, we can identify a real and—in many respects—rather solid collective public opinion.

If anything, public opinion concerning Social Security is actually more stable and more solid than opinion about most other policies. It rests on a firmer base of factual knowledge. In contrast to the apparent confusion about budget magnitudes, for example, the spring 1998 PSRA/ADSS survey found considerable clarity on other matters. Large majorities of Americans understand that Social Security is on a pay-as-you-go basis, with payroll contributions used to pay benefits for current retirees. Large majorities know that the program provides disability benefits for workers (84 percent), that retirees who work part time are still eligible for benefits (84 percent), that the program provides survivors' benefits for spouses (79 percent) and children (72 percent) of workers who have died, and that people can retire in their early sixties and still be eligible for benefits (69 percent).[11]

In their comprehensive study of what Americans know about politics, Michael Delli Carpini and Scott Keeter found knowledge about Social Security to be unusually high.[12] This should not surprise us, since the program is uniquely important to so many people.

In this review of public opinion concerning Social Security I will first briefly consider the level of general support for the system and the extent to which people perceive impending problems. I will then explore the public's reactions to various proposed program changes, grouping them under the general headings of benefit reductions, tax increases, and privatization.

Support for the System

The present Social Security system gets extraordinarily broad support from the American public, support that has varied little for decades. The best general measures of support, asked repeatedly over the years, concern the amount of money that the government should be spending on Social Security. The General Social Survey (GSS), for example, twelve times since 1984 has asked whether we are spending "too much" money on Social Security, "too little" money, or "about the right amount."[13] The National Election Study (NES) at the University of Michigan has repeatedly asked whether federal spending on Social Security should be "increased," "decreased," or "kept about the same."[14] Gallup (for the Chicago Council on Foreign Relations—CCFR) has repeatedly asked whether the Social Security program should be "cut back," "expanded," or "kept about the same."[15]

The results of these and other surveys have been remarkably consistent over the years. Large fractions of the American public regularly say that too little is being spent, that spending should be increased, and that the program should be expanded. Only tiny fractions—nearly always less than 10 percent—of the public say that we are spending too much money on Social Security or that the program should be decreased or cut back.

This high, stable level of support is particularly evident in a graph that shows, over time, the combined proportion of Americans who want to increase spending on Social Security or keep it about the same. In every one of its biennial surveys since 1984, for example, the NES found well over 90 percent favoring constant or increased spending (see figure 9–1.)[16]

There have been some shifts between "increase" and "keep the same" responses; the proportion of the public wanting to expand the program dipped a bit around the end of the 1980s, while the proportion for keeping it the same rose. But more recently that trend has reversed. In the spring of 1998, for example, GSS found that 56 percent of the public said we are spending "too little" money—up 12 percentage points since 1993—while 32 percent said about right and only 6 percent said too much.[17] Similarly, Gallup/CCFR found in autumn 1998 that 66 percent of the public wanted to expand Social Security—up fully 17 percentage points since 1994—while 27 percent said keep the same and only a miniscule 3 percent wanted to cut back.[18] If the "too little" or "expand" responses in these two surveys are combined with the status quo responses, as was done for the NES data in figure 9–1, then the support levels reach 93 percent and 97 percent, respectively.

Policymakers cannot get much specific budgetary guidance from these questions because they do not specify *how much* more spending people favor—not even whether or not respondents want to increase spending beyond the rates of inflation or growth in the population of retirees. But these survey items establish the fundamental fact of strong public support for the present Social Security system, which involves contributions through payroll taxes

Figure 9-1. *Stability in Support for Social Security*[a]

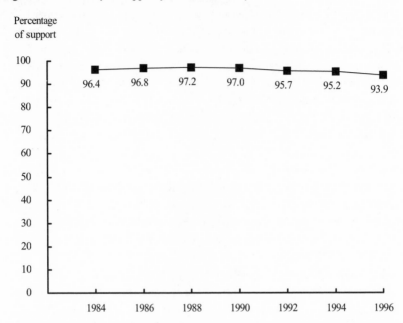

Source: Figure supplied by Fay Lomax Cook and Jason Barabas from National Election Studies (NES) data.
a. Support is defined as the percentage of respondents who want to see spending increased or maintained on these programs.

and defined benefits (their magnitude partly determined by peoples' earnings) provided by the federal government.

Further, since GSS and Gallup regularly ask similar questions about a variety of other government programs, the results also make clear that far more Americans want to spend more on Social Security than want to expand spending on such programs as defense, military aid to other nations, foreign aid, or the space program. The level of support for increasing Social Security approaches that for the highly salient and popular programs of education, health care, and combating crime.[19]

Recognition of Problems

Most Americans understand that Social Security faces challenges in the coming century; most are aware of the projected increase in number of retirees relative to the number of workers. Most of the public refuses to endorse the language of "crisis" surrounding Social Security, and few cite fixing Social Security as the "most important problem" facing the country.[20] But alarmist rhetoric in the media, together with general distrust of government, may have undermined confidence in the system beyond what is actually warranted. For many years expressions of confidence in the future of the system have been low: the 65 percent "very" or "somewhat" confident in 1975 dropped sharply to 32 percent in 1982 and rebounded only moderately thereafter.[21] A substantial number of citizens (26 percent in one survey) even suffer from the extraordinary fear that they themselves will not get any benefits from the program—surely the result of excessive doom-saying by politicians and commentators.[22]

In any case, most Americans understand that program changes must be made. In two 1997 surveys 83 percent of the public agreed that "major changes" will be necessary at some point to guarantee the future financial stability of the system.[23] The question is, just what sorts of changes win popular approval? Some do, but some definitely do not.

Opinion about Benefit Reductions

The public's general support for the Social Security system is accompanied by substantial resistance to most sorts of benefit cuts, whether in the form of direct, across-the-board cuts in benefit levels or of less direct cuts that focus on cost-of-living adjustments (COLAs) or the retirement age. This resistance is evident in many surveys over many years. The level of opposition to cuts has apparently held steady even in the face of apocalyptic rhetoric about the program's future and even when survey questions focus attention on problems with the program. We should not assume that such opposition will be easy to change. This does not mean that no benefit cuts whatsoever are now or will ever be acceptable to the American public, but it does suggest that any reform package might do well to look largely or entirely in other directions. Benefit cuts of any sort will be a very hard sell.

Across-the-Board Benefit Cuts

The "expand" and "spend more" responses discussed above have made public opposition to across-the-board benefit cuts so clear that rather few survey questions have asked explicitly about such cuts. Those that have done so in the context of budget cutting and deficit reduction have generally come up empty, even when they tried hard to elicit pro-cutting responses with biased question wording. An egregious 1981 Harris question, for example ("if the only way to have a chance to balance the federal budget by 1984 was to make sharp cuts in Social Security benefits, would you favor. . .?") found only 18 percent favoring such cuts and an overwhelming 82 percent opposed.[24] Questions about deficit reduction in the 1990s have elicited similarly high levels of opposition to cutting Social Security, on the order of 83 percent and 88 percent against cuts.[25]

A few survey questions that have invoked the need to save Social Security itself and focused on somewhat more vague future benefit cuts have elicited less opposition. But such findings should be interpreted with caution. A much publicized 1997 survey that seemed to show 69 percent support for reducing future spending on Social Security "to preserve Social Security for future generations," for example, appears to have generated this result by creating an artificial contrast: respondents were asked whether they would favor or oppose reductions in future spending "for each of the following purposes," and preserving Social Security beat deficit reduction or tax cuts hands down. In addition, the "to preserve" wording implied that such cuts would preserve the system and would be necessary for doing so; no alternative remedies were mentioned.[26]

Reducing Cost-of-Living Adjustments

On at least eight occasions in the last two decades various survey organizations have asked whether, in order to reduce the size of the federal budget deficit, the government should reduce scheduled cost-of-living increases in Social Security. (Different surveys asked whether respondents "favor[ed]" such a move, or thought it a "good idea," or would be "willing" to have it happen.) In every case large majorities of the public said no, it was a bad idea, they opposed it or were unwilling to have government do it. Even when questions rather blatantly pushed for a favorable response, and even in peak years of program cutting and antideficit rhetoric (like 1982 and 1995), no more than 34 percent of the public favored cutting COLAs. In every survey, 61 percent or more of the public opposed such cuts.[27]

To be sure, opposition to reducing COLAs looks less overwhelming when questions are put in terms of technical changes to the Consumer Price Index (CPI) that would slow down Social Security benefit increases as a side effect. Two surveys at the end of 1996 actually found narrow pluralities of the public favoring such changes. But one of these involved a starkly one-sided Harris question that put the weight of "a commission" and "most experts" behind the idea that the CPI currently overstates inflation, and the other confusingly asked about "reduc[ing]" the government's official measure of inflation—which may have been taken to mean reducing inflation itself.[28] A better balanced but still confusing question asked three months later by NBC/*Wall Street Journal* found a substantial majority, 53 percent to 37 percent, opposing the change.[29] This suggests that there is opposition to adjusting the CPI but that expert consensus and strong evidence might lead to public approval.

From the point of view of political feasibility it is no doubt true that painful policy changes can more easily be slipped by the public if they are put in the guise of "technical" adjustments, whether or not scientifically justified. But I would not advise policymakers to count heavily on this. Social Security is a highly visible, hotly contested issue. We should expect any and all policy changes to be scrutinized closely. The public considers COLA reductions to be cuts in benefits, and most Americans are very skeptical about benefit cuts.

Extending the Retirement Age

Similarly, there is a long history of public opposition to the idea of forcing people to delay retirement beyond age sixty-five in order to receive full Social Security benefits. Those of us who love our professional work and cannot imagine wanting to retire would do well to apply the "callus test"—asking someone who does arduous physical labor whether he or she would like to postpone retirement.[30] Or, for that matter, we might ask someone who is stuck in a boring, routine white-collar job.

The fact is that many people feel strongly about being free to retire when they get old. The trend in the industrialized world has been toward earlier retirement rather than later.

At least eighteen different surveys during the last two decades have asked about increasing the retirement age for Social Security, and all but two have found majorities opposed—usually very large majorities. (The two deviant questions from the early 1980s began with leading phrases: "To save money . . .," and "Congress has passed. . . . Do you favor. . . .?)[31] At the beginning of 1997, for example, PSRA—when asking about a series of proposals to "keep the system financially sound in the future"—found 64 percent opposed and only 31 percent in favor of "gradually increasing the retirement age for Social Security from 65 to 69 without affecting people now receiving benefits."[32]

In thinking about the political feasibility of stretching out retirements, of course, one might object that "we have already done it" in 1983, without major electoral repercussions. But one should ask, have we indeed, in the eyes of the public, already done it? The scheduled shift from age sixty-five to sixty-seven for full benefit eligibility has not yet occurred. I am not sure that we know what proportion of the population as a whole is aware of this change or how people will react as the new reality sinks in.

One sort of reform proposal that I have not seen explored in surveys might win considerably more public favor than postponing Social Security benefits. That is to *encourage* later retirement and increase opportunities for older people to work, through such measures as actively recruiting the elderly to help with teaching and day care, arranging special transportation to jobs, giving tax credits for the first few thousand dollars earned, enforcing laws against age discrimination, and altering our public rhetoric—and, ultimately, our social norms—in order to put high value on work by old people who are able to do it.

Adjusting Benefit Formulas

Technical proposals that would indirectly cut Social Security benefits—such as the proposal to average more past years (with lower earnings) into the baseline for calculating benefits, which is apparently a great favorite among policy experts—are entirely off the radar screen of most ordinary Americans. Very few have heard of such proposals. Even so, carefully designed survey questions that clearly explained the proposals might elicit meaningful responses. But if such questions have been asked I do not know about them. We should try to learn more about this in the future.

Again, from the point of view of political feasibility it is undoubtedly true that technical-sounding changes have a relatively good chance of slipping by without major objections from the public, particularly if they are small enough to remain obscure and escape public notice. Again, however, I would caution against the assumption that no one will catch on. Any policy changes that are big enough to matter may well attract scrutiny and noisy opposition. And once again, if we care about what the public wants as well as what policymakers can get away with, it would be helpful to remember that a disguised benefit cut is still a benefit cut.

Cutting Benefits for the Well-to-Do

Americans do not, however, simply oppose all benefit cuts. One of the most popular of all Social Security reform proposals—although it seems to have received little attention from policymakers—is to reduce the benefits of wealthy or well- to-do Americans.

In the context of proposals to reduce the budget deficit, for example (the same context that revealed strong opposition to cutting benefits across the board or reducing COLAs), at least four surveys during the past decade found that substantial majorities of Americans favored "increas[ing]" taxes (or imposing "new taxes") on Social Security benefits for "the wealthy" (or "upper income recipients"). In each of these surveys at least 56 percent of Americans supported the idea and no more than 40 percent opposed it.[33]

Even more to the point, a 1997 survey found that in order to "keep the Social Security program financially sound in the future," fully 64 percent of the American public favored "[r]educing benefits paid to upper-income retirees in the future." Only 34 percent opposed the idea.[34]

To be sure, excessive cuts in the benefits of upper-income retirees could undercut the social insurance rationale of the program. A large majority of Americans feel that everyone who contributes to Social Security should receive benefits.[35] But it is clear that the public supports a tax/benefits structure that is progressive. As most Americans see it, everyone who pays into the program should get benefits, but not everyone need receive benefits in identical proportion to their contributions. Policymakers who are interested in doing what the public wants—or simply interested in finding new, politically acceptable sources of revenue to bolster the program—might well want to consider some method of reducing the benefits or increasing the contributions of upper-income people.

Opinion about Tax Increases

It is often assumed by policymakers and pundits that the American public will not stand for tax increases to bolster Social Security. Extensive survey data, however, indicate that this is not correct. While substantial majorities resist the idea of a general rise in payroll taxes, there are indications of willingness to use general tax revenues to help the Social Security system. Even more clearly, large majorities of the public favor increasing taxes on the benefits of people with high incomes. Certain kinds of tax increases, in other words, appear to be acceptable to the public and indeed to be more popular than benefit cuts.

Raising Payroll Taxes

There is substantial resistance to the idea of a general increase in payroll taxes, even when the question is posed in terms of preserving the Social Security system. A survey in 1996, for example, found 52 percent opposed to paying higher Social Security taxes to strengthen the program's financial future.[36] When a 1997 poll included "having everyone pay more in Social Security taxes" in its list of proposals to "keep the Social Security program financially sound in the future," 61 percent opposed the idea; only 37 percent favored it.[37] Clearly a general payroll tax increase is not a popular measure for dealing with Social Security's problems.

At the same time, public opposition to a payroll tax increase should not be viewed as set in concrete; it could alter as the magnitude of financial shortfalls and the unattractive features of alternative proposals sink in, particularly if the facts are agreed upon and are clearly communicated by experts and prominent leaders of both political parties. Much opposition to tax increases seems to arise from perceptions that officials would "mismanage" the funds, "waste" them, or spend them on other government programs.[38] This public perception—when Social Security is actually quite efficient and well run—sometimes provokes puzzlement or disdain among policy experts, but we might want to acknowledge a possible grain of truth to it. It is not an entirely unreasonable interpretation of the 1980s and 1990s that the 1983 payroll tax increase, touted as "fixing" Social Security, was actually used to substitute for general revenues (particularly those lost through the 1981 income tax cuts), and that payroll taxes helped fund the Reagan military buildup and conceal the full extent of budget deficits.

If (and I emphasize *if*) it should become apparent to the American public that it is essential to increase payroll taxes in order to preserve Social Security benefits, and if it is clear that the revenue will actually be used for that purpose, I suspect that the public will go along. One important sign of this is the survey finding that, when forced to choose between benefit cuts and tax increases, a large majority of Americans—63 percent to 32 percent in one 1997 survey—chose payroll tax increases.[39] But other reform options are considerably more popular.

Using General Tax Revenues

Surveys do not generally ask direct questions about the possible use of general revenues to assist Social Security through the temporary emergency caused by the baby-boom bulge of retirees, but there are at least some indications that this might be acceptable to the public. Most of the indirectly relevant survey questions involve alternative ways to "use the budget surplus"—a peculiar notion, of course, when the current surplus consists mostly of payroll taxes not needed to pay current benefits and supposedly already saved in the trust fund for the future. Still, the public's reactions tell us something. More Americans say the top priority for any surplus money should be strengthening Social Security (39 percent in one survey) than say reducing the national debt (29 percent), cutting income taxes (16 percent), or increasing spending on other domestic programs (14 percent).[40] Given a straight choice at the beginning of 1998 between Republican leaders' proposal of tax cuts and President Clinton's proposal of no tax cuts until Social Security problems are resolved, 60 percent of Americans said they preferred President Clinton's approach; only 28 percent preferred the Republican proposal.[41] Similarly, the president's 1999 proposal to forbid non-Social Security uses of the payroll-tax-produced portion of budget surpluses won broad public support.

The public's reluctance to use real or hypothetical budget surpluses for purposes other than Social Security may or may not imply a willingness to use general tax revenues to bolster the system. More survey data are needed on this issue.

Increasing Taxes on High-Income People

One reform proposal that may have public support is to increase taxes on high-income people. In several surveys at the end of the 1980s and beginning of the 1990s, substantial majorities of Americans said that in order to reduce the budget deficit they would favor increasing the tax on Social Security income or benefits for "upper income" people or "the wealthy."[42] A 1994 question that did not mention deficit reduction came up with a similarly solid 57 percent to 38 percent majority in favor of requiring Social Security recipients with higher incomes to pay federal income taxes on a larger share of their benefits.[43]

None of this, of course, tells us anything definite about payroll taxes on regular earned income. It does, however, suggest that there may be public sentiment for tax structure less regressive than it is now perceived to be. (Such sentiment might well increase if more working people came to realize that income above a certain point is not now subject to the payroll tax.)

Raising or Removing the Cap on Earnings Subject to Tax

One prominent reform proposal, which the Social Security actuary has estimated would eliminate 68 percent of the anticipated Social Security revenue shortfall over the seventy-five-year forecasting period, is to remove the "cap" on earnings subject to the payroll tax.[44] This would bring in a lot of tax revenue but would, because of the somewhat progressive benefit formula, pay out only part of that revenue in benefits.

I have been unable to find survey data directly addressing this proposal. The public's approval of increasing taxes or cutting benefits for wealthy Social Security beneficiaries suggests that it might well be popular. This is an important area for new data collection.

Opinion about Privatization

The idea of wholesale privatization, abolishing—or making voluntary—the publicly managed and publicly funded Social Security system, is unpopular. This idea would probably sink any major political figure who openly espoused it, just as it damaged Republican presidential candidate Barry Goldwater in 1964. The only privatization proposals that seem politically feasible are those that involve partial privatization and compulsory participation.

Many Americans are attracted by the idea of getting higher returns on their payroll contributions, and many like the idea of managing some of their own investments. At the same time, awareness of the increased risks associated with equities rather than Treasury Bills and of the need for benefit cuts or tax increases during transition to a funded system undercuts support for even partial privatization. The public has more to learn about the possible costs and benefits of various privatization plans. Opinions are less fully formed and more subject to change than they are on other aspects of Social Security.

Abolishing Social Security or Making it Voluntary

Complete abolition of Social Security, or making it voluntary, is a non-starter with the public. Although the word *voluntary* has appealing connotations of choice and freedom, even survey questions that ask about "voluntary participation" in Social Security without mentioning any possible harm often find majorities opposed. A Public Agenda Foundation survey in early 1997, for example, found 55 percent opposed (36 percent "strongly"), with 42 percent in favor. In response to a follow-up question, fully 81 percent of the respondents indicated agreement with the concern that if participation is made voluntary, "the very people who need it most might drop out and get themselves into trouble."[45]

Private Investment Accounts

Two surveys for the CATO Institute in 1996 appeared to show strong (about two-thirds) support for using some payroll tax revenues for private individual retirement accounts, but their results should be interpreted with caution because they made no mention of risks or other possible negative factors and instead asked a series of questions that tended to lead the respondent toward approval. Similarly, a 1997 PSRA survey that found 71 percent favored "letting individuals decide how some of their own Social Security contributions are invested" gives a useful indication of Americans' enthusiasm for individual choice and for maximizing investment returns, but it is far from conclusive because of the failure to mention the pros and cons of concrete proposals for private accounts.[46]

As soon as the issue of investment risk is mentioned, expressions of enthusiasm for private accounts diminish. Two NBC/*Wall Street Journal* polls at the beginning of 1997, for example, that mentioned that investment of contributions in stock could produce returns that are "higher or lower," found the public about evenly divided between favoring and opposing the idea. When explicitly asked to weigh the "risk of losing money" against the "potential of higher returns," 57 percent said the risks outweigh the potential gains while only 37 percent said the opposite.[47]

Support for private accounts drops further when the transitional costs of honoring commitments to current retirees are mentioned, as in an NBC/*Wall Street Journal* question that mentioned an increase in payroll taxes and an increase in the federal budget deficit: 61 percent concluded that the costs outweigh the benefits while only 22 percent said the opposite.[48]

The difference in responses to these differently formulated questions suggests that public opinion about privatization is only partially formed and that it may change as public debate continues. But the same responses also suggest that further discussion of possible costs of and limits to privatization—not only investment risks and transition costs but also administrative expenses and restrictions on private investment choices—may well further reduce public support for the idea. This is an important topic for future surveys to explore.

President Clinton's 1999 proposal of subsidized "Universal Savings Accounts" supplemental to the Social Security system (and not affecting its guaranteed benefits) wins much higher public approval.

Trust Fund Investment in Equities

The idea of investment by the government (that is, by trust fund administrators or others) of some payroll tax revenue in equities rather than treasury obligations, which shares the goal of increased investment returns but lacks the element of individual control of investments, has initially received a fairly cool public response. Three recent questions about "investing some of the Social Security trust fund in the stock market"—which balanced the possibility of "more money" or "higher returns" with "greater risk" or "unpredictab[ility]"— revealed that substantial majorities (as high as 69 percent) opposed this or thought it a bad idea.[49] Two surveys also indicated that if some Social Security tax funds are invested in the stock market, large majorities favor allowing individuals to invest part of their portion "however they would like," rather than having the government invest in a broad index fund.[50]

Again, however, opinions may change as debate continues and the options are fleshed out. The general distrust of government that seems to underlie these responses, for example, might be alleviated by creation of an investment entity that is firmly separated from politics. And concerns about risk might be met by clearly defining the extent and nature of equity investments. Similarly, if public acceptance of the idea of private accounts diminishes because of increased concern over their possible costs, public opinion might move toward the idea of equity investment by the trust fund. But this is speculative. Continued and deeper surveying of the public will be needed to discover informed, deliberative opinions about privatization.

Conclusion: What the Public Wants and What It Will Put Up With

We should not always take current or past opinion surveys as showing definitively which Social Security reform proposals are or are not acceptable to the public. Reactions to certain options have been studied little or not at all. Opinions about some options are less firmly rooted than those about others and may change as new information is disseminated.

At the same time, the many available polls and surveys tell us quite a lot. The public's reactions to various policy alternatives are summarized in table 9-1.

First, the available survey data underline the high level of public support for the Social Security system as it now exists. Wholesale privatization or making Social Security voluntary is simply not politically feasible.

The data also make clear that there is considerable public reluctance to cut Social Security benefits, either directly or indirectly, by extending the retirement age, slowing COLAs, or the like. Some of the more obscure technical-sounding changes provoke less immediate resistance, but one should not assume that lack of public awareness of their consequences would continue if they were actually adopted. Of all proposed benefit cuts, only those targeted on well-to-do retirees win clear public approval.

General increases in payroll taxes also arouse substantial opposition, although there are some indications that tax increases might prove acceptable if they were shown to be necessary and if it were made clear that the revenues would not be "wasted" on other programs. There is strong support for using budget surpluses to preserve Social Security. There are indications that the use of general tax revenues might be acceptable, as might be the raising or removal of the cap on income subject to tax. The idea of extracting more revenue from the well-to-do seems to have solid public support.

Table 9-1. *Summary of Public Opinion and Social Security*

Policy alternative	Public reaction
Present Social Security system	Very strong and stable support
Benefit cuts	Substantial resistance over many years
Across-the-board cuts	Clear opposition
Reducing COLAs	Large majorities repeatedly opposed
Adjusting consumer price index	Present opposition but approval possible given strong scientific justification
Extending retirement age	Long history of opposition
Adjusting benefit formula	Opinion unformed but opposition likely
Cuts for well-to-do	Approval
Tax increases	Support for some, opposition to others; preferred over benefit cuts
Raising payroll taxes	Substantial resistance but approval possible if clearly needed
Using budget surpluses for Social Security	Strong approval
Using general revenues	Might be acceptable
Increases on high-income people	Approve higher taxes on benefits
Raising or removing cap on earnings subject to tax	Approval suggested by opinion on related issues
Privatization	Opinion less fully formed
Abolishing social security or making voluntary	Strong opposition
Private investment accounts	Skepticism; enthusiasm fades when risks, administrative costs, and other items are mentioned. (Universal Savings Accounts approved)
Trust Fund investment in equities	Initial skepticism. Possible approval if risks limited and decisions insulated from politics

Another option that might win public approval involves investing some retirement funds in equities. There are signs of initial enthusiasm for workers making some investments of payroll tax money on their own, though this enthusiasm tends to disappear when the question of risk is raised. Opposition might be expected to increase still further as people are made aware of possible administrative costs, restrictions on investment choices, and return-reducing obligations to earlier cohorts of retirees that are inherent in various private savings plans. For similar reasons we might expect increased support for trust fund investment in equities of some payroll taxes, particularly if means are devised to insulate investment decisions and the proceeds from political influences.

What proves to be acceptable to the public may be partly a matter of public relations packaging. As I have noted, obscure and technical-sounding changes in the CPI or in benefit formulas that just happen to reduce benefit levels or COLAs may possibly slip by the public without stirring up a major outcry, especially if they rest on sound scientific justification. Once again, however, I would suggest that decisionmakers not count too heavily upon public acquiescence based upon lack of awareness of policy consequences. Any policy changes that are big enough to make a difference in the Social Security financial picture may also be big enough to spark political debate, particularly if opinion leaders (politicians or interest group leaders, for example) choose to make a fuss about them.

Similarly, what proves to be acceptable to the public will partly be a function of which political actors, institutions, and processes are involved in the decisionmaking and what part they play. Conventional wisdom is probably correct, for example, that policy leadership by a carefully selected bipartisan commission along the lines of the 1982–83 model could dampen public controversy, lessen the role of ordinary citizens in the process, and widen the range of politically feasible policy alternatives. If both major political parties are thoroughly implicated in making an unpopular decision, neither party is likely to take much heat for it—at least not from the other major party.

Before acting upon this conventional wisdom, however, it might be well to examine both the desirability and the feasibility of this sort of use of the bipartisan commission model. Even if it were feasible to do so, would we in fact want to shut the public out of decisions concerning major changes in the largest, most important federal government program? To a political scientist it seems odd that some professional economists, who in the economic realm cherish consumer sovereignty and favor free competition in order to maximize consumer satisfaction, turn to the political realm and counsel collusion between the two major parties in order to stifle political competition. If consumer sovereignty is good, why not citizen sovereignty as well?

In any case, whatever we may think of the desirability of bipartisan collusion to enact unpopular policies, it may simply not be feasible. Politics at the end of the 1990s are not the politics of 1982–83, when a conservative Republican president, backed by a highly unified business community, faced an intimidated and confused set of congressional Democrats. Now, when the two parties are at roughly equal strength and are sharply polarized on policy matters (with impeachment memories fresh), it would be surprising if all leaders of the Democratic Party should choose to collude against parts of their own core constituency. If even one or two nationally prominent Democrats refused to do so and blew the whistle on others, then any nascent bipartisan deal for unpopular Social Security changes might be blown away by a gale of public outrage. Or, if consummated, such a deal might provoke a third-party rebellion.

So what is the policymaker to do, if the wide gap between projected Social Security benefits and revenues simply must be closed, if public opinion should or must be taken into account, and if the American public seems to oppose many proposals for benefit cuts or tax increases? Survey data alone cannot answer this question, but they do suggest certain guidelines.

First, policymakers might want to avoid the least popular options— especially benefit cuts—insofar as it is possible to do so, and focus their attention on the policy alternatives that are most acceptable to the public. These appear to include restricting non-Social Security uses of budget surpluses, raising caps on the income subject to payroll taxes, and taking advantage in some way of investment in equities.

Second, policy experts and survey researchers should explore more fully how the American public feels about the options that have not so far been thoroughly surveyed. These include raising or removing the income cap and the merits of individually managed versus government-managed equity investments, in the light of various possible administrative arrangements and costs, restrictions on investment choices, benefit reductions in the current program, obligations to help fund future benefits, and the like.

Third, everyone involved should work to provide the public, in the most easily accessible form, the best possible information about Social Security problems and possible solutions. (A broadly representative and noncollusive bipartisan commission might be helpful in providing such information and facilitating policy consensus.) My research over the years has convinced me that the average American is generally quite sensible about politics and will take into account whatever credible, well-documented, and widely authenticated information is made available. The public is perfectly capable of accepting painful policy prescriptions, so long as they are no more painful than necessary and so long as the necessity for accepting them is made clear by those whom citizens trust.

In short, I believe that the American public is ready for Social Security reform, if reforms are clearly articulated and justified and are shaped in response to the public's preferences. But not all proposed Social Security reforms are ready for the American public.

Notes

1. Benjamin I. Page and Robert Y. Shapiro, *The Rational Public: Fifty Years of Trends in Americans' Policy Preferences* (University of Chicago Press, 1992).

2. See Michael Delli Carpini and Scott Keeter, *What Americans Know About Politics and Why It Matters* (Yale University Press, 1996). The authors show that

political knowledge is greater than conventional wisdom has indicated, but it remains limited.

3. Philip E. Converse, "The Nature of Belief Systems in Mass Publics," in David E. Apter, ed., *Ideology and Discontent* (Free Press, 1964), pp. 206–61; Philip E. Converse, "Attitudes and Non-Attitudes: Continuation of a Dialogue," in Edward R. Tufte, ed., *The Quantitative Analysis of Social Problems* (Addison-Wesley, 1970), pp. 168–89. But see Christopher H. Achen, "Mass Political Attitudes and the Survey Response," *American Political Science Review* 69 (1975), pp. 1218–31.

4. Page and Shapiro, *Rational Public*, chaps. 1, 10. See also Benjamin I. Page, *Who Deliberates? Mass Media in Modern Democracy* (University of Chicago Press, 1996), esp. chaps. 1, 5.

5. Page and Shapiro, *The Rational Public*, chap. 2. The mass media, fond of stories involving drama and change, sometimes exaggerate opinion volatility by such means as chopping the bottom off graphs, which makes small changes look big. Impressions of fluctuating public opinion also arise from attention to presidential popularity and other attitudes that are more volatile than the collective policy preferences discussed here.

6. Benjamin I. Page, Robert Y. Shapiro, and Glenn R. Dempsey, "What Moves Public Opinion?" *American Political Science Review* 81 (1987), pp. 23–43; Page and Shapiro, *The Rational Public*, chap. 8.

7. The contention that many Americans hold incompatible opinions about taxes and spending (wanting something for nothing), for example, ignores public acceptance of certain kinds of tax increases and certain kinds of spending cuts (for example, on the military), as well as the possibility of principled acceptance of budget deficits. See Page and Shapiro, *The Rational Public*, pp. 160–61.

8. The capacity of collective public opinion to make sharp distinctions among alternative policies is well established (see the entries under "distinctions" in the index to Page and Shapiro, The *Rational Public*, pp. 471–72). This contrasts especially sharply with images of a confused and ignorant citizenry.

9. A January 21, 1999, Oppenheimer Funds/Third Millennium poll in which "Smith" said that the money going to Social Security "comes out of his own hard-earned paycheck" and that he has a "right to control" how it is spent, while "Jones" said Social Security had worked well for sixty years, "radical change" is "too risky," and the current system "should stay the way it is," found that 65 percent of young people considered "right-to-control" Smith closer to their own view and only 31 percent picked "stay-the-way-it-is" Jones. But a July 24, 1998, poll by 2030 Center in which Smith wanted to "reform and modernize" Social Security by letting workers invest part of their payroll taxes in "private accounts of their choice" to "encourage more savings and provide a better return," while Jones wanted to "strengthen and protect" Social Security, which has been a "great success" for sixty years and opposed private accounts as "too risky" and undermining the idea of a "decent" guaranteed retirement income, found only a slight 49 percent to 45 percent plurality among young Americans for the privatizer Smith. Beth Kobliner, who neatly presented this contrast at the National Academy of Social Insurance conference upon which this volume is based, also pointed out that a more straightforward August 1998 Princeton Survey Research Associates (PSRA) poll for Americans Discuss Social Security (ADSS) found that 60 percent of young people (age eighteen to thirty-four) favored "keeping Social Security . . . with a *guaranteed* monthly benefit based on a person's earnings," while only 36

percent said it was more important to "[let] workers invest some . . . contributions *themselves* even though an exact benefit would not be guaranteed."

10. PSRA/ADSS survey, press release, April 13, 1998, pp. 7, 9.

11. PSRA press release, April 13, 1998, p. 9. Lawrence R. Jacobs and Robert Y. Shapiro, "Myths and Misunderstandings About Public Opinion Toward Social Security: Knowledge, Support, and Reformism," paper delivered to the tenth annual conference of the National Academy of Social Insurance, Washington, D.C., January 29–30, 1998. Their table 3 shows the proportion of correct responses to a number of information questions about Social Security asked through 1997; table 2 shows the level of knowledge about financing.

12. Delli Carpini and Keeter, *What Americans Know*, chap. 2, esp. p. 80.

13. See Jacobs and Shapiro, "Myths," table 9; Jennifer Baggette, Robert Y. Shapiro, and Lawrence R. Jacobs, "The Polls: Social Security—An Update," *Public Opinion Quarterly* 49 (1995), pp. 429–30.

14. See Fay Lomax Cook and Jason Barabas, "Public Support for Social Welfare Programs, 1984–1996: Description and Explanation," Institute for Policy Research, Northwestern University, 1998, p. 11; Fay Lomax Cook, "The New Politics of Social Security," paper presented at the annual meeting of the Gerontological Society of America, Philadelphia, November 22, 1998; Baggette et al., "The Polls," p. 430.

15. See John Rielly, ed., *American Public Opinion and U.S. Foreign Policy 1999* (Chicago Council on Foreign Relations, 1999).

16. See Cook and Barabas, "Public Support," figure 1, and Cook, "The New Politics," figure 5 and p. 11.

17. Preliminary 1998 General Social Survey data provided by Tom Smith to Fay Cook, autumn 1998. Compare Jacobs and Shapiro, "Myths," table 9.

18. Data provided by the Chicago Council on Foreign Relations.

19. Rielly, ed., *American Public Opinion 1999*, p. 9.

20. See Jacobs and Shapiro, "Myths," p. 23.

21. Jacobs and Shapiro, "Myths," table 7.

22. *Los Angeles Times (LAT)*, January 1998. But the much ballyhooed "less likely than UFOs" comparison was concocted from misinterpretation of a Third Millennium survey. See Jacobs and Shapiro, "Myths," pp. 12–13.

23. Hart/Teeter, January 1997 and September 1997. Other surveys have found that "radical" change is embraced by much smaller proportions of the public.

24. The tendentious addition of "President Reagan wants to balance. . . ." to this question the following month garnered only 4 percent more pro-cutting responses (Harris, August 1981, September 1981). See Robert Y. Shapiro and Tom W. Smith, "The Polls: Social Security," *Public Opinion Quarterly* 49 (1985), p. 569.

25. Kaiser/Harvard November 1994; LAT January 1995. See Baggette et al., "The Polls," pp. 430–32; Jacobs and Shapiro, "Myths," table 11.

26. *Washington Post (WP)*/Kaiser/Harvard, March 1997.

27. Surveys between May 1982 and May 1995 by CBS/*New York Times*, Analysis Group, ABC/*Washington Post*, *Time*, Kaiser/Harvard, Roper, Yankelovich Partners (YP)/CNN/*Time*, and NBC/*Wall Street Journal*. See Jacobs and Shapiro, "Myths," table 13.

28. The former question was asked in a Harris poll, December 1996, with 49 percent favoring changing the Consumer Price Index (CPI) to a "more accurate" system, and 41 percent opposed. The latter was asked as part of an NBC/*Wall Street Journal* poll,

December 1996, with 47 percent favoring "reduc[ing]" the CPI, and 43 percent opposed. See Jacobs and Shapiro, "Myths," p.28 and endnote 24.

29. NBC/*Wall Street Journal*, March 1997. This item kept the "reduce . . . CPI . . ." format and mentioned that "some" economists think the CPI is inaccurate; it suggested that a change would reduce cost-of-living adjustments (COLAs), reduce the federal deficit, and "raise some future income taxes." See Jacobs and Shapiro, "Myths," p. 28 and endnote 24. Some surveys have found plurality support for the ambiguous idea of "postpon[ing]" COLAs.

30. Ben R. Page of the Congressional Budget Office has emphasized this point, which he attributes to Senator Phil Gramm (R-Texas).

31. CBS/*New York Times* July 1981; Audits & Surveys, April 1983. See Jacobs and Shapiro, "Myths," table 19 and notes c and n.

32. PSRA, January 1997. See Jacobs and Shapiro, "Myths," table 19 and note q.

33. Surveys between February 1988 and December 1994 by *Time*/Yankelovich, Clancy Shulman (YCS), Harris, *Newsweek*, and YP. A January 1993 survey by *U.S. News and World Reports (USNWR)* seemed to find only a narrow 49 percent to 46 percent plurality in favor of increasing taxes on upper-income beneficiaries (in contrast to the 67 percent to 31 percent margin that *Newsweek* found the same month), but *USNWR* used a defective question invoking newly elected Bill Clinton in a way that apparently increased opposition to the proposal among Clinton friends or foes. For the question wordings, see Jacobs and Shapiro, "Myths," table 14.

34. *Time*/CNN/*WP*, March 1997. See Jacobs and Shapiro, "Myths," table 14.

35. See Jacobs and Shapiro, "Myths," pp. 17–18.

36. CBS/*New York Times*, February 1996. See Jacobs and Shapiro, "Myths," p. 28 and endnote 25.

37. *WP*/Kaiser/Harvard, March 1997.

38. A February 1997 Public Agenda survey, for example, found that 69 percent thought funds from benefit cuts or tax increases would be "wasted" and the program would be in trouble again in ten or fifteen years; only 24 percent thought additional funds would be "put to good use" to get the program back on track. PSRA (for Pew Charitable Trusts), March 1998, found that 45 percent thought the main reason the Social Security program might be headed for financial troubles was that the government "spent Social Security reserves on other programs," while only 26 percent cited the growth in number of older people.

39. Employee Benefit Research Institute, 1997. See Jacobs and Shapiro, "Myths," p. 28.

40. ABC/*Washington Post*, January 1998.

41. *LAT*, January 1998.

42. *Time*/YCS, February 1988, 56 percent to 39 percent; Harris, October 1992, 58 percent to 40 percent; *Newsweek*, January 1993, 67 percent to 31 percent. The January 1993 *USNWR* survey found only a bare 49 percent to 46 percent plurality for taxing wealthy recipients more, but its question was marred by an unfortunate prologue about the "tough choices" that newly elected Bill Clinton "might make." See Jacobs and Shapiro, "Myths," table 14.

43. YP, December 1994.

44. Social Security Advisory Board, *Social Security: Why Action Should Be Taken Soon* (Washington, D.C., July 1998), p. 26.

45. Public Agenda Foundation, February 1997, 19 percent "somewhat" and 23 percent "strongly" favored making participation voluntary; 53 percent called the concern about dropouts "very close" to their own view and 28 percent said "somewhat close," with only 10 percent saying "not too close" and 7 percent "not close at all." Between 1981 and 1994, however, several surveys found narrow majority support for making Social Security voluntary. Baggette et al., "The Polls," p. 427.

46. Jacobs and Shapiro, "Myths," pp. 23–24.

47. NBC/*Wall Street Journal*, December 1996, 46 percent to 44 percent; January 1997, 48 percent to 46 percent. See Jacobs and Shapiro, "Myths," p. 25 and endnotes 21 and 22.

48. NBC/*Wall Street Journal*, January 1997. Jacobs and Shapiro, "Myths," p. 25 and endnote 23.

49. CBS/*New York Times*, February 1996; *Time*/CNN, December 1996, *WP*, March 1997. See Jacobs and Shapiro, "Myths," table 17.

50. *Time*/CNN, *WP*. See Jacobs and Shapiro, "Myths," pp. 26–27.

Comment by William Spriggs

The Public's Stake in Social Security Reform

Benjamin Page's work is fascinating and timely. As his analysis of public opinion polls shows, people deeply believe in social security and those of us in Washington would do well to understand what the public thinks about the various policy proposals.

It is clear that people are informed about the Social Security program and generally act in a rational way—from the economist's perspective—toward the program's benefits. For instance, when you look at those who choose early retirement as opposed to waiting until they can retire with full benefits, those people tend to be making reasonable decisions.

What will be difficult to get at in this debate, however, is the complexity of the program. It is difficult for the public to understand how the different components of Social Security interrelate. The agenda that some people have for reforming the program shows that they do not understand the complexity of the program either.

For instance, the public knows that people get disability from the Social Security program and they know that there are survivor's benefits. Yet the reform experts talk about rates of return on Social Security as if retirement benefits were the only thing citizens receive from the program. They tell the public that we are going to deal with one part of the program without upsetting the balance of the rest of the program. This is misleading and confusing.

The discussion has centered far too much on the intergenerational debate about retirement and not enough about other intergenerational aspects of the program. This is particularly true as it affects minority participants. For this set of workers it is clear that for various reasons there are real probabilities of dying too young or becoming disabled at a young age, and it is clear that we need to educate the younger public, in particular, about these probabilities and about the insurance aspect of the program. Retirement is not real to a lot of young people.

Page's work also makes it clear that the public might choose a tax increase to pay for meeting the 25 percent deficit that we know we will have after 2034. But, politicians, having been lobbied by other politicians, start the debate by ruling out tax increases. (I worked on Capitol Hill and I never thought about people lobbying lobbyists, but this does happen in this very fascinating arena.) The accepted perspective is that we start the discussion with, "Obviously you do not want us to increase taxes, and since that is not what you want, let us talk about how we are going to cut benefits."

Page's article is informative in pointing out the importance of the perception of what is and is not a benefit cut. He cites the example of increasing the retirement age to sixty-seven as a benefit cut reform that has been masked for most people. While the public strongly opposes increasing the retirement age, it may be that most people are not aware of the retirement age changes that were legislated in 1983. The complexity of the program creates a kind of "free ride" for some benefits cuts that appear not to be benefit cuts.

Even though the changes that can be made to save the program actually only have to be minor ones in the scheme of the entire program, this is not always acknowledged by those advocating total restructuring of the program. It will be interesting to see whether those who want more dramatic change will be able to make some of the finer points in order to advocate more radical changes to the program. An example would be a Martin Feldstein program. Feldstein has advocated programs that introduce individual retirement accounts as a component.

Page has made clear that people—Generation Xers and others—have long-term stable beliefs about certain programs, including Social Security. He has given us a good piece to think about where people really are. With respect to Generation Xers, his analysis makes it clear that we need to think about the spin given survey findings by the advocacy groups that fund these surveys.

The belief in Social Security cuts very deeply and, for obvious reasons, this is the one program where people care deeply for the beneficiaries and look them in the face, at least every holiday, if not more often. Social Security is a universal program and people understand the need for it at a very human level. There is a moral aspect to reforming this program; it is not something that we should take lightly and it is not something where we should act as if there is only a scientific answer to the dilemma.

People like the Social Security program because there is a deep commitment, both in terms of how they view themselves as citizens and how they view themselves as family members—how they view themselves as children and how they will view themselves as parents and grandparents. We need to take heed of this moral aspect as we go about making policy changes.

Comment by Bill Gradison

Polls, Politics, and Social Security Reform

Benjamin Page's article is excellent and thought-provoking. His main question, as I read it, was: Is the public ready for reform of Medicare and Social Security? I would answer, no. Then I would ask as the next question: Will the public ever be ready for reform of Medicare and Social Security: I would answer, probably not.

Then I would ask another question: Is that a problem? I would suggest it is not really much of a problem. In fact, I seriously doubt the public was all that engaged in the specifics of Social Security when it was adopted in the 1930s. They wanted a program. My hunch is, however, that had today's modern polling techniques been in place, broad public support would have been found for adding a health benefit, which was not added at that time.

Even though the enactment of Social Security was in the distant past, this does not mean that we cannot learn something from at least speculating about what was done then, why it was done, and what influence public opinion had on the structure that we have today.

It is unrealistic to expect there to be a public judgment on the details of such public policy proposals, then or now. Of course, what is a detail and what is basic, rockbed, important principle is obviously an important question.

There have been a lot of suggestions for changes in Social Security that, while they would not totally solve the seventy-five-year actuarial shortfall, would go a long way toward it. Many of these changes can properly be described as technical. They include changes in the bend points, using a longer time period for averaging earnings, even changing the inflation adjustment if it is not just done for Social Security; that is, if it is done across the board and based upon some true analysis rather than just as a gimmick to try to cut federal expenditures.

As I see this—from the perspective of someone who spent more than thirty years in elective office—I think the fact that the public has an opinion does not mean that the issue is salient to them. In other words, if you ask people, do you have an opinion on who should win the World Series, they are going to have an opinion, but it does not mean that they will march in the streets if the outcome differs from what they have in mind.

My experience is that legislation that reasonably seeks to achieve a desirable public goal is likely to have public acceptance. I had the feeling during my years in elective office that as long as I was focused on what my constituents cared about, they were willing to cut me some slack in terms of how I went about trying to achieve that goal.

I am not convinced, for example, that the issue of individual accounts, at least at the moment, is a salient issue to the public. It might become one, but I doubt if we are there at this point.

The recent history of Social Security suggests to me that legislators are not going to jump off the cliff alone on this issue, but they may be willing to jump off holding hands, and if they do, the chances of having a soft landing are good.

I think this is a good thing for the country and a very good thing for the program. There is much to be said for waiting until there is broad, bipartisan support for reforms in this program, which everyone in this country and for generations to come, depends upon. The necessary and desirable permanence and consistency of the program is greatly assisted if its broad outlines are not changed every time a different party takes control in Washington. It is not a political cop-out to say, "Let's wait until we can get both sides to agree." I think that is very healthy.

Most of my experience on this issue was based upon the fact that I served on the Social Security Subcommittee of the Committee on Ways and Means— during the 98th Congress (1982–1983). And I survived it. In fact, most of us that were a part of that process managed to survive. At that time the committee chairman was Democrat Jake Pickle of Texas, the ranking Republican member was Bill Archer, also of Texas, who is now the chairman of the Ways and Means Committee.

We developed a bipartisan approach. There was no partisan disagreement within the subcommittee or, as I recall it, in the full Ways and Means Committee. We were facing an immediate crisis—the Old Age Trust Fund was going to run out of money and it did, actually, in the spring of 1983. Ironically, it had to borrow from the Hospital Insurance Trust Fund, which is the one we are most worried about today, but that is history—and the checks did go out on time.

But there clearly was a sense of urgency about this and a sense of crisis, without which I doubt if anything much would have happened. Even with the environment that I outlined, even with the bipartisan nature of things, it was necessary to create what later became known as the Greenspan Commission. In fairness, I do not think they came out with a lot that was original, but they did give the recommendations that had been developed by others and that they gave their blessing to, a degree of credibility, which made it possible for action to be taken.

My view of the work of the Greenspan Commission is that it was not so much what they said that carried the day but who said it. After this whole thing was over I saw Chairman Alan Greenspan and I congratulated him. I said, Mr. Chairman, as a result of your performance with this commission, I am going to nominate you for the Nobel Prize. And he asked, the Nobel Prize in economics? And I said no, the Nobel Peace Prize.

I think that really reflects the nature of the issue that we are dealing with here. It is not so much the analysis as the politics of it that really counts.

Even with the support of the Greenspan Commission, when this issue came before the House of Representatives there was an attempt to strike some of the provisions. The one I remember most clearly was the provision to increase the retirement age. This was a Democratic House of Representatives.

As I remember it, Speaker Tip O'Neill (D-Mass.) actually spoke in the well—which he very seldom did—in opposition to that provision. And so did the late and very distinguished Claude Pepper (D-Fla.), who was truly the most effective spokesman for the elderly in our time.

They lost by an almost two-to-one vote. I think this is remarkable when you think about it, and particularly when we look at survey data that suggests the public was outraged by the notion. Now it is possible to say, "Well they did not know about it or it did not take effect until later."

But that same thing could be said of changes that might be proposed today. They do not have to take effect right now. I am not trying to glorify keeping the public in the dark. What I am trying to say is that there are other things in people's lives than those amendments that are being considered on the floor of the House of Representatives every day.

I once worked out a hierarchy based upon the fact that I got elected by knocking on doors and knocking off an incumbent in a rather difficult year, the Watergate year—not a great time to be a Republican. People's main concerns are their family, health, job, home, neighborhood, the schools, the church, and– where I come from–whether the Reds are going to win the pennant. Somewhere further down the line is what the city council or the legislature or Congress is going to do to them.

I am not aware of any polls taken back in 1982 or 1983 showing public support for or opposition to what happened. But my hunch is that the things that we actually did—raising the retirement age, increasing Social Security tax, and cutting back on benefits—would not have run very well in the surveys then any more than they do today.

I am well aware of the political impact of the debate about the Social Security cost-of-living adjustments, particularly the vote on the floor of the Senate. I believe it did have political implications and was an important explanation of the twenty-six or so House seats Republicans lost that year and in the turnover in control of the Senate.

It is easy to understand what happened. It became a partisan issue and, of course, it did not pass into law. But people have learned from this and that is why they are not about to jump off the cliff without holding hands. It was not that long ago. For better or worse, politicians have long memories.

I have a few contrarian views to share with you about some current proposals. First, with regard to Medicare, it is remarkable how quiet the discussion has been in recent days about the use of general revenues in Medicare.

Traditionally, I thought what I was hearing was that some of the strongest supporters of the program—as an entitlement, as an earned right—were opposed to the use of general revenues, feeling that it would be a step toward means testing of that program, that is, converting it from a social insurance program into a welfare program. I am still waiting—and maybe my ear is tin— to hear that point being made today. I think it should be made, actually.

With regard to Social Security, again a contrarian view. I think the notion of a modest carve out, a couple of percentage points, for private accounts might paradoxically increase support for the system. There are a lot of young people out there who are skeptical that they will ever get anything out of Social Security. They are wrong, but there are many people who have that belief.

They might feel more secure if a piece of that account was their own— vested, theirs—and they would not have to worry about what might happen in the future with regard to benefits. After all, they can put it into government bonds if they have an individual account. They do not have to put it into equities. That would be their choice.

I would expect that absent bipartisan, bicameral, White House agreement nothing will happen. The last thing Congress is going to want is a vetoed Social Security bill.

I doubt that there would be a political price to pay for inaction since the system is not in immediate financial crisis. I believe something can happen in the 106th Congress; the proposals now on the table are openers, not final positions, and not cast in concrete.

In conclusion, if Page's assertion about the importance of collective preferences for Social Security is correct, then people should have been marching on the Capitol when fundamental changes were made back in 1982–83. They were not.

It may seem quaint to say this, but I suspect there is strong support in this country for representative government. This will trump polls and focus groups once the powers that be in Washington decide that there is a greater political price to pay for inaction than for action.

Comment by Beth Kobliner

Generation X, Social Security, and Public Opinion Polling

Increasingly, the mass media have been addressing the question of what young adults think about Social Security reform. As a result, an informal conventional wisdom of sorts has sprung up that holds that "Generation X"—people born between 1965 and 1976—is leading the charge to replace the current Social Security system with one featuring individually directed accounts and a greater degree of stock market investment.[1] As a financial journalist who specializes in financial issues affecting young people, I have followed this discussion with interest.

As Benjamin Page points out, survey responses are highly dependent on the wording of the questions. In preparing for this discussion, I reviewed some of the recent polls and studies related to Generation X's views on Social Security reform. What I found is that, on closer inspection, the views of Generation X are neither simple nor obvious, and may actually be far closer to the views of the general public than we have been led to believe.

By way of example, I would like to contrast the findings of two polls that were recently released in connection with two different Generation X advocacy groups: the 2030 Center, which believes in maintaining the traditional defined-benefit character of the Social Security system, and Third Millennium, which favors privatization. The first poll was co-conducted by the 2030 Center and the National Committee to Preserve Social Security and Medicare; the second was conducted by Oppenheimer Funds in conjunction with Third Millennium.

Although created separately, the polls both contain a question positing two individuals with differing positions on the future of Social Security and asking respondents to choose between them. The two polls' questions are similar in most respects but differ subtly and crucially in tone.

The Oppenheimer/Third Millennium question is as follows:

> Mr. Smith says that the money that goes into Social Security comes out of his own hard-earned paycheck and he has the right to control how it's spent. Mr. Jones says that Social Security has worked well for the past 60 years, that radical change right now is too risky, and that the current Social Security system should stay the way it is. Which comes closer to your view?

Hard-working Mr. Smith—the privatizer—won the support of 64.7 percent of eighteen- to twenty-nine-year-old respondents in this poll, while just 31.3 percent agreed with risk-averse Mr. Jones.[2]

The 2030 Center version of the question uses a similar framework, but comes at it from a slightly different angle:

Candidate Smith says that we need to reform and modernize Social Security in order to make it work for future generations. He believes that workers should be allowed to invest part of their Social Security taxes in private accounts of their choice to encourage more savings and provide a better return on people's contributions. Candidate Jones says that we need to strengthen and protect Social Security, which has been a great success for 60 years, so that it works for both current and future retirees. He opposes private accounts which he says are too risky and would under-mine Social Security's ability to provide a decent, guaranteed lifetime retirement income. All things being equal, who do you like better, Smith or Jones?

Generation X respondents to the 2030 Center question were almost evenly split. This time around, Smith appealed to just 49 percent of respondents, while support for Jones jumped to 45 percent.[3]

Clearly, subtle choices in wording can make an important difference in poll results. This constitutes a significant problem when those results are subse-quently alleged to reflect the opinions of Generation X. To get a true sense of Generation X's opinions on complex issues, we may need to ask more complex questions—questions that clearly disclose the advantages and drawbacks of the various alternatives involved.

A poll conducted by the Princeton Survey Research Associates, on behalf of a group called Americans Discuss Social Security, found that 60 percent of young people—those eighteen to thirty-four—said that they favored having some portion of their Social Security payroll tax put into an individual investment account.[4] Since the general public favored this option by a consid-erably lower margin (52 percent), this finding would seem to suggest that Generation Xers are indeed in the vanguard of the push for privatization.

But in a separate question in the same Princeton poll, the same group of respondents were asked to choose which Social Security objective was more important—maintaining a guaranteed monthly benefit based on earnings or letting workers invest some of their own Social Security contributions themselves with no exact benefit guaranteed. A strong majority (59.8 per-cent) went for the guaranteed benefits here, compared with just 35.6 percent who came out for the investment option. In other words, these respondents seemed to reverse themselves: 60 percent said that they believed in indi-vidual accounts, but when asked a slightly more complicated version of the same basic question 60 percent said that they preferred the guaranteed benefit after all.

One conclusion to be drawn from this apparent contradiction could be that Generation X's allegedly fervent support for privatization is in fact relatively soft support. The views of Generation Xers on this matter may be more similar to those of the general public than has been generally acknowledged, and their apparent interest in privatization may stem in part from media-inflated misperceptions and unfounded fears.

For example, in preparing this discussion I asked someone in my office, a smart twenty-three-year-old, to find statistics on Social Security. One of the things she found was the fact that Social Security will "go broke" in 2030. I asked her if she knew what that meant. Yes, she said, it meant that there would be no Social Security after the year 2030. She was shocked to learn that, in fact, 75 percent of promised benefits would still be in place after 2030. And she is far from alone. A 1997 poll conducted by PaineWebber found that 33 percent of those aged eighteen to thirty-four think they will get no Social Security benefits *at all*.[5]

There is no factual basis for this belief, but it informs the polling data nonetheless. People who believe that Social Security is completely disappearing are more likely to favor individual accounts, because the alternative is no Social Security at all. Additionally, Generation Xers have come of age during a period in which the Dow Jones Industrial Average literally tripled in six years. The traditional assumption that privatization involves risk has been turned on its head.

It is easy to see how misperceptions about the future of Social Security gain cultural currency. Polls, as we have seen, can be crafted to produce results; the ensuing press releases pump the findings into dramatic language. Journalists on weekly or daily deadlines do not have the time or interest necessary to delve into details or challenge analysis. The ambiguities—and there are many—can get lost in the shuffle.

Ultimately, despite the claims of the press releases, it is nearly impossible to come up with a consistent take on Generation X. One reason for this is that Generation X is a deeply diverse economic group. In real, inflation-adjusted dollars, people between the ages of twenty-five and thirty-four actually earned 3.8 percent less in 1997 than their age bracket did in 1977. But that decrease has not hit everyone evenly. Those who completed at least four years of college earned 8.6 percent more in 1997 than in 1977. By contrast, Generation Xers with only high school degrees earned substantially less in 1997 than their 1970s counterparts.[6] These increasingly stratified groups have radically different stakes in the Social Security debates.

Some analysts have argued that lower-income groups benefit from the redistributive aspects of the current Social Security system, which suggests a rational incentive for lower-income Generation Xers to stick by the current defined-benefit system. A 1998 paper by the Employee Benefit Research Institute, for example, argues that the transition costs associated with moving to a partially privatized system could make it a worse option for all but the wealthiest Generation Xers.[7]

On the other hand, the better-educated, better-off wing of Generation X may feel it has little to lose, and much to gain, from privatization. PaineWebber's 1998 survey of "investor confidence" found that 92 percent of investors aged eighteen to thirty favored a private account system, far more than other age groups—but this particular group of Generation Xers is hardly representative.[8]

It is therefore wise to be cautious when trying to pigeonhole Generation Xers as fervent believers in individual accounts or in any one policy option. The divisions within Generation X seem far more substantial than the alleged differences between Generation X and other generations. Partial privatization may yet be a good option for reform. But it seems clear to me that some sort of guaranteed-benefit component will remain essential to a significant part of every segment of the population—including Generation X.

Notes

1. For the sake of convenience, I will use the term *Generation X* here despite my reservations about the phrase and its implications.

2. "Social Security Survey," conducted by the Luntz Research Companies and Mark A. Siegel and Associates for Oppenheimer Funds, January 10–12, 1999. Random telephone polling of 804 Americans. Third Millennium was Oppenheimer's partner and cosponsor for a Washington, D.C., panel discussion held January 21, 1999, entitled "Retirement Roundtable Discussion," at which the results of this survey were released. Much of the poll's press release deals with intergenerational differences in perceptions of Social Security. In the eighteen to twenty-nine age bracket, 132 people answered the "Smith vs. Jones" question.

3. "Social Security Survey," conducted by Peter D. Hart Research Associates for the National Committee to Preserve Social Security and Medicare and the 2030 Center, July 6–13, 1998. Random telephone polling of 326 Americans ages eighteen to thirty-four. Of those surveyed, 162 people answered the "Smith vs. Jones" question.

4. "Making Hard Choices: Public Opinion on Options for Social Security," conducted by Princeton Survey Research Associates for Americans Discuss Social Security, August 6–27, 1999. Random telephone polling of 2,008 Americans over the age of eighteen.

5. "The Index of Investor Optimism," conducted by the Gallup Organization for PaineWebber, November-December 1998. The poll asked questions of 1,001 ran-

domly selected "investors" (defined as the head or spouse of a household with total savings or investments of $10,000 or more).

6. U.S. Census Bureau, Historical Income Tables P-27 and P-28B. In 1991 the Census Bureau changed its education attainment questions, complicating direct comparison between high school graduates in 1977 and 1997: before 1991, the "high school only" category included people who had attended some college but had not completed a full year, whereas those people are now included in the "some college" category. This change accounts for some of the comparative decrease in real income for the "high school only" group, although almost certainly not for the full differential of 14.3 percent. It should also be noted that various social factors (such as the rise in college attendance and the increased presence of women in the workforce) hinder our ability to draw strict conclusions from these statistics.

7. Kelly A. Olsen and Dallas L. Salisbury, "Individual Social Security Accounts: Issues in Assessing Administrative Feasibility and Costs." Employee Benefit Research Institute Special Report SR 34/issue brief no. 203 (November 1998).

8. "The Index of Investor Optimism," conducted by the Gallup Organization for Paine Webber, November-December 1998. The poll asked questions of 1,001 randomly selected "investors" (defined as the head or spouse of a household with total savings or investments of $10,000 or more).

Contributors

Kenneth Apfel is commissioner of the United States Social Security Administration.

Robert M. Ball is a consultant on Social Security, health, and welfare policy to many organizations and elected officials.

Edward D. Berkowitz is a professor in the Department of History at George Washington University.

John Breaux is a three-term senator from Louisiana and the ranking Democrat on the Special Committee on Aging.

Sheila Burke is the executive dean at the John F. Kennedy School of Government at Harvard University.

Stuart Butler is currently vice president and director of domestic and economic policy studies at the Heritage Foundation.

Sharon Canner is vice president of entitlement policy with the National Association of Manufacturers.

Paul R. Carey is commissioner of the United States Securities and Exchange Commission.

Nancy Ann DeParle is the administrator of the Health Care Financing Administration.

Bill Gradison is a former nine-term Republican representative from Ohio and currently with the law firm Patton Boggs LLP.

Janice M. Gregory has directed legislative affairs for the ERISA Industry Committee (ERIC) since 1984.

Edward M. Kennedy is a seven-term senator from Massachusetts and the ranking Democrat on the Labor and Human Resources Committee.

Eric Kingson is professor of social work at Syracuse University.

Beth Kobliner is a journalist and commentator who has been writing and speaking on personal finance for more than a decade.

George F. Loewenstein is professor of economics and psychology at Carnegie Mellon University.

James Lubalin is a senior health services and policy researcher in the Research Triangle Institute's Washington, D.C., office.

Theodore Marmor is professor of public policy and management at the Yale School of Management and professor of political science in the Department of Political Science at the Institution for Social Policy Studies at Yale University.

Karen Matherlee is codirector of the National Health Policy Forum, a freelance writer and editor, and an adjunct faculty member in health policy and management at the John Hopkins University.

Marilyn Moon is a senior fellow in the Health Policy Center of the Urban Institute and a public trustee of the Social Security and Medicare trust funds.

William A. Niskanen has been the chairman of the Cato Institute since 1985 and the former acting chairman of the Council of Economic Advisers for President Ronald Reagan.

Benjamin I. Page is the Gordon Scott Fulcher Professor of Decision Making at Northwestern University, where he teaches in the departments of political science and communications studies.

Uwe Reinhardt is the James Madison Professor of Political Economy at Princeton University, where he has taught since 1968.

Robert D. Reischauer is a senior fellow at the Brookings Institution.

John Rother is the director of legislation and public policy at the American Association of Retired Persons.

Kathleen Sebelius is the Kansas insurance commissioner.

David Smith is the director of the Public Policy Department at the AFL-CIO.

William Spriggs is the director of research and public policy at the National Urban League.

Bill Thomas is an eleven-term Republican representative from California and chairman of the Subcommittee on Health of the Ways and Means Committee and of the House Oversight Committee.

Fredda Vladeck is a senior health policy consultant to the National Council of Senior Citizens.

Mark J. Warshawsky is the director of research for the TIAA-CREF Institute, the research and education arm of TIAA-CREF, a financial services organization and pension system for workers in U.S. educational and research institutions.

Conference Program

National Academy of Social Insurance
11th Annual Conference

Social Security and Medicare: Individual versus Collective Risk and
Responsibility
January 27–28, 1999

Wednesday, January 27, 1999

9:30 a.m.   Welcome and Introduction
                             Opening address
                             Robert Reischauer

10:00 a.m.–12:00 p.m. Session I. Is the Public Ready for Reform of
                             Medicare and Social Security?

    Policymaking by public opinion poll sometimes
seems the mechanism of government today. Yet
these polls may shed little light on the kinds of
policy choices and tradeoffs the public will support
and sustain in Medicare and Social Security reform.
How does "public judgment" come about? What is
its role in policymaking on health care and income
security? How might citizens view government risk
pooling versus compulsory individual responsibility?

Moderator: Eric Kingson, Syracuse University
Presenter: Benjamin Page, Northwestern University
Discussants:
    William Spriggs, National Urban League

Bill Gradison, Patton Boggs LLP
Beth Kobliner, author of *Get a Financial Life*

12:00 noon   Luncheon Dialogue: Individual Choices and Shared
                      Responsibilities
                      Two views, one that favors more individual
                      choice and one that supports more collective
                      responsibility, debate how this question has evolved
                      into a key one in the current debates about Medicare
                      and Social Security reform.

                      Moderator: Marilyn Moon, Urban Institute
                      Debaters: Stuart Butler, Heritage Foundation
                      Theodore Marmor, Yale University

1:15–2:30 p.m.   Session II. Why Do We Have Social Insurance?
                      Social Security and Medicare reflect a particular
                      set of answers to fundamental values questions of
                      individual choice, risk-bearing, and the relationship
                      between the individual and society. How did we as a
                      nation arrive at the answers embodied in our existing
                      programs? Why are these fundamental questions
                      being asked anew in today's debate on how to shape
                      retirement policy and health care for the future? Are
                      there lessons of the past that ought to influence the
                      choices we make for the future?

                      Moderator: Uwe Reinhardt, Princeton University
                      Presenter: Edward Berkowitz, George Washington
                          University
                      Discussants: Robert M. Ball, commissioner of Social
                          Security, 1960–72
                      Janice M. Gregory, ERISA Industry Committee

3:00–5:00 p.m.   Session III. How Do People Make Decisions?
                      Reforms contemplated for both Social Security
                      and Medicare involve a much greater role for
                      individual decisionmaking and a responsibility to
                      choose wisely. How do people make decisions about
                      health care and retirement security? What influences

those decisions?   What kind of information do they use (or not use) in making a choice?

Moderator: Henry Aaron, Brookings Institution and academy chair

Presenter: George F. Lowenstein, Carnegie Mellon University

Discussants: James Lubalin, Research Triangle Institute

Mark Warshawsky, TIAA-CREF

Fredda Vladeck, consultant to labor organizations

6:45–8: 30 p.m.   Dinner and 1999 Heinz Award ceremony
                         Speaker: Uwe Reinhardt

Thursday, January 28, 1999

9:00 a.m.   Roundtable Discussions
                         Introducing Funded Pension Programs: How Did They Do It in Canada and Sweden?

Moderator: Dalmer Hoskins, International Social Security Association

Do Medicare and Disability Benefits Work Together to Encourage Independence?

Moderator: Patricia Owens, UNUM Life Insurance Company of America

Welfare Reform: Implications for Social Insurance

Moderator: Janet Shikles, Abt Associates

Challenges to Educating the Public about Medicare Reform

Moderator: Drew Altman and Diane Rowland, Henry J. Kaiser Family Foundation

Long-term Care Lessons to Be Learned from Other Countries

Moderator: Robyn Stone, International Longevity Center

10:30 a.m.   Opening Address
                        The Honorable Edward M. Kennedy (D-Mass.)

11:00 a.m.   Session IV. What Kind of Regulation Will Assure
                            That the Markets Deliver on Their Promise?
                        If Medicare reforms continue to go in the direction
                        of market-based choices, what regulation is
                        necessary to make those markets work in ways that
                        allow them to fulfill their purpose of promoting
                        health security? If mandatory retirement accounts
                        are added to the U.S. Social Security system, what
                        rules will make them deliver retirement security? In
                        both reform scenarios, what mechanisms will be
                        needed to protect consumers? What will their
                        information needs be? Should individuals be
                        protected from making bad choices, and to what
                        extent?

                        Moderator: Gail Wilensky, Project HOPE and the
                            Medicare Payment Advisory Commission
                        Panel: Paul R. Carey, commissioner, Securities and
                            Exchange Commission
                        William Niskanen, chairman, Cato Institute
                        Kathleen Sebelius, insurance commissioner, Kansas

12:30 p.m.   Session V. "Current Events"
                            How do things stand after the recent White House
                        Conference on Social Security and with the
                        upcoming report of the Medicare Commission? This
                        conference panel will feature key players and
                        analysts from these two reform discussion efforts.

                        Moderator: Sheila Burke, Kennedy School of
                            Government
                        Luncheon speakers: Senator John Breaux (D-La.)
                        Representative Bill Thomas (R-Calif.)

After-lunch panel: Kenneth Apfel, Social Security Administration
                        Nancy Ann DeParle, Health Care Financing
                            Administration

Sharon Canner, National Association of
   Manufacturers
John Rother, American Association of Retired
   Persons
David Smith, AFL-CIO

2:45 p.m.   Conference Highlights: Wrap-up
                    Sheila Burke
                    Eric Kingson
                    Uwe Reinhardt

Index